Democracy and Education in Namibia and Beyond
A critical appraisal

EDITED BY

Elizabeth Magano Amukugo

UNAM PRESS

UNIVERSITY OF NAMIBIA

University of Namibia Press
www.unam.edu.na/unam-press
unampress@unam.na
Private Bag 13301
Windhoek
Namibia

First published:	2017
Cover design:	Nambowa Malua
Copy-editing:	Tara Elyssa, Cynthia Murray, Sarah Taylor
Design and layout:	Vivien Barnes, Handmade Communications
Printed by:	John Meinert Printers, Windhoek

ISBN 978-99916-42-30-7

Distribution
In Namibia by Namibia Book Market: www.namibiabooks.com
Internationally by the African Books Collective: www.africanbookscollective.com

Contents

Foreword

I welcome this contribution to the literature on education and democratic emancipation in society, with special reference to Namibia. It is an important reflection on the essential elements of democracy and differing philosophical approaches to education, providing context for a broad-based assessment of key aspects of the Namibian education environment.

Education creates knowledge, and knowledge is empowering. When people have the knowledge to emancipate themselves, they can articulate and advocate for their democratic human rights. In fact, education plays a critical role as an instrument of democracy the world over – in our homes, societies and governments. Education nurtures, promotes, and facilitates rational thinking during the process of soul-searching to solve individual, societal and national challenges.

UNESCO's World Conference on Higher Education, held in October 1998, unanimously recommended that societal challenges should define the missions of higher education institutions, to enable those societies to attain sustainable economic and social development based on human rights, democracy, tolerance and mutual respect (UNESCO, 2003). Structural challenges within Namibia, inequality, and high levels of poverty inherited from the colonial period, are reflected in all aspects of our society, including the education system. Thus, a holistic approach is required to maximise the impact of efforts to change those structures.

Namibia's education system faces some critical challenges that need to be dealt with to ensure that we achieve the best for our students/learners and teachers alike. Most of these challenges date back to the time before the country attained its independence. Since then, education has enjoyed particular attention from government, in terms of dismantling the previous, ethnically based education system and setting forth a uniform national system based on the principle of Education for All.

At the tertiary level, the government established the University of Namibia in 1992, with the clear focus of producing internationally competitive graduates and ensuring that it is part of the international networking family of institutions of higher learning. The Polytechnic of Namibia, established in 1996, was transformed into the country's second university, the Namibia University of Science and Technology (NUST), in 2016.

Enrolment of Namibian children at primary and junior secondary level is high, but it is important that the provision of universal primary education and universal secondary education does not emphasise the quantity of learners before the quality of graduates. Similarly, our universities need to be careful not to produce graduates who are insufficiently trained and cannot find employment. The family also has a role in grooming children within our homes, to develop a culture of curiosity, of wanting to read and discover more of the world around them.

It is prudent that we continue to undertake targeted interventions to expedite further reform in the education system. It is in this respect that a new Education Bill will be tabled before the National Assembly in 2017; this Bill takes stock of the issues highlighted in this book in addition to other challenges within our education sector.

The proposed new Bill covers key elements of the Sustainable Development Goals (SDGs) and includes, *inter alia*: benchmarking on national and international policies and legislations that guarantee inclusive quality education for all children; targeted intervention for learners with disabilities and special needs; ensuring a comprehensive and compulsory provision for Early Childhood Development (ECD) and pre-primary education; and appropriate educational infrastructure including accommodation for both learners and teachers, as well as Information and Communication Technology (ICT).

The issues discussed by the editor and authors in this book speak directly and indirectly to the challenges we face in Namibia. This is an important contribution to the Namibian education landscape, and it will certainly stimulate further debate and highlight key deficits that we must deal with to ensure meaningful reform in our education system.

An educated person is likely to interrogate and seek a better governed environment. Therefore, children who receive good education are more likely to strive for good governance and democracy. In this regard, it is worthwhile remembering the words of one of the world's greatest philosophers, Plato, when he said: 'If you do not take an interest in the affairs of your government, then you are doomed to live under the rule of fools'.

I commend the editor and authors for their efforts in producing this book and the manner in which they have reflected upon various classical and contemporary writings on education and democracy. This is indeed worthwhile reading for all those who aspire to empower themselves and advocate for a democratic existence for themselves and the wider society.

Hon. Prof. Peter H Katjavivi, MP
Speaker of the National Assembly of the Republic of Namibia
Founding Vice Chancellor of the University of Namibia (1992–2003)
Chancellor of the Namibia University of Science and Technology (2016–)

Reference

UNESCO. (2003). *The African University at the threshold of the new millennium: potential, process, and prospects.* Publication from the Meeting of Higher Education Partners, Paris, 23–25 June 2003, p. 14.

Acknowledgements

A book of this nature which focuses on the three broad concepts of democracy, education and social justice, would not have been possible without many hands that contributed in one way or another. Thus, although this book was initiated and coordinated by me, its wide-ranging topics required me to draw on the knowledge and expertise of colleagues who produced several information-rich chapters. Their ingenuity, co-operation and encouragement provided much needed inspiration throughout the production of this work. The late Professor Pempelani Mufune needs a special mention. In addition to producing one chapter, he agreed with much enthusiasm to serve as co-editor of this book. Although ill-health and eventually his passing prevented him from taking his passion for this project to its final conclusion, his partial contribution deserves a distinctive credit. A scholar of note, Professor Mufune went too soon and left a vacuum not only in terms of this book's production, but even more importantly, at the University of Namibia and in the African academic fraternity as a whole.

I would also like to express my appreciation to UNAM Press staff under the leadership of the former Publisher, Mrs Jane Katjavivi and her successor Dr Jill Kinahan, for their advice, encouragement and untiring support for this project. I am indebted to my two sons Hainyeko and Tjivingurura Mbuende, whose steadfast support and reassurance throughout provided the necessary fortitude to me to make it through those long working hours. In the final analysis, however, I owe my work ethics to my late parents, Rev. Armas and Hilma Amukugo.

Elizabeth Magano Amukugo
Associate Professor, University of Namibia
Windhoek, April 2017

Abbreviations and acronyms

ART	Action Research Team
BETD	Basic Education and Teaching Diploma
CEQUAM	Centre for Quality Assurance and Management
CSIC	*Consejo Superior de Investigaciones Científicas*
ECD	Early Childhood Development
ETSIP	Education and Training Sector Improvement Programme
GRN	Government of the Republic of Namibia
HIGCSE	Higher International General Certificate of Secondary Education
HPP	Harambee Prosperity Plan
ICT	Information Communication Technology
IGCSE	International General Certificate of Secondary Education
IMF	International Monetary Fund
IUM	International University of Management
JSC	Junior Secondary Certificate
MBESC	Ministry of Basic Education, Sport and Culture
MEAC	Ministry of Education, Arts and Culture
MEC	Ministry of Education and Culture
MECYS	Ministry of Education, Culture, Youth and Sport
MoE	Ministry of Education
MoHSS	Ministry of Health and Social Services
MPs	members of parliament
NAMCOL	Namibia College of Open Learning
NANSO	Namibia National Students' Organisation
NANTU	Namibia National Teachers' Union
NBC	Namibian Broadcasting Corporation
NCHE	National Council for Higher Education
NDP	National Development Plan
NEPAD	New Partnership for Africa's Development
NIED	National Institute for Educational Development
NPC	National Planning Commission
NSSC	National Senior Secondary Certificate
NUST	Namibia University of Science and Technology
PSE	pre-school education
SADC	Southern African Development Community
SDGs	Sustainable Development Goals
SIAPAC	Social Impact Assessment and Policy Analysis Corporation
SWAPO	South West Africa People's Organization
UCLES	University of Cambridge Local Examination Syndicate
UN	United Nations
UNAM	University of Namibia
UNDP	United Nations Development Programme

UNESCO	United Nations Educational, Scientific and Cultural Organization
UNICEF	United Nations Children's Fund
UNPAF	United Nations Partnership Framework
VET	Vocational Education and Training

1

Introduction: Exploring democracy, education and social justice

Elizabeth Magano Amukugo

Readers are encouraged to engage as critical thinkers with the issues discussed in this book. Therefore you may use the following Focus Questions to stimulate your thinking about the issues coming up in this chapter and subsequent chapters:

1. In your view, to what extent is there equality and equity between races, genders, ability groups and social classes in your country?

2. To what extent do you think the historic struggle for democracy in your country has brought about equality and equity?

3. How would you rate your country's education system in terms of promoting equality and equity?

This book aims to explore, firstly, the meaning of the concept 'democracy' and its relationship to education; and, secondly, what democracy means for justice in a societal context. The idea for the book was a result of earlier research conducted (Amukugo, 2002; Amukugo, Likando, & Mushaandja, 2010; Government of the Republic of Namibia [GRN], 1999; World Bank, 2005) which depicts inequities within the Namibian educational system.

Notwithstanding the progress made, two questions can be raised:

1. How can educational disparities across regions and social classes be possible in independent Namibia despite a well-received government educational policy (Ministry of Education and Culture, 1993) that cleared the way 'From Elite Education to Education for All' only three years into independence?

2. How do inequities and problems of poor quality continue to haunt the Namibian educational system, despite an internationally acclaimed Namibian Constitution, in which Article 20, Chapter 3 on 'Fundamental Human Rights and Freedoms', stipulates that 'All persons shall have the Right to Education'?

Given the diverse meanings of democracy as presented, it can be argued from the outset that the concepts of democracy and education can mean different things to different people, depending on their different world views.

In light of the historically varied concepts of democracy, there is an urgent need first to come to terms with the different concepts of the term democracy and specifically its meaning for education. Secondly, assuming that Namibian society subscribes to a certain concept of democracy, there is a need to pose the question of whether or not Namibian educational objectives and practices do develop and help sustain a democratic culture in Namibia. Put differently, there is a need to ascertain whether there is a harmonised relationship between theory and practice. This book therefore aims to achieve the following:

1. To contribute to a better understanding of the relationship between democracy, education and social justice;
2. To create a knowledge of the strengths and limitations of education as an instrument of social change;
3. To contribute to the existing knowledge/literature about the role of education in a democratic society; and
4. To explore the question of whether education needs a more solid philosophical base in order to enhance democracy.

Methodology

Social science literature has discussed the concepts of democracy, education and justice separately; some, including the classical works of John Dewey (2010), draw a link between education and democracy. Dowding, Goodin and Pateman (2004, p. 6) confirm this observation and point out that '[d]emocratic theorists, conversely, have been remarkably silent about justice' and that the relationship between the two concepts remains mostly unaddressed. Furman and Shields (2005) agree by suggesting that the issues of social justice and democratic communities in relation to schools (or education) have been ignored predominantly in mainstream literature. It is due to this gap that the book by Dowding et al. (2004) aims to draw a connection between democracy and justice. The authors do this by advancing the view that the state regulates the supply of private goods as well as enabling and delivering universal public goods, such as health and education, which are central to both democracy and justice. They point out that an adequate co-operation of these could be a prerequisite for a socially just society. Education, especially, plays a major role since '... some of the central concerns of a well-functioning democracy require an informed and active citizenry' (Dowding et al., 2004, p. 10). It can also be emphasised, however, that an informed and active citizenry also need food, clothing and a roof over their head. This should place the socio-economic conditions of the populace at the top of the state's agenda, although it does not always happen that way.

Recently, however, Allen and Reich (2013) went a step further by linking education, democracy and justice. Their book sets out to examine the way in which educational institutions and practices can advance justice and support democracy by generating favourable conditions for equal citizenship and empowerment. They proceed from the premise that policy debates tend to conceal, rather than help to explain, the educational aims, content and challenges. Their objective is, therefore, to seek clarity and content by developing an increased understanding and appreciation of what they see as fundamental ideals, namely, education, justice and democracy. They do this by placing the three concepts within a broader social, political and developmental context. However, the essays in Allen and Reich's book have been written from a generally egalitarian perspective. As Dowding et al. (2004) noted:

> Egalitarian debates are largely about what is to be equalized and maximized
> – utility, welfare, resources, opportunities, capabilities, power, real freedom –
> and all too often say little about the institutions which are to deliver the goods
> (Dowding et al., 2004, p. 29).

Our book presents chapters written from various points of view; predominantly liberal, egalitarian, libertarian and feminist perspectives. From the standpoint of the core discussion about democracy, education and justice, the book touches on the broader issues of distributive justice[1] as well as on social institutions that are crucial to ensuring that distributive justice takes place. This book aspires to present the material coherently and includes some unique features. The book advances some conclusions that are meant to stimulate the reader towards thinking through the implications of the chapter. This is also intended to encourage the reader to ask new questions and consider new issues. We believe that the chapters are intellectually rigorous enough to excite curiosity, while stimulating critical thinking as they lead readers to question the relationship between education, democracy and social justice which might have been taken for granted. The pedagogical design of the book focuses on controversies and debates to stimulate thinking and critical reflection on what is at stake in the presented issues. The book discourages a simple 'assimilation of facts', as such 'facts' differ from situation to situation and are ever changing.

This book was developed from the teaching and research experience of the authors. We have taught educational and social science subjects in a number of universities. We have also interacted with university lecturers and researchers who have an extensive interest in educational issues. The problems associated with education and democracy have been widely discussed. It was generally agreed that there was a need for a book that debated the education-democracy nexus in the southern African context in general and in Namibia specifically, and which resonated with researchers within the region. As scholars and lecturers, we have also over the years been confronted with a lack of appropriate literature, especially for post-graduate students, making the writing of this book both necessary and timely.

---

[1] The [socio-economic] framework that each society has – its laws, institutions, policies, etc. – results in different distributions of economic benefits and burdens across members of the society. These [socio-economic] frameworks are the result of human political processes and they change constantly over time, both across and within societies. The structure of these frameworks is important because the economic distributions resulting from them affect people's lives fundamentally. Arguments about which frameworks and/or resulting distributions are morally preferable constitute the topic of distributive justice. Principles of distributive justice are therefore best thought of as providing moral guidance for the political processes and structures that affect the distribution of economic benefits and burdens in societies (Lamont & Favor, 2016).

The recent work by Allen and Reich (2013) has ably linked the three concepts of justice, democracy and education, placed within an American context. Thus, there is still a shortage of literature that unites all three concepts from an African perspective. This book is an attempt to fill that lacuna. It is intended to be a primary text for courses in education, politics and sociology. It may also be useful as a supplementary text to students of social studies. In general, it will benefit researchers, post-graduates and undergraduates, and can serve as background reading or reference material for those interested in Namibian studies.

The Organisation of the Book

Chapter 2 sets the tone for this book, by outlining theoretical perspectives on the relationship between the concepts of democracy, education and social justice. The author defines these three concepts and shows how they are interlinked. She further delineates the philosophical foundations for education which are portrayed from various philosophical points of view in answer to the question of whether education needs a philosophical base in order to augment democracy and contribute to the course of social justice.

Chapter 3 outlines general conceptual issues related to democracy, education and social justice. The chapter attempts specifically to determine the relationship between education and democracy. To achieve this, Mufune interrogates existing literature that argues from three different positions, namely:

1. That more education leads to more democracy at societal level;
2. That the argument above is prejudiced; and
3. That school is hierarchical and non-democratic and can therefore not promote democracy.

The ensuing process of analysis leads him to confirm the observation made in Chapter 2, that there are many forms of democracy, including the elitist, pluralist and republican. In light of the contending views, he concludes that it would be more meaningful to think in terms of different types of democracy and link them to the concept of education as a way of understanding the relationship between the two notions.

Chapter 4 serves to delineate the aims of education in a democratic society by examining the views of selected educational thinkers from both the western world and the Southern countries respectively. In this context, the author considers the works of Greek philosophers, other western philosophers and African theorists. The analysis provides varied concepts of the role and place of education for the individual and society respectively. Just as the issue of justice was important to Plato, who lived in a highly undemocratic Greek society, the post-colonial African educational thinkers have been preoccupied with the issue of how education could contribute to socio-economic development.

Chapter 5 focuses on the relationship between democratic values, norms and education in post-colonial societies. Like the previous authors, Iijambo acknowledges the existence of differing views on democracy and apportions these differences to distinct cultures, norms, values and aspirations. His point of departure is a view that democracy, as a political system separate from the economic system, must include basic principles of participation, transparency, flexibility and tolerance. In general, he places his trust in the capacity of education to improve democratic practices within society, by instilling values of responsibility, tolerance and moral judgement.

Chapter 6 scrutinises the aims of education in pre-colonial, colonial and post-colonial Namibia. It becomes clear that a particular historical juncture, coupled with the political, economic and cultural reality of any given society, contributes to the shaping and determining of the aims of education in society.

When Namibia moved towards consolidating its political independence in the 21st Century, the aims of education changed further towards making a contribution towards the development of an aspiring knowledge-based economy – what Amukugo sees as a move fuelled by a technocratic view of education.

Chapter 7 addresses the importance of democracy, human rights and freedoms in education. Citing Plato, who saw the ends of democracy as being liberty, equality and variety, and Aristotle, who emphasised that democracy should be manifested in any democratic education (Rusk & Scotland, 1979), Lilemba argues that it is through democratic education that people are encouraged to participate in the running and decision-making exercises of the schools.

The author proceeds from the premise that democracy is about adhering to the common values of society, while at the same time respecting the 'freedom' of others. He interprets human rights as entitlements that encapsulate civil and political rights on the one hand, and economic and cultural rights on the other hand. Placing education under the latter, Lilemba argues that democracy, human rights and education are intertwined and together help to create an environment conducive to developing learners into responsible citizens.

The author also discusses in detail how Namibia reflects what he sees as the contradictions between democracy, human rights and education, and suggests alternatives to minimise those contradictions.

Chapter 8 makes a case for democratic education and how its fundamentals can bring to bear a more inclusive education through creating opportunities for all. Advancing a social-psychological view of the term, Brown and Haihambo define inclusive education as a value system that recognises and appreciates diversity in its multiple forms – a moral issue of human rights and values that can contribute to the creation of an inclusive society.

The authors point out that a general problem of attitudes within society represents a real threat to moving towards a more inclusive educational system. They believe that changing attitudes, especially of teachers, can help to improve the situation. Thus, success towards change presupposes that the school system be reformed in a way that enables teachers to accept diversity more readily as well as to learn to cherish it.

Chapter 9 deals with the issue of institutionally based violence with special emphasis on sexual harassment in institutions of higher learning in general and the University of Namibia in particular. Edwards-Jauch and Namupala observe that many people do not understand why sexual harassment specifically and sexual violence in general are related to social justice. They reduce the issue of sexual violence to an issue of safety, dressing modestly and an avoidance of strangers on the part of women. But sexual violence and harassment is more profound than that. Sexual harassment is a social justice issue because it violates human rights and rests on disparities in power which are tied to the subordinate position of women in society. According to McDonald and Flood (2012), sexual harassment is a diverse form of gendered mistreatment, which reflects and reinforces inequalities between men and women at places of work and learning. As such, sexual harassment should be seen as a profound and damaging injustice in the workplace. In this context, sexual violence and sexual harassment in particular against females form only part of broader social injustices. This chapter is included because the combating of sexual violence and sexual harassment at places of work and learning is crucial to achieving social justice. Using a Feminist Action Research method, the authors proceed from the view that sexual harassment, as a form of gender-based violence, not only reflects broader social inequalities, but also exposes how aspects of silence, fear and intimidation represent undemocratic and patriarchal cultures within universities.

Chapter 10 concludes by highlighting major suppositions made by different authors on pertinent issues addressed in the various chapters.

Rationale behind the Focus Questions preceding each chapter

In line with the main theme of this book, readers are encouraged to engage with the ideas presented as critical thinkers. Therefore, to avoid a situation where readers simply accept prescribed facts, through these focus questions readers can be engaged inductively, and thereby encouraged to participate in the process of analysing and evaluating the issues related to democracy and education.

In order to achieve this engagement and stimulate critical thinking, the questions are designed to invoke the higher order critical thinking skills such as application, analysis, comparison and contrast, synthesis and evaluation. This empowering approach is designed to help students and educators think creatively through and beyond what is presented here, and in line with the book's aims, to become agents of change and improvement in the education systems in their countries after reading this book.

Since the material presented in the book is profoundly academic, and the vocabulary will be complex to some readers, these Focus Questions have purposefully been designed with a light approach, starting with readers' opinions and what they already know and care about, in order to peak readers' interest, make the material relevant to their experience and needs, and warm up their thinking to the more challenging concepts and terminology in the chapters. Furthermore, the Focus Questions serve to point out to readers some of the main areas on which to focus their attention in each chapter. The questions become more and more challenging as the book progresses and should lead to animated group discussions.

References

Allen, D. & Reich, R. (Eds.). (2013). *Education, justice and democracy.* Chicago: University of Chicago Press.

Amukugo, E. M., Likando, G. N., & Mushaandja, J. (2010). Access and quality dilemma in education: Implication for Namibia Vision 2030. *Higher Education Forum (RIHE)*, 7, 101–112.

Amukugo, E. M. (2002). Education for all in independent Namibia: Reality or political ideal? In V. Winterfeldt, T. Fox and P. Mufune (Eds.), *Namibia, society, sociology.* (pp. 239–251). Windhoek: University of Namibia Press.

Dewey, J. (2010). *Democracy and education: An introduction to the philosophy of education.* Lexington, KY: BLN Publishing.

Dowding, K., Goodin, R. E., & Pateman, C. (Eds.). (2004). *Justice & democracy*. Cambridge: Cambridge University Press.

Furman, G. C. & Shields, C. M. (2005). How can educational leaders promote and support social justice and democratic community in schools? In W. A. Firestone & C. Riehl (Eds.), *A new agenda for research in educational leadership* (pp. 119–137), New York, N. Y.: Teachers College Press.

Government of the Republic of Namibia [GRN]. (1999). *Presidential commission on education, culture and training*. Windhoek: Gamsberg Macmillan.

Lamont, J. & Favor, C. (2016). "Distributive Justice". In E. N. Zalta (Ed.), The Stanford encyclopaedia of philosophy (Winter 2016 ed.). Retrieved from http://plato.stanford.edu/entries/justice-distributive/

McDonald, P. & Flood, M. (2012). *Encourage. Support. Act! Bystander approaches to sexual harassment in the workplace*. Retrieved from http://ro.uow.edu.au/cgi/viewcontent.cgi?article=2968&context=artspapers

Ministry of Education and Culture, Namibia [MEC]. (1993). *Toward education for all: A development brief for education, culture, and training*. Windhoek: Gamsberg Macmillan.

Rusk, R. R. & Scotland, J. (1979). *Doctrines of the great educators* (5th ed.). New York: St. Martin's Press.

World Bank. (2005). Namibia – Education and Training Sector Improvement Program (ETSIP). Washington D. C.: World Bank Group. Retrieved from http://documents.worldbank.org/curated/en/142631468062936389/Namibia-Education-and-Training-Sector-Improvement-Program-ETSIP

2

Democracy, education and social justice: Theoretical perspectives

Elizabeth Magano Amukugo

Before you read this chapter, examine your own thinking by answering these questions:

1. How important is it for education in Africa to do the following?

(Write Very/Not Very/ or Moderately)

a. be relevant enough to all learners that it will help them gain sustainable livelihoods.
b. be available to and provide equally and equitably for all learners in society regardless of gender, race, economic group, or ability level
c. be monitored and accountable to all public groups in the society
d. develop the mind, thinking capacity and critical consciousness of youth
e. train citizens to take action based on an informed position
f. focus on all round development of the human being
g. prepare youth for life in the future
h. be an instrument of liberation by awakening learners' capacity to fight for justice and change what is wrong in society
i. teach youth to question existing knowledge

2. In your opinion which three of the above educational goals are most important for your country?

3. Add two additional goals you think are critical to your country's education system.

HOW DEMOCRACY RELATES TO EDUCATION AND SOCIAL JUSTICE

> Normative thinking around democracy often emphasises the supremacy of electoral politics, underplaying the salience of education as a defining feature to produce a more meaningful, engaged, inclusive form of democracy. (Paul R. Carr, 2010, p. 2)

It is a common understanding that democracy is a system of governance in which members of an institution/organisation or society partake directly or indirectly in a decision-making process and through their participation, can exercise control over decision-making on issues that affect their lives. This definition is, however, limited and raises more questions than answers. Who participates; what are the terms of such participation; to what extent does such participation influence the decisions taken on behalf of those being led; and, more importantly, of what benefit is that participation to those who are not directly part of the decision-making group? Ake (2000, p. 185) regards this concept of democracy as '... a simple liberal democracy based on a multi-party electoral competition'. This, he argues, is not only the least appropriate type of democracy that corresponds to African social reality, but it would also be less helpful, unless it is accompanied by structural democratisation, including reorganisation of the state in a way that guarantees democratic outcomes emanating from the democratic processes. The most important outcomes, he suggests, are concrete economic rights, as opposed to abstract political rights, and addressing economic inequalities which limit the democratic participation of the poor.

Amukugo (2013) observed that liberal democracy accompanied by market economic models spread like wildfire in Africa during the 1990s and into the 21st Century. Its introduction, however, was seen by various social scientists such as Ake (1993, 1996, 2000), Amukugo (1998, 2013), Mafeje (2002) and Sankatsing (2004), as having been responsible for much social wretchedness across Africa. In this respect, Mafeje (2002) points out that:

> ... While liberal democracy upholds the principle of equality of all citizens in front of the law, it does not address the question of social equity. Accordingly, it is unable to deal with some of the major issues that have come to haunt contemporary society such as increasing poverty globally and intolerable social injustice within nations and among nations. Indeed, it is highly handicapped because the theory of laissez-faire on which it is founded obliges it to accept such phenomena as poverty and social inequality among citizens and nations as a natural outcome of the right of the individual to choose (Mafeje, 2002, p. 11).

Amukugo (1998) shares a similar view to Mafeje by suggesting that liberal democracy's thrust to uphold equilibrium within society without achieving equality in the economic sphere, coupled with a tendency to present facts in a fragmented way instead of providing an integrated, holistic picture, impedes society's capacity to change in a comprehensive manner. Shivji (2003) goes a step further by suggesting that social change is not just a matter of explication, but is essentially a matter of real life. Thus, while he criticises liberal democracy's discourse as being based on pretence rather than reality, he emphasises the fact that the struggle for democracy is ultimately embedded in the life-conditions of the people.

Focusing on the issue of socio-economic development, Ake (2000), who sees liberal democracy and the market as having the same core values that place the market over the state and economics over politics, also holds the view that liberal democracy played a role in preventing socio-economic development in Africa. As such, Ake (1996, p. 1) rightly observes that '… by all indications, political conditions in Africa are the greatest impediment to development…'. Ake (2000) argues further that liberal democracy not only repudiates popular power, it also ensures the rights of the individual, something that appeases the emerging African bourgeois. He delineates the concept of democracy from a historical perspective. According to him, the pluralist view that argues against the viability of 'classical democracy' and 'representative democracy' suggests that ordinary people cannot exercise substantive influence in politics due to ignorance, apathy and lack of power and resources. At the same time, people's political representatives mostly lead as they wish, manipulating and dominating the led instead of representing their interests. Consequently, democracy in pluralistic terms is reduced to a mere pursuit of competitive interest groups.

Another school of thought, according to Ake, is the protectionist view, which expounds the idea of a minimal state and government. In this, the state is regarded as a threat to the people's freedom while civil society is seen as a vibrant force, the purpose of which is to protect the people from the state. Airing a critical view against the protectionist stance, Ake (2000, p. 21) suggests that the implication of the protectionist theory is that democracy ceases to be '… about active self-determination or involvement in the collective enterprise of democratic citizenship but about securing immunities against [state] threat'.

Another theory of democracy is the economic notion, which suggests that democracy is mainly about '… the struggle for wealth, power, and office, and that any social outcome in politics is incidental', since those who compete/participate in democratic politics have their focus and interest on 'utility outcomes' rather than realising an ideal or public policy (Ake, 2000, p. 210). Moreover, Ake argues that the development of capitalism and, by consequence, monopoly capitalism, led to a situation whereby liberal democracy did away with political participation in a significant way and instead promoted competitive elitism. Yet, as Amukugo (2013) explains, democracy can contribute to social change if people are provided with more possibilities for participation in governance and thereby influence policy decisions affecting their lives, instead of merely voting every five years. Given the above, can modern representative democracy help to curb the shortcomings of a democratic system?

Sankatsing (2004) argues that the democratic appropriation of power in a liberal democratic set-up does not necessarily translate into a democratic exercise of authority or governing in the people's interest. To the contrary, historically liberal democracy has meant that:

> … individual-endorsed control of governance and rule over all by vested or new elites derived from the mobilization of existing allegiance or from induced consent. It authorizes control of collective assets and command of the destiny of society through individualized electoral process, based on the tenet that a society can be represented fairly by the aggregate of its individual and the arithmetic sum of their votes …. Under the banner of democracy, individual-based majority rule typically combined elite affluence with widespread misery asphyxiating any real option for development … (Sankatsing, 2004, p. 4).

The above analysis suggests that an alternative to liberal democracy needs to be found in order to achieve social equity and combat 'widespread misery' or poverty, which is still evident in most African countries today. This is crucial in the light of what Ake (2000) understands as the yearning of the ordinary African to achieve democracy as 'the second independence' from their own leaders, which would offer them political empowerment, get the economic agenda on track and bring about concrete economic and social rights. Ake (1993), for example, implores that for African democracy to be relevant, it has to '... de-emphasize abstract political rights and stress concrete economic rights, because the demand for democracy in Africa draws much of its impetus from the prevailing economic conditions within'.

The demand for concrete economic rights places the notion of social justice at the centre of democracy. This holds true if one defines the concept of 'state' as a social collective, the major aim of which is to promote socio-economic development. In this regard, democracy would be about the state's capacity to create a socially just society, where citizenship does not mean voting rights only but also other fundamental human rights, such as legal and socio-economic rights. Thus, democracy should not be an end in itself, but rather a process by means of which the goals of equality,[1] equity[2] and justice in a given society are realised. This in turn presupposes the active participation of citizens.

Education is at the core of such participation as it raises people's capacity to realise their full potential. Therefore, if and when education serves as a tool for developing critical consciousness about social reality, and when such awareness is used to act and bring about social change, then education would have a real meaning for democracy as it would both increase democratic participation as well as contribute to socio-economic development. This critical concept of education generates a link between knowledge, action and social change as observed by Giroux (2009, p. 46), and a more applied concept of education and democracy as suggested by Carr and Hartnett that:

> The task of cultivating in pupils the knowledge, skills and attitudes necessary for public participation requires a curriculum which fosters those forms of critical and political knowledge which allow pupils to reappraise existing social norms and reflect critically on the dominant social, political and economic institutions of contemporary society. Pedagogically, it requires participatory rather than instructional teaching methods in order to cultivate skills and attitudes which democratic deliberation requires (Carr & Hartnett, 1996, p. 42).

In other words, both content and practice are crucial if education is to serve as a tool for democracy. But would education, so perceived, serve to promote social justice?

It is important at this juncture to take note of a caution by Brian Barry (as cited in Dowding, Goodin, & Pateman, 2004, p. 5) that a democratic system would not necessarily be a just one. Barry elaborates his point by suggesting that:

---

[1] From a liberal democracy viewpoint, the term equality means 'sameness' in legalistic terms. Not only is everyone equal before the law, but also equal in terms of the opportunity to succeed or fail in a societal context.

[2] Equality in legalistic terms would, in our understanding, be insufficient without equity, which, as Arnaud, cited in Herrera, 2007, p. 323, suggests: '... call[s] for deliberate efforts to reduce inequalities, to deal with factors that cause or perpetuate them, and to promote a fairer sharing of resources'.

> ...there is nothing inherent in democracy that necessarily makes it just. Democracy is a procedure for formally capturing the views of the citizens and translating them into outcomes. That procedure has only tangential connections to the outcomes being just. Furthermore, the justification of... 'the majority principle' should lead us to accept its results even when we think the outcomes [are] unjust.

This means that constitutional provision for democratic representation does not automatically lead to achieving social justice, as the latter depends mainly on the social structure of a given society.

Dowding (2004) nevertheless concludes by saying that in the final analysis, democratic procedures are more likely to maintain a socially just society. Dowding observes further that '[t]heories of justice tend to set out conditions of distribution of rights, welfare, resources, primary goods, capabilities or whatever (hereafter the "distributandum")' (Dowding, 2004, p. 28). In this respect, theories of justice basically focus on 'just institutions of society'. Dowding cautions, however, that just as in the case of democratic procedures, just institutions do not always secure 'just outcomes' (2004, p. 32). Thus, injustices that result from the way in which these institutions function will ultimately necessitate 'legitimate arguments' for changing these institutions. In the main, Dowding holds that the basis for justice lies in developing 'the basic structure of society and political institutions' (2004, p. 29). He observes further that while 'liberalism' has succeeded in defining universal practices for equal treatment, it fails to develop a theory of the state. This apparent gap, argues Dowding, is the reason why liberals, for example, find it difficult to deal with conflicts in divided societies (2004, p. 23). It can be said, therefore, that since it is possible for a democratic society to produce injustices through institutions of the state, education can also be an unjust institution. To borrow from a conflict viewpoint, education can serve '...the interests of the powerful. It maintains their power, justifies their privilege and legitimizes their wealth' (Haralambos & Holborn, 2008, p. 602). These views suggest that the concepts democracy, education and social justice are indeed complex.

Sen (2009) suggests that teaching, learning and graduate formation is a crucial location for '...advancing justice or reducing injustice in the world' (Sen, 2009, p. 337). As Marginson (2011) observed, Sen (2009) identified two distinct approaches to social justice based on notions of 'fairness' and 'inclusion' respectively. Tikly (2011) agrees with this distinction, and using insights from Sen's (2009) capability approach, identifies three interrelated principles for evaluating social justice in education systems:

1. The first is that 'education should be inclusive', not only in terms of 'access to the necessary resources to learn but also to overcoming economic, social and cultural barriers that prevent individuals and groups from converting these resources into desired outcomes or functioning'.
2. The second principle is that 'a quality education must be relevant, i.e. that learning outcomes must contribute to sustainable livelihoods and wellbeing for all learners, must be valued by their communities and consistent with national development priorities in a changing global context.'
3. The third principle is that 'education should be democratic in the sense that learning outcomes are determined through public debate and ensured through processes of accountability.'

The above principles encapsulate key aspects that bind democracy, education and social justice, namely: access, equity, quality and relevance. Moreover, these principles also link the idea of capability, education and social justice. Sen (2009, p. 326) argues that the two concepts of justice and democracy share discursive features. Sen insists on the role of public reasoning in determining what constitutes social justice. He argues that the demands of justice can only be assessed through public reasoning since the formation of values is both reasoned and interactive. Thus for Sen, there is really no justice without discussion. According to Walker (2010, p. 494), 'Sen (2009) gives some indirect helpful curriculum and pedagogical guidance in that he ascribes a central role to our powers of "public reasoning" as a moral and political imperative. The advancement of justice depends on democracy – deepening democracy depends on discussion and collective reasoning that injects more information and knowledge, diverse perspectives and plural voices into debates'. This is where education comes in. Universities and school systems are crucial to developing capabilities that enable individuals to engage in public reasoning. It is through the school system that individuals and groups of individuals develop capacities to scrutinise and assess how society performs. This implies open debate on the values and principles underlying societal processes. As Walker (2010, p. 494) puts it 'discussion and voice are important because understanding the demands of justice is not a solitary exercise'. 'When we try to assess how we should behave, and what kind of societies should be understood to be patently unjust, we have reason to listen and pay some attention to the views and suggestions of others' (Sen, as cited in Walker, 2010, p. 494). Thus, 'critical inquiry/discussion practices ought to produce justice or at least reduce injustice, for example by developing graduates with critical knowledge, critical self-reflection and the capacity to act in the world' (Walker, 2010, p. 494).

One important question for this book is whether education needs a solid philosophical base in order to enhance democracy. The following sub-section discusses various philosophical bases for education, democracy and justice.

Philosophical foundations for democracy, education and social justice

Materialism

From a materialist perspective, democracy is viewed as bourgeois terminology – a system of power that officially subjects the minority to majority will, and asserts equality and freedom for all, without necessarily linking these formal attributes to prevailing socio-economic reality (Saifulin & Dixon, 1984). From this standpoint, the aim of education would be twofold: firstly, to produce 'fully developed human beings' by linking education with productive work and thereby narrowing the gap between intellectual activity and manual labour; and secondly to systematically develop consciousness (the capacity to perceive things the way they are in reality, including societal injustices). Consciousness is perceived in this context as providing human beings with the curiosity to search for knowledge and with the ability to understand the 'root causes' of matter (reality); and using that awareness to take action based on an informed position (Castles & Wüstenberg, 1979; Volkov, 1982).

Amartya Sen, mentioned earlier, is a recent materialist philosopher and economist, and a 1998 Nobel Prize winner. His famous book, *The Idea of Justice*, set out to scrutinise what he termed the 'realization-based comparisons', based on the key question of how justice was to be advanced (Sen, 2009, p. 8). In Sen's view, such a consideration would facilitate the 'realization-focused' understanding of justice, and by consequence, necessitate the need to focus on 'actual realizations and accomplishments' in society. This is, to him, contrary to the question of what perfectly just institutions would be. The latter question reflects what he calls the 'transcendental-focused' comprehension of justice, which centres on 'the establishment of what are identified as the right institutions and rules' (ibid., p. 9). In Sen's view, the transcendental approach fits in with current political philosophical tradition which places emphasis on the 'just society' – a perfectly just social arrangement (institutions, regulations and behavioural rules), spearheaded by John Rawls. Sen's approach to justice on the other hand, bears comparison with classical 'social realization' theorists such as Adam Smith, Karl Marx and John Stuart Mill, among others, whose common thread compared existing societies, and even what might be emerging in society, including the sort of life that people could actually live (ibid., pp. 7–10).

What implications would the above philosophical viewpoint have for education? The father of transcendentalism, Ralph W. Emerson, emphasised the concept of 'Self-Reliance'. At the centre of this concept lies the significance of the individual (a commonality with liberalism) and his/her intellectual development. In this, he supported individualism. He viewed most citizens as being conformists, who sacrifice their liberty and culture to gain security. To the individual therefore, '[n]on-conformity to society is the ultimate action of a self-reliant person, while conformity is the converse of self-reliance' (Carbone II, 2010).

If individualism is at the centre of transcendentalism, and given Emerson's emphasis on 'self-reliance', it would not be wrong to conclude that in terms of educational philosophy, the individual should be a master of his/her own learning. The right-based approach to education would also be appealing to transcendentalists. As argued by Rajapakse (2016), 'the right-based discourse to education is perceived as a human right, in keeping with their liberal, democratic political and social systems, [and] Anglo-Saxon education models'. This model further embraces the 'human capital' theory of education, in accordance with which, education is meant to provide knowledge and skills as an investment that yields both private and social returns.'

On the other hand, on the basis of Sen's analysis of the transcendental-focused theory of justice, transcendentalism would encourage the development of educational institutions that focus on learners' behaviour, moral uprightness and the promotion of equal rights for all.

Contrary to the transcendental line of thinking, the realization-focused approach to justice, of which Sen is a stern advocate, would put emphasis on achieving not only equal rights, but more importantly, equity and fairness, and an educational content that promotes critical consciousness and all-round development of learners (skills, aesthetic appreciation and inculcation of core social values). Physical development through sports and physical education would add to the all-round development of learners. Thus, whilst transcendentalism places education within a narrow scope with the individual at the centre, the realization-focused approach places education within the broader socio-economic context. In summary, a materialist educational philosophy would address access (universal education for all) as well as the development of critical consciousness as opposed to mere intellectual development, and the role of education as an instrument of social change for the common good rather than for the individual.

Idealism

Idealism is said to be the oldest western systematic philosophy. It can be traced back to ancient Greece. As a metaphysical theory of the nature of reality, idealism is based on an ideological position that all things in the universe are an expression of the mind and that ideas are the only true reality. The father of idealism, Plato, suggested in *The Republic of Plato* that true reality exists in the realm of ideas, which is beyond the material world (the world of physical things). To Plato, education is about rediscovering what is already within an individual, and we should hence build on that innate capacity – turning the eye of the soul from darkness to light (Plato, Book VII: 518 c-e). He believed that society would be better off with enlightened leaders, developed through education (Plato, Book V: 473 d-e). From an idealist perspective, therefore, the primary purpose of education should be to develop the individual's capacity to think and shape his/her personality. Democracy would then be about achieving 'equality of opportunity' in the socio-economic sphere, of which education is a part. The notion of 'equality of opportunity' originated from an idealist view in accordance with which it signifies enjoying inherent equal rights and receiving equal treatment before the law.

In the context of education, equality of opportunity would be achieved by giving each child access (in legal terms) to education; and thereby creating an opportunity for all to realise their innate potential. But, as Evetts (1970) points out, the notion of 'equal educational opportunity' raises more problems. Referring to the English education system during the 20th Century, she suggests that the term has been used to support an educational elite – 'the nation's intellectual resources' – at the expense of the majority who, by virtue of attaining low level IQ[3] results, were channelled into practically oriented study lines (Evetts, 1970). Another critic of the 'equality of opportunity' view, Demaine (2001), terms this a weak liberal definition of justice. He quotes Lynch, who points out that '[u]nequal results are justified if everyone has an equal opportunity to succeed' (as cited in Demaine, 2001, p. 52). Lynch further points to the limit of the above concept in that it fails to address key issues of 'hierarchies of power, wealth and other privileges' (as cited in Demaine, 2001, p. 52). One can argue, therefore, that equality of opportunity-based policies can be discriminatory. In terms of education, idealism serves to address the aspects of access and equality (sameness) in education without addressing the notion of equity (equitable redistribution of resources – financial, human and material). This shortcoming is in turn reflected in both the level and quality of educational outcome across socio-economic barriers.

In view of the above supposition one can conclude that whilst materialism regards the concepts of equity and justice as a pre-condition for democratic practice in the socio-economic realm, idealism underscores 'equality of opportunity' in legalistic terms as an indication of democracy. Both views have consequences for educational policy and practice.

The second major philosophical thought in this context is that of 'modern idealism', which dates from the 15th Century and was characterised by 'systematisation' and 'subjectivism'. Major exponents of modern idealism include René Descartes, George Berkeley and Immanuel Kant, among others.

Descartes's most outstanding works include *Discourse on Method of Rightly Conducting One's Reason* and *Meditation on First Philosophy*. In *Discourse*, Descartes coined his famous words in 1637: *cogito, ergo sum* (Latin), which means 'I think, therefore I am'. Descartes regarded this as

---

[3] Intelligence quotient (IQ) tests refer to a genetically based 'ceiling' of ability and have been used for centuries as a means of channelling students into practical versus theoretical pathways within a given educational system.

the first principle of philosophy he was seeking (Descartes, 1637, Part 4). In this, he explored the 'methodical doubt' by means of which he doubted himself and everything else and, through that exploration, arrived at *cogito, ergo sum*, which basically means that our existence depends on our thinking capacity – without thinking, you are not a human being. It can then be argued in this respect, that the major aim of education is to develop the mind and, by consequence, the thinking capacity.

Berkeley's major ideas have been developed through his treatises on philosophy. One prominent treatise is *The Principles of Human knowledge* (Berkley, 1710/2004). In this he contends that all existence hinges on the mind to know it; and that nothing exists unless the mind perceives it. By this, Berkeley challenged the materialist view that the materialist world exists in reality irrespective of whether the mind perceives it or not.

Kant developed his philosophy of idealism in two major works, namely *The Critique of Pure Reason* (Kant, 1781/2007) and *The Critique of Practical Reason* (Kant, 1788/2014). In *The Critique of Pure Reason*, Kant challenged the 'rationalist view in accordance with which knowledge could be deduced from universal truths'. In *The Critique of Practical Reason*, he criticised the empiricists' emphasis on experience as the source of knowledge. In Kant's understanding, the two distinct views, the rationalists' analytic position and the empiricists' synthetic thinking, were not useful. It is from a critical analysis of the two positions that he developed a system of 'human thought processes based on *a priori* (analytic) and *posteriori* (synthetic) reasoning. In this way, he argued, reliable knowledge of human experience can be developed firmly based on scientific laws of nature. Both philosophical thoughts then could be combined into one unified system.

Kant's idealism differed somewhat from that of Descartes's and Berkeley's in that Kant did not focus only on the mind, but sought to combine the abstract (*a priori*) with empiricism. Nonetheless all three philosophers are united in placing the mind above matter, which qualifies them to belong to the philosophy of idealism.

In general, however, all idealist philosophers agree on one thing: that the aim of education is first and foremost to develop the mind and character of the individual. This differs from the materialist philosophers who stress the all-round development of a human being (Castles & Wüstenburg, 1979; Volkov, 1982).

Pragmatism

Pragmatism as a philosophical approach developed in the latter part of 19th Century America through the works of Pierce, James and Dewey. It is based mainly on a principle that 'meaning' and 'truth' depend on the applicability of ideas, and that 'an ideology or proposition is true if it works satisfactorily', provided that the proposition's meaning will be located in the 'practical consequence' of its acceptance, and that unpractical ideas be rejected (Pragmatism, 2006). This stance bears similarity to the positivist/empiricist doctrine, which, according to Auguste Comte (as cited in Lenzer, 1997, p. x) holds that true knowledge is that which can describe and explain observable phenomena.

Although James is credited as the first person who used the term pragmatism (Pragmatism, 2006; 2008), it was, in our view, John Dewey who perfected the term and finally became known as the father of pragmatism. Dewey (1916/2010) developed the term further and suggested among other things that:

> Plasticity or the power to learn from experience means the formation of habits ....
> Active habits involve thought, invention and initiative in applying capacities to
> new aims. They are opposed to routine which marks an arrest of growth (Dewey,
> 1916/2010, p. 36).

Dewey's concept of growth, for example, added more depth to the simple analogy between ideas and practice. It is from the observation above that Dewey built the notion of education as growth, a theory he later developed into the concept 'education as experience'. In *Experience and Education* (1938/1997), Dewey posited that:

> ... amid all uncertainties there is one permanent frame of reference: namely,
> the organic connection between education and personal experience ... (Dewey,
> 1938/1997, p. 25).

He was, however, quick to caution that not all experiences result in education, since some experiences may be 'miseducative'. As is clear in Dewey (1916/2010), the purpose of education is not to prepare the young for life in some distant future, but rather to help reorganise their experience in such a way as to add meaning and create continued growth.

With regards to democracy, Dewey argued that the link between democracy and education was strong in that more education helps to improve democratic governance. To this end, Dewey (1916/2010, p. 56) professed that:

> The devotion of democracy to education is a familiar fact. The superficial
> explanation is that a government resting upon popular suffrage cannot be
> successful unless those who elect and who obey their governors are educated.
> Since a democratic society repudiates the principal of external authority, it must
> find a substitute in voluntary disposition and interest; these can be created only
> by education.

In Dewey's view, education contributes to the continued growth of the individual as a member of society and it can enhance democracy if education is made available to all members of society. Dewey obviously sees the role of education as developing the individual's personality, shaping character and developing awareness of important issues. Thus, through education, citizens develop the ability to make informed decisions – a practical utility of education. This would, in our view, depend on whether education functions as a socialisation agency that assists individuals in internalising sets of democratic ethos, norms and values, in addition to creating capacity through knowledge and skills.

Critical theory

Critical theory is a social theory which applies 'critique' as a mode of investigation. Its major aim is to create a better understanding of social reality and thereby create conditions for social change. Its roots originate from a philosophical and social theoretical tradition known as the Frankfurt School. Founded in the early years of the 20th Century, its primary aim was to make a meaningful contribution to the struggle against all forms of domination (Darder, Baltodano, & Torres, 2009). Horkheimer, who coined the term 'critical theory', suggested that a theory qualifies as critical if it strives for 'human emancipation' (as cited in Bohman, 2005). However, this view is limited, as human emancipation in itself is not enough to bring about social justice unless it is accompanied by practical action. As Bohman rightly observed, however, three criteria must be met in order to make critical theory suitable for the purpose: namely, that it should be explanatory, practical and normative. In other words, it should explicate the shortcomings within existing social reality, establish the actors for changing the situation, and offer both standards and attainable goals for social change (Bohman, 2005). Thus, critical theory's main aim is not merely social critique but more importantly to interpret contemporary social reality and to suggest alternatives based on an insightful depiction of the current situation.

In his analysis of 'citizenship education', a major proponent of critical theory, Giroux (1980, p. 331), articulated the difference between 'old rationality' and 'new rationality' and suggested that in order for citizenship education to contribute to the creation of a just society, the relationship between school and broader society needs to be redefined. This implies moving away from stressing issues of 'technique, objectivity and control' (a positivistic scientific approach) to a rationality that leans on 'understanding and critique' (Giroux, 1980, p. 331). In this context, Giroux criticises the traditional and liberal concept of education for emphasising the aspect of 'historical continuities and development'. He instead proposes that the critical mode of inquiry provides an alternative view of education that is placed firmly in a historical context, that '…stresses the break, discontinuities and tensions in history, all of which become valuable in that they highlight the centrality of human agency and struggle while simultaneously revealing the gap between society as it presently exists and society as it might be"' (Giroux, 2009, p. 47). In other words, the mode of critique not only helps us to better understand human activities, including education, it also presents us with an opportunity to look critically at the current socio-economic reality with a view to planning for a better future.

An eminent critical theory voice from the South is that of the Brazilian educator, Paulo Freire, whose first-hand experience with hunger during the Great Depression of the 1930s helped to shape his genuine association with and concern for the disadvantaged within society. His famous book *Pedagogy of the Oppressed* expanded its reach throughout the world, as it succinctly elucidates how education can serve as both an instrument of oppression (banking concept of education) as well as of liberation (education for 'conscientisation'). He explains clearly that:

> Whereas banking education anesthetizes and inhibits creative power, problem-posing education involves a constant unveiling of reality. The former attempts to maintain the submersion of consciousness; the latter strives for the emergence of consciousness and critical intervention in reality (Freire, 1996, p. 62).

He illuminates the above point further by saying that:

> 'conscientisation' is viable only because men's consciousness, although conditioned, can recognize that it is conditioned. This 'critical' dimension of consciousness accounts for the goals men assign to their transforming acts upon the world (Freire, 1985, pp. 69–70).

In Freire's view, education can enhance that critical dimension of consciousness. Placing education firmly within a social context, Freire (1996) illustrates how illiteracy and banking education are products of an unjust social order where injustice, exploitation, poverty and despair dehumanise the poor and rob them of their humanity. Education, he proposes, can restore a people's humanity by providing tools for people to critically analyse and perceive reality and thereby take action to change material reality rather than being conditioned by it. In this way democracy and justice are augmented through education for 'conscientisation' that provides many with the capacity to develop both 'self-knowledge and knowledge of the world'; and to use that knowledge in both democratic participation as well as in fighting for justice.

In this respect, Torres (n.d.) attempts to analyse the relationship between education and social justice from a Freirean perspective. In accordance with this view, democracy implies conceptualising 'democratic citizenship' in a way that allows citizens to participate in the democratic process as active beings, who are at the same time knowledgeable in democratic politics and fully aware of their democratic rights and obligations.

It can be said, therefore, that Freire's educational philosophy incorporates economic, social and educational issues upon which his ideas on democracy and justice rest. As McLaren and Leonard (1993, p. 25) observed:

> This pedagogy challenges teachers and students to empower themselves for social change, to advance democracy and equality as they advance their literacy and knowledge. His [Freire's] critical methods ask teachers and students to question existing knowledge as part of questioning habits appropriate for citizens in a democracy.

Education for critical consciousness then is a fundamental concept within the educational philosophy of critical theory because it is expected to enhance both democracy and social justice, since it leads to action that is crucial to achieving social change (social, economic, political and cultural).

The feminist perspective

Feminism developed out of recognition that, historically, women have been oppressed. It is a broad term covering a multitude of ideas about male and female relations within society. As Mannathoko (1992) noted:

> Feminism questions and challenges the origins of oppressive gender relations and attempts to develop a variety of strategies that might change these relations for the better. All feminism pivots around the recognition of existing women's oppression and addresses the prevailing unjust and discriminatory gender relations. Feminism does not just deal with issues of justice and equality but also offers a critique of male-dominated institutions, values and social practices that are oppressive and destructive (Mannathoko, 1992, p. 71).

The feminist theories and critiques have been based mainly on Marxist, liberal and radical philosophical traditions. Marxist feminists focus on women's oppression and inequalities within society in general, by linking gender inequality and social class, and seeing inequalities within the education system as reflecting class struggle in a capitalist society. As such they downplay the issue of gender, highlighting the notion that inequalities within education come about as a result of the socio-economic structure of a capitalist society. Since liberalism is about granting 'equal opportunity' for all within society, liberal feminists argue for equal rights between women and men and between girls and boys, with regard to education, among other rights. In terms of education, they emphasise access at the expense of equity. Radical feminists on the other hand focus on the biological difference between men and women as a source of oppression of women. As Kibera and Kimokoti (2007) observed, the resultant reproductive differences have consequently led to a segregated division of labour whereby women took care of home and child maintenance, while men worked outside the home – occupying positions in most sectors of society where these social structures support and maintain male dominance. This is why radical change should be effected mainly at the level of social institutions, including education, and the patriarchy system of male dominance at large. It is in this context that Chapter 9 ('Sexual harassment in institutions of higher learning') becomes relevant. In the said chapter, Edwards-Jauch and Namupala argue from a standpoint that conceptualises sexual harassment as a form of gender-based violence that reflects broader societal inequalities; besides being an international phenomenon that affects universities and educational institutions around the world.

Some feminists go beyond biological differences between men and women. Thus those who use a social construction definition of gender, like Butler (1990), refuse to think of gender as a static description of a person – they reject essentialist explanations attributing gender differences to natural, biologically occurring differences. Butler in particular argues that gender is performed. She suggests that it is not enough to separate gender (cultural aspects) from sex (biological aspects). What is needed is to move away from building gendered norms of behaviour upon biologically determined male and female bodies. She argues that individuals perform masculinity or femininity, rather than being male or female. Thus gender is an identity that is continuously constructed and reconstructed in everyday actions. Schools are important agents of socialisation in that they teach learners about appropriate gender roles, but learners' agency is equally important in the process of acquiring gender. Learners can express and create their own gender systems through their interactions since gender identities are fluid and unstable. It is here that issues of social justice and democracy enter. From the point of view of Butler (1990), there is more scope for individuals to choose their identities and therefore resist hegemonic identities that might promote discrimination and harassment.

CONCLUSION

This chapter has shown that the concept of democracy can be interpreted differently, depending from which theoretical or ideological perspective one chooses to view it. The resultant divergent views also influence one's interpretation of the concept of education and of what constitutes social justice. The chapter examined different notions of democracy, including classical, pluralist, protectionist, liberal and economic democratic ideas. A constant critique of 'liberal democracy' and its meaning for Africa's socio-economic development became apparent from various African social scientists such as Ake, Mafeje, Shivji, Amukugo, among others. These analyses can be summed up by saying that liberal democracy is the least appropriate form of governance that can address pertinent African socio-economic issues such as poverty for various reasons, the most important being that it does not correspond to African reality as it is the least competent governing system that can address social inequities.

Its failure to address social inequities is mainly due to its focus on abstract political rights at the expense of economic rights and it repudiates popular power by emphasising individual rights at the expense of those of the majority, or, to borrow from Ake (2000, p. 210), it promotes 'competitive elitism'. As Cliffe (2003) argues in his review of Ake (2000), liberal democracy in Africa has not only eroded the principles of equality and participation, but '[t]he resulting patterns of competitive elitism and apoliticisation follow with the parallel development of capitalism, so that the core values of liberal democracy are essentially the same as those of the market: egotism, property, formal freedom and equality.' (ibid, 2003). This definition of liberal democracy resonates with the author's understanding of this concept as outlined in this chapter.

The above supposition does not only hold true for Africa but can be extended to other parts of the underdeveloped world. To paraphrase Sankatsing (2004), liberal democracy has often led to elite prosperity at the expense of the poor who live under widespread misery, stifling any significant development. In our view, therefore, within a liberal democratic framework education's capacity to promote democracy and social justice becomes limited because it is less concerned with developing learners'/students' critical consciousness of social reality, and their capacity to explore the root causes of that actuality so as to be able to improve the situation. This critical view of education not only helps to increase public participation, argues Giroux (1980), it also generates an important link between knowledge, action and social change. Nonetheless, for education to promote the values of democracy and social justice presupposes that education should be relevant to the needs of both the individual and society; it should be of good quality, and address the critical issues of equity and inclusiveness. Furthermore, as Sen (2009) suggests, the meaning of social justice should be assessed and determined through public reasoning, because values (as part of aesthetics) are acquired through both reasoning and interactivity (reciprocal action). In this regard, education not only helps to develop the critical capacity that enables us to participate actively in public debates and collective reasoning, but also the ability to assess how society and its various institutions are performing. This accords a central place to education and graduate formation as a medium through which justice can be advanced and injustices minimised.

References

Ake, C. (1993). *The unique case of African democracy*. Retrieved from http://facultyfiles.deanza.edu/gems/kaufmancynthia/Ake.pdf

Ake, C. (1996). *Democracy and development in Africa*. Washington: Brooking Institution.

Ake, C. (2000). *The feasibility of democracy in Africa*. Dakar: Council for the Development of Social Science Research in Africa (CODESRIA).

Amukugo, E. M. (1998). Can liberal democracy deliver equity in education? *Southern African Political and Economic Monthly (SAPEM)*, *11*(6), 11–14.

Amukugo, E. M. (2013). Liberal democracy, education and social justice in Africa. *Journal for Studies in Humanities and Social Sciences*, *2*(1), 144–157.

Berkeley, G. (2004). *The principles of human knowledge*. Retrieved from http://www.earlymoderntexts.com/assets/pdfs/berkeley1710.pdf.

Bohman, J. (2005). Critical theory. In *The Stanford encyclopedia of philosophy*, 2012. Retrieved from http://plato.stanford.edu/archives/spr2012/entries/critical-theory/

Butler, J. (1990). *Gender trouble: Feminism and the subversion of identity*. New York: Routledge.

Carbone II, S. A. (2010). American transcendentalism and analysis of Ralph Waldo Emerson's "Self-Reliance". *Inquiries Journal/Student Pulse, 2*(11). Retrieved from http://www.inquiriesjournal.com/a?id=329

Carr, P. R. (2010). Re-thinking normative democracy and the political economy of education. *Journal for Critical Education Policy Studies, 8*(1), 1–40.

Carr, W. & Hartnett, A. (1996). *Education and the struggle for democracy: The politics of educational ideas*. Buckingham: Open University Press.

Cliffe, L. (2003). The feasibility of democracy in Africa/disciplining democracy/the Congo from Leopold to Kabila. In *Leeds African Studies Bulletin, 65*, 64–67. Retrieved from http://lucas.leeds.ac.uk/review/the-feasibility-of-democracy-in-africa-disciplining-democracy-the-congo-from-leopold-to-kabila/

Castles, S. & Wüstenberg, W. (1979). *The education of the future: An introduction to the theory and practice of socialist education*. London: Pluto Press.

Darder, A., Baltodano, M. P., & Torres, R. D. (Eds.), (2009). *The critical pedagogy reader* (2nd ed.). London: Routledge.

Demaine, J. (2001). *Sociology of education today*. New York: Palgrave.

Descartes, R. (1637). *Discourse on the method of rightly conducting one's reason and seeking truth in the sciences*. Retrieved from http://www.earlymoderntexts.com/pdfs/descartes1637.pdf.

Descartes, R. (1641). Meditations on first philosophy. Retrieved from http://selfpace.uconn.edu/class/percep/DescartesMeditations.pdf

Dewey, J. (1997). *Experience and education*. New York: Touchstone. (Original work published 1938).

Dewey, J. (2010). *Democracy and education: An introduction to the philosophy of education*. Lexington, KY: BLN Publishing. (Original work published 1916).

Dowding, K., Goodin, R. E., & Pateman, C. (2004). *Justice and Democracy. Essays for Brian Barry*. Cambridge: Cambridge University Press.

Dowding, K. (2004). Are democratic and just institutions the same? In K. Dowding, R. E. Goodin, & C. Pateman (Eds.), *Justice and democracy. Essays for Brian Barry*. Cambridge: Cambridge University Press.

Evetts, J. (1970). Equality of opportunity: The recent history of a concept. *The British Journal of Sociology, 21*(4), 425–430. Retrieved from http://www.jstor.org/stable/588497

Freire, P. (1985). *The politics of education: Culture, power and liberation*. New York: Bergin & Garvey publishers.

Freire, P. (1996). *Pedagogy of the oppressed*. London: Penguin.

Giroux, H. A. (1980). Critical theory and rationality in citizenship education. In *Curriculum Inquiry. 10*(4). Retrieved from http://www.jstor.org/stable/10.2307/1179823

Giroux, H. A. (2009). Critical theory and educational practice. In A. Darder, M. P. Baltodano & R. D. Torres (Eds.), *The critical pedagogy reader* (2nd ed.) 27–51. London: Routledge.

Haralambos, M. & Holborn, M. (2008). *Sociology: Themes and perspectives* (7th ed.). London: Collins.

Herrera, L. M. (2007). *Equity, equality and equivalence – a contribution in search for conceptual definitions and a comparative methodology.* Retrieved from www.sc.ehu.es/sfwseec/reec/reec13/reec1312.pdf

Kant, I. (2007). *The critique of pure reason.* Retrieved from http://www.earlymoderntexts.com/assets/pdfs/kant1781part1.pdf (Original work published 1781).

Kant, I. (2014). *The critique of practical reason.* Retrieved from http://www.morelightinmasonry.com/wp-content/uploads/2014/06/Kant-Critique-of-Practical-Reason-Cambridge.pdf (Original work published 1788).

Kibera, L. W. & Kimokoti, A. (2007). *Fundamentals of sociology of education with reference to Africa.* Nairobi: University of Nairobi Press.

Lenzer, G. (Ed.). (1997). *The essential writing: Auguste Comte and positivism.* London: Transaction Publishers.

Mafeje, A. (2002). *Democratic governance and new democracy in Africa.* Retrieved from http://www.foresightfordevelopment.org/sobipro/download-file/46-222/54

Mannathoko, C. (1992). In R. Meena (Ed.). (1992). *Gender in southern Africa: Conceptual and theoretical issues.* Harare: SAPES Books.

Marginson, S. (2011). Higher education and public good. *Higher Education Quarterly, 65*(4), 411–433.

Mclaren, P. & Leonard, P. (Eds.) (1993). *Paulo Freire: A critical encounter.* London: Routledge.

Plato. (1991). *The republic of Plato.* (A. Bloom, Trans.). New York: Basic Books.

Pragmatism. (2006). In *The internet encyclopedia of philosophy.* Retrieved from http://www.iep.utm.edu/

Pragmatism. (2008). In *The Stanford encyclopedia of philosophy.* Retrieved from https://plato.stanford.edu/entries/pragmatism/

Rajapakse, N. (2016). Capitalism, education and research: The Anglo-Saxon model reconsidered after the financial crisis. C. Coron & F. Lauby (Eds.). LISA E-Journal. *XIV*(1). Retrieved from https://lisa.revues.org/8831

Saifulin, M. & Dixon, R. (1984). *Dictionary of philosophy* (2nd rev. ed.). Moscow: Progress Publishers.

Sankatsing, G. (2004). People's vote compatible with people's fate: A democratic alternative to liberal democracy. In *Political democracy, social democracy and the market in the Caribbean.* Retrieved from http://www.crscenter.com/Democracy.pdf

Sen, A. (2009). *The idea of justice.* London: Allen Lane.

Shivji, I. G. (2003). *The struggle for democracy.* Retrieved from http://www.marxists.org/subject/africa/shivji/struggle-democracy.htm

Tikly, L. (2011). Towards a framework for researching the quality of education in low-income countries. *Comparative Education, 47*(1), 1–23.

Torres, C. A. (n.d.). Paulo Freire, Education and transformative social justice learning. Retrieved from http://www.ipfp.pt/cdrom/Pain%E9is%20Dial%F3gicos/Painel%20A%20-%20Sociedade%20Multicultural/carlosalbertotorres.pdf

Volkov, G. N. (Ed.). (1982). *The basics of Marxist–Leninist theory.* Moscow: Progress Publishers.

Walker, M. (2010). A human development and capabilities 'prospective analysis' of global higher education policy. *Journal of Education Policy, 25*(4), 485–501.

3

Education and democracy: Some general conceptual issues

Pempelani Mufune†

Before you read this chapter, clarify your own opinions:

1. Which do you believe a teacher should emphasise more:
    a. encouraging learner participation OR training learners to be obedient and absorb a set of facts to repeat for examinations?
    b. allowing learners to express divergent opinions and questioning what they read in books OR to accept what recognised authorities have established to be the best ways and ideas?
    c. encouraging memorisation of prescribed information OR gaining the skills for discovering facts on their own?

2. Do you think schools are typically run on democratic principles? If not, is it still possible for them to promote democracy?

3. What are the characteristics of an education system that promotes democracy compared to the characteristics of an education system that promotes authoritarianism? Would you say your country's education system is more geared to promoting democracy or authoritarianism? Would you seek to change this, and if so, how?

INTRODUCTION

There are three basic positions on the relationship between democracy and education. The first is that there is a strong correlation between democracy and education. This is the position taken by writers such as Lipset (1959), Glaeser, Ponzetto, & Shleifer (2006) and Kamens (1988), among others. Their argument is that there is substantial empirical evidence that shows that countries that have more education are, on average, more democratic than countries with less education. This relationship stands, although it is sometimes confounded by the effects of economic development.

The second is that the relationship between democracy and education is spurious. Acemoglu, Johnson, Robinson and Yared (2005) have in particular challenged the hypothesis originally set by Lipset (1959) linking education to democracy. Acemoglu et al. (2005) argue that studies positing a correlation between education and democracy may be biased because they omit certain variables. When Acemoglu et al. (2005) looked at panel data model controlling for country-specific effects and then considered the relationship between education and democracy within specific countries, they found no relationship between an increase in education and an increase in the level of democracy. In other words, the supposed correlation between education and democracy could be spurious.

The third position is that the relationship between education and democracy is a myth. The argument is rather simple, and it is that schools in most societies are hierarchical structures that have little to do with democracy. How, then, could an institution that is not democratic in itself promote democracy? This cannot happen as the ideals and practices of democracy do not coincide with the purposes or practices of schooling.

What is the relationship between education and democracy (in terms of the level of political rights)? This chapter attempts to answer this question by interrogating the existing literature. The chapter starts by clarifying the focal concepts of education and democracy, before looking at the argument that says that education and democracy are highly correlated. Then it considers the argument that education and democracy are spuriously related, and finally, looks at the position that the link between education and democracy is mythical. It then tries to clarify the relationship between the two concepts by expanding on the meaning of democracy and clarifying its various types. These are then linked to education.

CONCEPTUAL DEFINITIONS

Education simply means the transmission of knowledge through formal or informal channels. In many cases we reserve the term education for schooling (i.e. formal education). The main function of formal schooling is to pass knowledge from generation to generation. Formal education is overtly designed to transmit general and specific skills necessary for the operation of a given society. It therefore serves as a stimulus to innovation and creative thinking and action, which contribute to changes in society. Thus education is essential to the development of cultures. In so far as education promotes creativity and innovation, it might stimulate productivity and increased standards of living for individuals and for societies in general. We can best see the role of education in democracy if we consider it as both a micro and a macro variable.

We usually think of education as a micro variable. That is, education is something that individuals achieve and possess and which enables them to get ahead in society. Evidence from around the world indicates that for many people the main reason for going to college is to get a good job and earn more. Economists talk in terms of 'returns to education'. The objective of having more education in order to have a good job and earn more is widespread around the world. It also seems to be realistic in most societies.

Mass education is a macro issue if we look at it from the perspective of the whole society. Thus we can look at education in terms of the number of eligible children in school; the proportion of literate adults within countries; the proportion of people with a certain level of educational attainment; the proportion of females with a certain level of education; the percentage of investments in research and development; etc.

As Kunczik (2001) argues, democracy is a very vague concept and at least since the American and the French revolutions there has been intensive debate about the question of what democracy is and how to achieve and maintain democracy. Gasiorowski and Power (1998, p. 742) define democracy as

> ... a type of political regime in which (a) meaningful and extensive competition exists among individuals and organized groups for all effective positions of government at regular intervals and excluding the use of force; (b) a highly inclusive level of political participation exists in the selection of leaders and policies, such that no major (adult) social group is excluded; and (c) a sufficient level of civil and political liberties exist to ensure the integrity of political competition and participation.

In the context of southern Africa, Berger (2002) argues that democratic functionality means

> ... decision-making power by majority principle, exercised by the way of a process that is based on equal rights of participants. There are other important associated principles (informed participants, freedom of expression, right of access to public information, rule of law, checks and balances on power, human rights, and respect for minorities) but these can also have a life outside democratic decision-making and are not quite as central (Berger, 2002, pp. 21–22).

Gasiorowski and Power (1998) argued that in practice this means that a country holds regular, free, fair and universal elections. According to West-Burnham (2009), democratic society can be said to have the following characteristics:

1. High significance is attached to individual freedom and personal liberties guaranteed by the rule of law.
2. In their personal and political lives, individuals are able to make choices which directly inform political and social systems, with the majority will prevailing, but minority rights being respected.
3. There is optimum participation in political and social processes with appropriate levels of influence. Representatives selected through the political process are answerable and accountable.
4. Democratic systems are open with maximum access to information and the sharing of knowledge to allow informed consent.
5. A primary function of governments elected by a democratic society is to protect the safety, well-being and economic and social security of its citizens.
6. Democratic societies work to ensure that their members lead lives which allow opportunities for personal growth, creativity, artistic expression and social fulfilment.

This is in line with Held (1995) who argues that democracy constitutes 'a cluster of rules, procedures and institutions permitting the broadest involvement of the majority of citizens, not in political affairs as such, but in the selection of representatives who alone can make political decisions'.

Argument 1: Democracy is linked to education

How does education affect democracy in given countries? Broadly speaking, there is a correlation between education investment and democracy. There is substantial empirical evidence linking education to democracy. Lipset (1959, p. 80) argued that if we cannot say 'that a "high" level of education is a sufficient condition for democracy, the available evidence does suggest that it comes close to being a necessary condition in the modern world'. Lipset's data showed a strong correlation between education and democracy. Lipset argued that modernisation leads to increasing wealth, which in turn leads to more literacy, education, urbanisation, and then to democratisation, because citizens are generally less amenable to oppression and authoritarian behaviour, and more willing to support democracy. Accordingly, 'education presumably broadens man's outlook, enables him to understand the need for norms of tolerance, restrains him from adhering to extremist doctrines, and increases his capacity to make rational electoral choices' (Lipset, 1959, pp. 83–84). Essentially Lipset argues that formal education provides political attitudes conducive to democracy. Almond and Verba (1963), in their analysis of survey data from five countries, also considered education as the most important factor in creating the attitudes and values vital for a participant culture.

Linking democracy to citizenship, Prah (2007) agrees:

> In a practical sense, citizenship is incapacitated if citizens are illiterate. Their ability to understand social policy processes is seriously curtailed. Subtleties of policy and politics are lost on many. For the teeming masses in Africa, Asia and Latin America who are politically and socially crippled by illiteracy, practically meaningful citizenship remains out of their grasp (Prah, 2007, p. 7).

On the other hand:

> The poorer a country and the lower the absolute standard of living of the lower classes, the greater the pressure on the upper strata to treat the lower as vulgar, innately inferior.... Consequently, the upper strata in such a situation tend to regard political rights for the lower strata, particularly the right to share power, as essentially absurd and immoral (Lipset, 1959, p. 83–84).

Barro (1999) compared several countries between 1960 and 1995, and found a strong link between democracy and education. Similarly Glaeser et al. (2006) found empirical support linking education and democracy. They found that democracy and education also go hand-in-hand in the 126 countries they studied. Similarly, they found that democracy varied inversely with primary school education in the 146 countries they considered. Castelló-Climent (2006, p. 1) observed that, 'all the countries with an average of at least 4 years of schooling in 1960 are nowadays stable democracies, whereas the countries with less than 1 year of education in 1960 remained authoritarian regimes during the period 1960–2000.'

One of the few studies in Namibia linking education to democratic values was done by Keulder, Nord and Emminghaus (2000/2010). They found that the importance allocated to democratic competition increased with a rising level of education among a sample of Namibians. They found that among those without formal education, less than half (45.3%) of the respondents regarded competition as very important. On the other hand, for 75% of respondents with a university degree, competitiveness in elections was very important. The opinions of primary and secondary school-leavers lay between these two extremes (Keulder et al., 2000/2010, p. 242–243). They concluded that education was the demographic factor with the strongest influence on the importance of competition. This result confirms the importance of education for the formation of a democratic culture. One may safely assume that an improved level of education in the population could also strengthen support for democracy in Namibia, indirectly (Keulder et al., 2000/2010, p. 243).

Keulder et al. (2000/2010) also compared the opinions of the various groups according to level of education. They found a correlation between an individual's level of education and their participation in politics. More respondents without formal schooling (37.4%) compared to those with a university degree (20%) prefer to leave politics to the politicians (Keulder et al, 2000/2010, p. 243).

Another study linked education to women's participation in decision-making (Ministry of Health and Social Services [MoHSS], Namibia and Macro International Inc., 2008, p. 242). It found that '[a]ccording to men, a wife's participation in decision-making increases with age, education, and wealth quintile.' It further found an inverse relationship between education and attitudes towards beating a wife as a punishment for (among other reasons) arguing with her husband. Fifty percent of women with no education, compared with 11% of women with more than secondary education said that husbands were justified in beating their wives for at least one of five specified reasons. There was also an inverse relationship between a man's level of education and his perception of wife beating. For example, 49.8% of men with no education said that a husband is justified in beating his wife for at least one of the specified reasons compared with 16.6% of men with more than secondary education (MoHSS and Macro International Inc., 2008). Similarly, the Social Impact Assessment and Policy Analysis Corporation (SIAPAC) (2009) found that people with lower education levels in Namibia (holding for males and females, and holding across age group) were more likely to agree with the statement that: 'A good wife obeys her husband even if she disagrees'. Both females and males with higher levels of education were more likely to have fought back when attacked in situations of domestic violence.

Barkan, Mattes, Mozaffar and Smiddy (2010) linked the individual education of political actors to democratic action. They asked members of parliament (MPs) in various African countries to estimate their fellow members' capacity to understand the legislation considered by the committees on which they served – in particular MPs' assessments of the capacity of the clerks assigned to parliamentary committees. They found considerable variation from a very low rating for committee clerks in Namibia to a high rating accorded committee clerks in Zambia. Whereas in Namibia, slightly more than five percent of legislation was reviewed by a legislative committee, in Zambia it was nearly 88%, and in South Africa all proposed legislation was reviewed by an appropriate committee. In Kenya, it was 59%. These differences were attributed partly to different educational levels among MPs.

All these appraisals of the linkage between democracy and education have been done from the perspective of modernisation. This perspective may be seen as a complex set of changes in the structure of society that take place as traditional societies become industrial societies. Thus modernisation is a dichotomous model in which certain features point to traditional society while others point to a modern state of affairs. Modernisation points to certain features which define social change. According to Gould (as cited in Miller, 1997) these include: individualisation of social behaviour; an increase in instrumental and utilitarian behaviour; increased secularism; the legal rationalisation of social management structures; increasing domination of humans over nature; and the predominance of the market in social relationships. Furthermore, as Gould claims, some authors state non-social economic variables as indicative of modernisation. These include personal liberties, accountability and democracy.

There is education that is general in nature. Mathematics and logical skills, communication techniques and practices, knowledge of business law and political processes are all essential to the production of many goods and services. In most of the world's economies, this kind of education and training is not only a tool but a requirement for participation in work. In less developed countries, this kind of education plays a crucial role in transferring people from agriculture to industry. The most able people, i.e. the most educated young rural people, simply move to the city to work in industry, although they do not always find employment. Historically, one condition for industrialisation (i.e. development) is the shift from agricultural to manufacturing employment. In general, the smaller the share of a country's employment sector that is involved in agriculture, the higher the rate of economic development. This is the case because once productivity in the agricultural sector has increased (e.g. if one farmer can feed 50 instead of three people), some of the people working on the farm must move into other sectors of the economy. These other sectors are non-agricultural and require more knowledge and skills (i.e. education).

There is also education that is specific in nature. This kind of education is particular to given occupations or enterprises, and includes specific instruction in business administration, data processing, etc. In fact, very few individuals enter jobs with the requisite skills. They have to undergo on-the-job training to enable them to know how things are done and the practices that surround a particular job. It is this kind of education that assures efficiency and effectiveness. According to Castelló-Climent (2008), it is general education, i.e. the education attained by the majority of the society that should be relevant for the implementation and sustainability of democracies across and within a country.

There are essentially three lines of reasoning linking education to greater democracy. The first was well summarised by Glaeser et al. (2006) who argue that individuals face weak incentives to support democracy – meaning that the costs to support democracy are high on individuals but the payoffs are shared among all citizens. It may be very costly for an individual to demand participation in the politics of the country (costs may include isolation, imprisonment or even death in some societies), yet when political participation is widespread in a given society, it is not limited to those who fought for it. Thus individuals face weak incentives to support democracy. Education raises the benefits of political participation and increases the number of people who support democracy. As such, democracy may be reinforced by primary education encouraging democratic attitudes, and the opinions of more educated people may favour democracy over other forms of governance.

On the other hand (and this is the second line of reasoning), democratically elected governments may have a greater incentive than authoritarian regimes to provide citizens with education, especially with primary schooling (Glaeser et al., 2006). The argument is that democratic governments have a greater incentive to provide basic public services in comparison to less democratic ones, because they depend on elections to win and keep power. Since they need the support of the general public in elections, they are more likely than not to spend on basic public services and education, especially primary education, as one of the most important basic services (Brown & Hunter, 2004).

The third argument is that societies that are educated have far more stable democracies than societies that are less educated. Kamens (1988), for instance, argues that the expansion of national educational systems affects the character of national political systems. How? Such an expansion creates 'citizens' (and not subjects). This especially happens via primary schooling and in turn legitimates citizen participation and the institutionalisation of formally democratic political regimes. What is more is that the creation of social and political elites through secondary and tertiary schooling also institutionalises formally democratic political regimes (Kamens, 1988). 'Citizenship', according to Kamens, involves 'membership in a national community with all the rights and responsibilities such a status entails' (Kamens, 1988, p. 117). It is only citizens who can question and challenge matters affecting them (a precondition for democracy). Education is the most important means for creating citizenship. According to Prah (2007):

> Modern citizenship is, at best, an educated condition, and democracy is its most credible and enabling condition. Thus citizenship is a requisite feature of a successful democratic system. When we say a socio-political system is democratic we are also saying that the system is sensitive and responsive to the interests of the citizenry and also that this citizenry operates the routinization of government through an institutionalized elective process which gives them a share in government, however removed they may be from the immediate area of political leadership and decision-making. Furthermore, modern citizenship eschews the idea of superior or inferior citizens. All are equal before the law, all have equal voting rights, without exception all are free to engage in the activities of citizenship, and all are in the expression of their political rights free to express both individual and group interests (Prah, 2007, p. 6).

The relationships involving education and democracy that flow from the modernisation thesis are captured in Inglehart and Welzel (2005) (Fig. 1).

Argument 2: Education and democracy have spurious links

Acemoglu et al. (2005), in particular, have challenged the Lipset hypothesis that education and democracy are intrinsically related. They argue that studies which find a high correlation between education and democracy are biased because they omit certain variables. Measurement imprecision is also said to be a major problem when it comes to such a complex concept as democracy (Hadenius & Teorell, 2005). In fact, when Acemoglu et al. (2005) controlled for country-specific effects and analysed the relationship between education and democracy within a country, they found no relationship between an increase in education and an increase in the

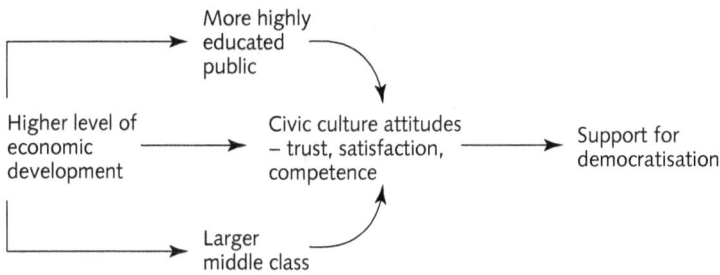

ECONOMIC DEVELOPMENT AS A FACTOR IN DEMOCRATISATION

Figure 1: Ronald Inglehart – How education links to democratization

level of democracy. This argument is bolstered by Weil (1985), who found that the relationship between individual education and politically tolerant attitudes varied widely among Austrians, Germans, French and Americans. Also related to this is research by Robinson (2006) indicating that the same factors that influence the creation of democracy (i.e. greater inequality, greater importance of land and other easily taxable assets in the portfolio of the elite, and the absence of democratic institutions) are also more likely to destabilise democracy.

What is emerging is that democracy is a multi-dimensional phenomenon that cannot be linked only to a single variable, such as education. Again, few studies in Namibia speak to links between individual educational attainment and political tolerance (a crucial aspect of democracy). Crush and Pendleton (2004) reported that negative attitudes in the anti-foreigners' 'troika' (South Africa, Namibia, Botswana) were pervasive and widespread across all personal attributes: educational groups, poor and rich, employed and unemployed, male and female, black and white, conservative and radical.

Argument 3: Education and democracy links are a myth

Societies and communities are either educated into subservience to authoritarianism or out of subservience into participatory democracy (Zulu, 2000, p. 162). Henry Giroux (1992) agrees by looking at the impaired relationships between democracy and education. He argues that neither the ideals nor the practices of democracy any longer characterise the purposes or practices of schooling; or, if they do, they are so weak as to be near insignificance (Fenstermacher, 2002, p. 1). Giroux says that focusing on educational outcomes, test scores and choice shifts the gaze away from addressing the importance of schooling for the improvement of public life. He views the hidden school curriculum of competitiveness, individualism and achievement as undermining the responsibility of public service, rupturing the relationship between schools and the community. West-Burnham (2009) agrees by insisting that the debate linking democracy to education must relate to the nature of learning in schools. He argues that schools promote shallow learning, i.e. the memorisation and replication of information in a process that is largely extrinsically motivated. To West-Burnham, the result of such schooling is the production of individuals who score high on compliance and dependency, yet this is the very antithesis of democracy. Education that is 'concerned with deep learning, the conversion of information into knowledge through a process of reflection, testing and application' is the one that promotes democracy (West-Burnham, 2009, p. 14).

Among those arguing that schooling is a vehicle for the delivery of curriculum through given subjects is Noam Chomsky (2000), who argues that school subjects structure the individual's experience of school. Most see assessment and accreditation as the reason why schooling exists. Few schools are in a position to teach democracy or impart democratic ideals:

> Any school that has to impose the teaching of democracy is already suspect. The less democratic schools are, the more they need to teach about democratic ideals. If schools were really democratic, in the sense of providing opportunities for children to experience democracy through practice, they wouldn't feel the need to indoctrinate them with platitudes about democracy (Chomsky, 2000, p. 27).

The best way to discover how a functioning democracy works is to practise it. However, it can be argued that schools don't practise democracy very well. A good measure of functioning democracy in schools and in society is the extent to which the theory approximates reality, and we know that in both schools and society there is a large gulf between the two (Chomsky, 2000, p. 28).

Educational institutions generally require people who are willing to adjust to the institution's power structure and accept the code of their discipline without asking too many questions (Chomsky, 2000). Chomsky argues that there is some process of indoctrination, socialising people into acceptable patterns of thought and behaviour. Higher education therefore can be one of the ways in which certain views and questions are suppressed.

The idea of school organisation as an obstacle to democracy has also been broached in the African context. Thus Sifuna (2000) argues that the organisational mode brought forth by western education is authoritarian, and the bureaucratised hierarchical nature of schools is not the best place for inculcating democratic virtues. Colonial-era schools taught unquestioned acquiescence to authority; the colonial education system encouraged rote learning; and the schools' discipline system, through the prefect system, was fashioned along military lines. Few teachers and principals listened to juniors, let alone pupils and students. This philosophy and practice has more or less continued after independence, and therefore continues to thwart democratic values and civic virtues.

CONCEPTUAL CONSIDERATIONS

In this section we look at the concept of democracy and link it to education, taking into account the many forms of democracy. One possible explanation for the equivocal evidence regarding the relationship between democracy and education is the failure of most researchers to specify the meaning of democracy in detail. Although speaking in the context of media and democracy, Baker (1998) argues that different concepts of democracy lead to different conceptions of how aspects of society function. Thus one's understanding of liberal democracy colours one's view and expectations of the desired role of education in society. Baker (1998) points to four conceptions of democracy that might influence the role of education: elitist, interest-group pluralist, republican and complex democracy.

Elitist democracy, in this context, stands for 'a political regime form in which, first, the legitimate exercise of power is effectively in the hands of relatively isolated, albeit competing elites and, second, the voters' choice between these elites at free and fair elections can only to a limited extent generate alternations in policies, especially economic policies' (Møller, 2007, p. 13).

In a nutshell, the rationale for this kind of democracy is that societal problems are necessarily complex and require some level of expertise. 'Good governments must routinely respond to problems that are technically complex' (Baker, 1998, p. 2). Politics and economics are too complex for the average person to comprehend and process into good policy. This implies that people with some expertise (i.e. elites of one form or another) should rule.

> Most people have neither the interest nor the ability to understand, much less to devise solutions for, the problems facing society ... experts and specialists at understanding the economic, human and natural environments must do the bulk of the government's decision-making work (Baker, 1998, p. 321).

Despite this, ordinary people have the right to choose their rulers. However, citizens elect between elites. This is necessary to assure legitimacy. Elections, in the manner of Pareto, increase the circulation of elites, further legitimising the system. Legitimacy is further boosted by the resultant efficiency in the running of government, economy and society. In an elitist democracy, there are arrangements for the separation of powers that ensure that one group of elites does not achieve total domination. It is in this context that school and schooling is crucial for it is the system that produces elites. Schooling promotes the rotation of elites. Educated elites are the ones who seek sufficient information to participate in the public sphere to function rationally and, of course, to perform a watchdog function (Price & Krug, 2006, p. 96).

As argued by Kurth-Schai and Green (2009), education in elite democracy is necessary to support government-centred institutions. It prepares citizens for orderly civic participation centred on obeying the law and voting in national, state and local elections. Education also promotes social stability to ensure political continuity and economic growth. Through schools, individuals acquire the knowledge, skills, and dispositions necessary for informed and responsible consumption of material goods (economic productivity) and non-material civic benefits (individual rights).

Contrary to elite democracy, interest-group or pluralist democracy sees differentiated groups vying with one another in the political arena. Thus, by definition, a pluralist democracy is a political regime form in which there is more than one centre of power. Competing interest groups check each other's power to ensure that none of them becomes too strong. Interest groups are then organised for competing groups that vie to represent different views of citizens. Interest groups thus protect citizens from centralised power. The whole system rests on the fact that the diversity of interests within society is recognised, protected and promoted. Whereas the legitimacy of the polity in elite democracy is merely sociological, i.e. 'people feel and treat their government as more legitimate – and thus are more prepared to obey its laws – if it is democratic' (Baker, 2001, p. 135).

On the other hand, in pluralist democracy real opportunity for participation is crucial for normative legitimacy. The claim is that 'participatory democracy is necessary for (normative) legitimacy of the framework on which peoples' flourishing depends' (Baker, 1998, p. 328). From the point of view of pluralist democracy, interest groups counterbalance one another's power and, through compromise, competition policy and indeed politics, ideally are created because 'democracy provides the mechanism most likely to take into account and properly weigh all interests' (Baker, 1998, p. 328). It is this participation that provides groups with the protection of their interests and rights (which drive them) as they affect policy, regardless of their resource endowments. Legitimacy for the political system is gained through bargaining and compromise.

What is the role of education in this context? Taking interest-group or pluralist democracy as rule by interest groups, where citizens form such groups to bargain and advance their interests, and since groups that exert the strongest pressure under fair rules should prevail, the role of education is to produce citizens who advocate for group interests, mobilise interest groups to protect and promote their interests and inform authorities on group interests (Althaus, 2011). Schools by definition should also reproduce society's diverse interests. Since pluralist democracy focuses on broad and active involvement in civic life, beyond mere voting during elections, the role of education is to ground individual citizens in democratic values (especially equality and social justice) and to inform them about central institutional structures and processes (Kurth-Schai & Green, 2009). This kind of democracy also envisages an education that goes beyond this to include critical enquiry of ideas and events.

Republican democracy stands for a political regime form in which there is rule by

> … deliberated consensus, [which is a system] designed to help citizens discover their common interests by communicating with one another across lines of difference. Different models of republicanism place different responsibilities on citizens, but all tend to lean heavily on citizens to articulate, defend and advance their interests in search of the best possible solution for the whole. In extreme forms of republicanism, such as those advanced by Rousseau and carried forward in the communitarian tradition, citizens might be expected to legislate for themselves, political representation by elected officials might be minimal or absent, and collective choices might be decided primarily by the force of the better argument (Althaus, 2011, p. 23).

It is on the issue of legitimacy for (and participation in) the political system that pluralism most differs from republican democracy. Whereas in pluralism, legitimacy is gained through bargaining and compromise, republicanism rejects such unabashed self-interest for some kind of common ground or public good resulting from overcoming self-interest. In republican democracy, legitimacy is due to the citizenry's commitment to and indeed agreement (through deliberations) on what is common.

Since republican democracy is rule by deliberated consensus in which citizens follow public affairs and deliberate upon them so as to discover common interests and to let the best argument prevail, the role of education is threefold: (a) to produce citizens with civic virtue; (b) to produce citizens who can understand and follow events sufficiently to expose corruption and other lapses in civic virtue; and (c) to create a common understanding for informed, objective, and inclusive debate (Althaus, 2011, p. 46). In republican democracy, education must serve as a foundation for democratic institutions that facilitates a deliberative process in which individuals and groups find common ground (Alonzo, 2006). In the understanding of republican democracy, educational institutions are the key institutions of enlightenment and nurturing of citizenship. Education and adult literacy are necessary to cultivate webs of public communication among well-informed citizens. The role of education is to provide individuals with practices of collective civic engagement. Young citizens learn to increase their deliberative competence, social imagination, and inclusive participation in social transformation (Kurth-Schai & Green, 2009).

Complex democracy, the last concept of democracy discussed by Baker (1998), is a hybrid or amalgamation of republican (with its emphasis on common good) and pluralist (with its emphasis on self-interest) democracy. It borrows from Habermas (1996). 'This system combines pluralism and republicanism and calls for numerous public sphere[s], including some media channels open to everyone and designed to encourage public discourse, and other channels used by individual interest groups to build internal consensus' (Alonzo, 2006, p. 765).

What is the role of education in the context of complex democracy? Paraphrasing Baker (1998, p. 393), education should perform both a 'republican societal wide discourse role' and 'provide for a liberal pluralist role' with different aspects of education (or different schools) relating to different societal groups. Multi-cultural education designed to teach people to respect differences within diverse societies is ideal for complex democracy. Adult education may be crucial to this process.

Democracy and education in Namibia

The present regime in Namibia is undeniably more democratic than its predecessor, the apartheid state. It is more accountable; it is more accommodating to alternative political parties; it is more responsive to the rule of the law; it pays more attention to civil and human rights; and it engages in periodic elections. In southern Africa, Namibia is ranked among the more democratic states. Unlike neighbouring Angola and Zimbabwe, it has consistently held free and fair elections every five years. It is among the few countries that has never been a one-party state since its independence. It has one of the freest media (if not the freest) in southern Africa.

Despite the positives, Namibia has been dominated by one political party – SWAPO. The link between media exposures and policy reform is weak and unreliable. Thus, in Namibia, 'while the Office of the President has launched some 17 commissions of enquiry over the past decade, mostly relating to corruption – including investigations into the Social Security Commission, the Namibian Development Corporation and the Ministry of Fisheries – the reports, or at least the recommendations, have never been made public' (Friedrich-Ebert Stiftung, 2009, p. 20). In Namibia, radio talk shows[1] *Open Line, Chat Show, Ewi Lya Manguluka* and *Silozi* have been stopped, because politicians did not like the issues they raised. In Namibia 'most government websites, including that of the state broadcaster NBC, are outdated and not functional in terms of providing current public information' (Friedrich-Ebert Stiftung, 2009, p. 19). Thus, what exists in Namibia is in line with Baker's (1998) notion of an elitist democracy. There is a kind of elitist democracy in which certain (and limited) groups participate meaningfully. These groups include people with secondary and university education who are mostly found in urban areas. The school system produces people who aspire to join the lifestyle of the elites, a lifestyle of upper-level occupations, houses in suburban areas, two or so cars and authority at the workplace. Many of them have benefited and are still benefiting from the affirmative action policies that replaced whites with blacks in upper level jobs. Few of them are interested in working in rural areas where transformation needs are greatest. As we have argued above, schooling in an elitist

---

[1] Most of these radio talk shows, however, were opened again in 2016 due to popular demand.

democracy promotes the rotation of elites. Educated elites are the ones who seek sufficient information to participate in the public sphere to function rationally and, of course, to perform a watchdog function. Many graduates of the Namibian school system aspire to participate in this rotation. In August 2014, the ruling party SWAPO held its congress to elect its next set of leaders. This congress witnessed the emergence of these people in the party, and they form the bulk of the parliament sworn in in March 2015.[2]

Given entrenched bureaucracies and status hierarchies, moderate levels of economic growth, high levels of inequality and traditional family structures and the like, education has little chance of contributing to republican or complex democracy as described by Baker (1998) in Namibia. At present, the school system is not (a) producing citizens who are concerned with civic virtue; (b) producing citizens who can understand and follow events sufficiently to expose corruption and other lapses in civic virtue; and (c) producing citizens with a common understanding for informed, objective and inclusive debate. In complex democracy, the role of education is to provide a multi-cultural education designed to teach people to respect differences within diverse societies. This seems far from what the Namibian school system is doing. Our schools are not creating enough space for criticism, deliberation and responsibility.

CONCLUSION

The American philosopher John Dewey argued that education is an important site for the reproduction of society. It cultivates skills and capacities, qualities of character, and habits of mind that enable members of a society to live and work in a manner that maintains its definitive economic, political and cultural features. This is the conservative aspect of education. Education, however, also has a progressive possibility of contributing to society's further democratisation. It is our contention that although there is a relationship between education and democracy, it is not always straightforward. Thus, although there is empirical evidence showing that countries with more education are on average more democratic than countries with less education, it is easy also to point out countries with more education that falter when it comes to democracy (Singapore of the 1970s, 1980s and 1990s being a prime example). Even in developing countries, such as Namibia, there is no conclusive evidence linking individual education to democratic values of openness and tolerance. It is also not clear to what extent the relationship between education and democracy is confounded by economic development. It is much more productive in our view to think in terms of different types of democracy and then link them to education. This is because education plays different roles in different versions of democracy.

---

[2] The 2015 Namibian Cabinet, while including a few members without secondary school certificates, consists of a majority who possess secondary education qualifications and above. The same can be said about Deputy Ministers. In this respect, Baker's (1998) notion of 'elitist democracy' as described above does apply to the Namibian situation. Against the backdrop of an aspired 'knowledge-based economy' however, a minimum requirement of a Master's degree for Cabinet ministers and Permanent Secretaries, and an undergraduate degree for deputy ministers would be ideal for Namibia.

References

Acemoglu, D., Johnson, S., Robinson, J. A., & Yared, P. (2005). From education to democracy? *American Economic Review Papers and Proceedings, 95*(2), 44–49.

Almond, G. & Verba, S. (1963). *The civic culture: Political attitudes and democracy in five nations.* USA: Princeton University Press.

Alonzo, J. S. (2006). *Restoring the ideal marketplace: How recognizing bloggers as journalists can save the press.* Retrieved from http://www.nyujlpp.org/wp-content/uploads/2012/11/Joseph-S-Alonzo-Restoring-the-Ideal-Marketplace.pdf

Althaus, S. (2011). *What's good and bad in political communication research? Normative standards for evaluating media and citizen performance.* Retrieved from faculty.las.illinois.edu/salthaus/Publications/althaus_Sage_HPC_chapter%20FINAL.pdf

Archibugi, D. & David, H. (Eds.). (1995). *Cosmopolitan democracy: An agenda for a new world order.* Cambridge: Polity Press.

Baker, C. E. (1998). The media that citizens need. *University of Pennsylvania Law Review, 147,* 317–408.

Baker, C. E. (2001). *Media, markets, and democracy.* Cambridge: Cambridge University Press.

Barro, R. J. (1999). Determinants of democracy. *Journal of Political Economy, 107*(S6), 158–183.

Barkan, J. D., Mattes, R., Mozaffar, S., & Smiddy, K. (2010). *The African legislatures project: First findings.* (CSSR working paper No. 277). UCT: Democracy in Africa Research Unit.

Berger, G. (2002). Theorizing the media democracy relationship in southern Africa. *The International Journal for Communication Studies, 64*(1), 21–45.

Brown, D. S. & Hunter, W. (2004). Democracy and Human Capital Formation: Education Spending in Latin America, 1980–1997. Retrieved from http://journals.sagepub.com/doi/pdf/10.1177/0010414004266870

Castelló-Climent, A. (2008). On the distribution of education and democracy. *Journal of Development Economics, 87,* 179–190.

Chomsky, N. (2000). *Chomsky on miseducation.* Maryland, USA: Rowman & Littlefield Publishers.

Crush, J. S. & Pendleton, W. C. (2004). *Regionalizing xenophobia? Citizen attitudes to immigration and refugee policy in Southern Africa.* Cape Town: Southern African Migration Policy (Series 30).

Dewey, J. (1916). *Democracy and education.* New York: The Macmillan Company.

Fenstermacher, G. D. (2002). *Democracy and education: Are the connections a myth?* Retrieved from http://www-personal.umich.edu/~gfenster/ovpesms.PDF

Friedrich-Ebert Stiftung. (2009). *The African Media Barometer (AMB) country reports.* Retrieved from http://www.fesmedia-africa.org/home/what-we-do/africa-media-barometer-amb/amb-country-reports/

Gasiorowski, M. J. & Power, T. J. (1998). The structural determinants of democratic consolidation: Evidence From the third world. *Comparative Political Studies, 31*(6), 740–77.

Giroux, H. (1992). Educational leadership and the crisis of democratic government, *Educational Researcher. 21*(4), 4–11.

Glaeser, E. L., Ponzetto, G, & Shleifer, A. (2006). *Why does democracy need education?* NBER working paper: No 12128.

Habermas, J. (1996). *Between facts and norms: Contributions to a discourse theory of law and democracy.* Cambridge, UK: Polity Press in association with Blackwell Publishers.

Hadenius, A. & Teorell, J. (2005). Cultural and economic prerequisites of democracy: Reassessing recent evidence. *Studies in comparative international development, 39* (4), pp. 87–106.

Held, D. (1995). Democracy and the new international order. In D. Archibugi & H. David (Eds.), *Cosmopolitan democracy: An agenda for a new world order.* Cambridge: Polity Press.

Inglehart, R. & Welzel, C. (2005). *Modernization, cultural change and democracy: The human development sequence.* New York and Cambridge: Cambridge University Press.

Kamens, D. H. (1988). Education and democracy: A comparative institutional analysis, *Sociology of Education, 61*(2), pp. 114–127.

C. Keulder, C. (Ed.). (2010). *State, society and democracy: A reader in Namibian politics.* Windhoek: Macmillan Education Namibia. (Original work published 2000).

Keulder, C., Nord, A. & Emminghaus, C. (2010). Namibia's emerging political culture. In C. Keulder (Ed.), *State, society and democracy: A reader in Namibian politics.* Windhoek: Macmillan Education Namibia. (Original work published 2000).

Kunczic, M. (2001). Media and democracy: Are western concepts of press freedom applicable in new democracies? In P. Bajomi-Lázár & I. Hegedűs (Eds.), *Media & politics. Conference papers on the interplay of media and politics.* Budapest: New Mandate Publishing House.

Kurth-Schai, R. & Green, C. (2009). Education and democracy. In E. F. Provenzo, Jr., (Ed.). *Encyclopedia of the social and cultural foundations of education.* Thousand Oaks, CA: SAGE.

Lipset, S. M. (1959). Some social requisites of democracy: Economic Development and political legitimacy. *American Political Science Review, 53*(1), pp. 69–105.

Miller, M. (1997). Why Darwinism fails in explaining social and cultural evolution – Comments on Peter J. Richerson and Robert Boyd. In W. Schelkle, W. Krauth, M. Kohli, & G. Elwert (Eds.). *Paradigms of social change: Modernization, development, transformation, evolution.* New York: St. Martin's Press.

Ministry of Health and Social Services (MoHSS), Namibia and Macro International Inc. (2008). *Namibia demographic and health survey 2006–07.* Windhoek, Namibia and Calverton, Maryland, USA: MoHSS and Macro International Inc.

Møller, J. (2007). *Elitist Democracy and the rise of populism in East-Central Europe. Has Pareto been proved right?* Retrieved from http://www.jhubc.it/ecpr-riga/virtualpaperroom/016.pdf

Prah, K. K. (2007, August). *Democracy, education, literacy and development.* Keynote Address; 10th Year Jubilee Celebrations of the Centre for International Education, University College of Oslo. Retrieved from http://www.nvit.ca/docs/democracy_%20education_%20literacy%20and%20development.pdf

Price, M. E. & Krug, P. (2006). The enabling environment for free and independent media. In M. Harvey (Ed.), Media matters: Perspectives on advancing governance and development. *The Global Forum for Media Development,* 95–102. Retrieved from http://repository.upenn.edu/asc_papers/143

Robinson, J. (2006). Economic development and democracy. *Annual Review of Political Science 9,* 503–527.

SIAPAC-Namibia [Social Impact Assessment and Policy Analysis Corporation]. (2009). *Knowledge, attitudes, and practices study on factors and traditional practices that may perpetuate or protect Namibians from gender based violence and discrimination: Caprivi, Erongo, Karas, Kavango, Kunene, Ohangwena, Omaheke and Otjozondjupa regions.* Windhoek: Ministry of Gender Equality and Child Welfare.

Sifuna, D. N. (2000). Education for democracy and human rights in African schools: The Kenyan experience. *Africa Development XXV* (1&2), 213–239.

West-Burnham, J. (2009). *Rethinking educational leadership and democracy*. London: Bloomsbury Publishing.

Weil, F. D. (1985). The variable effect of education on liberal attitudes: A comparative historical analysis of anti-Semitism using public opinion survey data. *American Sociological Review, 50*(4), 458–474.

Zulu, P. M. (2001). Education as a precondition for democracy. *Democracy, Reality and Responsibility*. Pontifical Academy of Social Sciences, Acta 6, Vatican City. Proceedings of the Sixth Plenary Session of the Pontifical Academy of Social Sciences, February, 2000. Retrieved from http://www.pass.va/content/dam/scienzesociali/pdf/acta6/acta6-zulu.pdf

4

The aims of education: Some general conceptual issues

Elizabeth Magano Amukugo

Before you read this chapter, clarify your own thoughts and conclusions:

1. Choose three of the following statements which most closely express your own beliefs. Then choose three of the following statements which are least important in your opinion:

Education in my country should:
   a. equip people to perform their function in serving society
   b. produce leaders who can guide others
   c. be an equalising force between men, women, rich and poor, all cultures
   d. be a stabilising political force within the state
   e. turn the young into responsible citizens
   f. be a system for discovering learners' aptitudes and training them for society's use
   g. prepare people to govern themselves and participate in their society's governance
   h. involve individuals in the process of critical enquiry
   i. make learners self-reliant
   j. instil the social goals of living for the common good
   k. train people to think for themselves and make informed decisions
   l. increase tolerance for human diversity
   m. equip people for economic gain
   n. transmit and preserve cultural traditions
   o. serve as a transforming social force
   p. serve as a tool for achieving social justice

2. For education in your country to achieve the three most important of the aims that you chose above, what would need to change or improve?

INTRODUCTION

As is the case with the definitions of democracy and justice, and as argued in chapters two and three, education can mean different things to individuals or social groups depending on the worldviews of those concerned. Historically, however, the purpose of education for both the individual and society has long occupied the minds of educational thinkers from the pre-20th Century (Plato, Aristotle and Rousseau) through the 20th Century and beyond (Pestalozzi, Froebel and others). Robert Owen's utopian socialist educational ideas and the Marxist educational thoughts built on the views of Karl Marx and Friedrich Engels in the 19th Century preceded those of Maria Montessori in Europe and John Dewey in America. We recognise Montessori and Dewey as the 20th Century's foremost exponents of what were then 'progressive educational ideas' in western Europe (Montessori) and United States of America (Dewey) (see Bowen, 2003), and feel their impact even today. In fact, most of the above names featured in the *Doctrines of the Great Educators* by Rusk & Scotland (1918/1979), while conspicuously absent from the list were African educational thinkers such as Dr James Africanus Horton (1835–1883), Edward Wilmot Blyden (1832–1912) and Henry Carr (1863–1945), who belonged to the 20th Century educational thinkers (Akinpelu, 1981, pp. 78–112).

As Africa began to rid itself of colonial subjugation during the 1950s through the 1960s, 1970s and the 1990s, African educational thinkers including, but not limited to, Nyerere (1967), Ishumi (1978), Thompson (1981), Datta (1984) and Moyana (1988) began to articulate the role that education could play in social development.

Arguing from a critical theory viewpoint, the purpose of this chapter is to examine the aims of education in a democratic society, partly through the eyes of selected educational thinkers. By exploring the role and place of education both in the life of the individual and in society, we begin to understand the connection between democracy, education and social justice. The chapter will examine the aims of education from western perspectives on the one hand and perspectives from the southern countries on the other hand.

Democracy, education and social justice: Plato and Dewey revisited

To understand the aims of education in a democratic society as outlined by educational thinkers and ourselves, presupposes that we first comprehend what we mean by the terms democracy and justice, as this will determine our views on the role and function of education in society.

Educators and thinkers today generally accept the view that the term democracy has its roots in the political history of Greece in the 5th Century BC, and regard the city of Athens as the world's first democracy. In fact, the literal meaning of the term means 'rule by the people' in Greek (Arendt, as cited in Fotopoulos, 2005) calling attention to the fact that Athenian democracy was the first historical example of identifying the sovereign with those exercising sovereignty. Fotopoulos augmented this point by suggesting that Athenian democracy was founded on the belief that citizens themselves should directly exercise sovereignty – a practice we refer to today as direct democracy. At the same time, both Arendt and Fotopoulos point to Athenian democracy as having been a partial democracy due to the exclusion of the vast majority of its citizens. This view is shared by, among others, Birch (2007, p. 109), who stresses that the right to political participation was granted only to a small minority in Athens. However, the partial democracy notion does not fit entirely into the idealist viewpoint which classical Greek's most prominent philosophical and educational giant, Plato, espoused. His treatise *The Republic* suggests otherwise. As Plato explains in *The Republic* (Book VIII: p. 557 a):

> ... [D]emocracy, I suppose, comes into being when the poor win, killing some of the others and casting out some, and share the regime and the ruling offices with those who are left on an equal basis .... Then I suppose that in this regime especially, all sorts of human beings come to be .... It is probably the fairest of the regimes .... Just like a many-colored cloak decorated in all hues, this regime, decorated with all dispositions, would also look fairest .... (As cited in Bloom, 1991, p. 235)

Notwithstanding the autocratic social organisation of Greek society at that particular historical juncture, Plato's own words cited above point to a view of democracy that seems to be more inclusive than the partial democracy which Arendt and others expressed. An Athenian philosopher, Plato, partly reacting to the death penalty verdict of his teacher, Socrates, contributed to the broader understanding of the term democracy by theorising about 'absolute justice'. This type of justice, in his view, was not only higher than the public will, but should also be placed outside the limits of human manipulation (Bowen & Hobson, 1974). In *The Republic*, Plato further argued that the fundamental value of justice would be better secured and maintained if the state were to take charge of the activities of all its citizens (Plato, 1991/360 BCE). As Bloom (1991, p. vii) contends in the preface to his second edition of Plato's work: 'No other philosophic book so powerfully expresses the human longing for justice.'

Placing the responsibility of funding education squarely on the state's shoulders, Plato also felt the state was responsible for organising the division of labour, based on individual talent and in accordance with the expertise it required. Through state-financed education, he argued, citizens would be most well-equipped to perform the functions of the division to which they belonged. To him, therefore, justice was defined in terms of the responsibilities that citizens owed to the state (Akinpelu, 1981; Bowen & Hobson, 1974). Moreover, Plato was convinced that the state would be competently governed if rulers were to attain the level of 'philosopher kings' – an idea he borrowed from his teacher, Socrates. As Plato clearly suggests in Book V of *The Republic* (as cited in Bowen & Hobson, 1974, p. 50):

> [t]he society we have described can never grow into reality or see the light of day, and there will be no end to the troubles of states, or indeed, my dear Glaucon, of humanity itself, till philosophers become kings in this world, or till those we now call kings and rulers really and truly become philosophers, and political power and philosophy thus come into the same hand ...

An idealist philosopher who dreamt big, Plato clearly believed in the power of education and knowledge in guiding decision-making, which he suggests by his basic principle that 'knowledge is virtue' and 'ignorance is vice' (Akinpelu, 1981; Bowen & Hobson, 1974). One can argue, therefore, that Plato's concept of justice, which partly entailed each person doing his/her job without encroaching on another's area of expertise or responsibility, and his idea of equality between men and women in terms of the provision of education and the division of labour, not only reflect his idealist stand, but also express a yearning for a more just and inclusive society. At the same time, Plato's idealist worldview put limitations on the practical utility of some of his ideas. Some (e.g. Karl Popper (n.d.), in his *The Open Society and its Enemies*) criticise Plato's political programme as totalitarian justice, as justice in Plato's Republic implies what is in the interest of the state and the preservation of 'a rigid class division and class rule', whereby the wise rule and the ignorant obey; and that the individual exists in order 'to maintain the stability of the state'. Others, (e.g. Takala (1998) in *Plato on Leadership*), who regard Plato as a great philosopher, interpret Plato's stable, ideal state as one that depends on the leader's (philosopher king's) 'transcendental abilities' and 'mystical skills', which Platonian education not only provided, but which served as a means through which the young were to be turned into responsible citizens. As such, says Takala, Platonian education had a political basis. In *Plato on Leadership*, Takala (1998) suggests, however, that Plato's idea of philosophy kings as rulers failed as Plato came to accept that this idea may remain an ideal rather than become reality.

John Dewey's reading of Plato is somewhat different from that of the other critics. To Dewey, although Plato contributed valuable knowledge to the world, the conditions under which he worked limited the realisation of his ideas. Dewey (1916/2010) points out that:

> Education proceeds ultimately from the patterns furnished by institutions, customs, and laws. Only in a just state will these be such as to give the right education ... (Dewey, 1916/2010, p. 57).

Moreover, he commends Plato's concept of the division of labour and the role of education in that process, and clearly spells out the role and function of education to both the individual and society by suggesting the following:

> No one could better express than did he [Plato] the fact that a society is stably organized when each individual is doing that for which he has aptitude by nature in such a way as to be useful to others (or to contribute to the whole to which he belongs); and that it is the business of education to discover these aptitudes and progressively to train them for social use (Dewey, 1916/2010, p. 57).

Dewey's 'equilibrium' perspective of society (as expressed above) notwithstanding, he recognised the limitations imposed on Plato's thinking by the historical and social conditions under which the latter lived. As an example of such limitations, Dewey (1916/2010, p. 57) argued that it would be impossible to determine the '... limits and distribution of activities – what he [Plato] called justice – as a trait of both individual and social organization'.

In other words, Plato's understanding of democracy was, in Dewey's view, useful but restricted. Hence, Dewey observed that it was almost impossible for the individual to reach 'consistency of mind' since 'self-consistency' was only possible under a complete whole. Dewey, while appreciating Plato's outstanding ability to carve out the role of education for both the individual and society, as well as the latter's contention that birth or wealth should not decide the individual's place in society, sympathised with Plato's incapacity to figure out the 'uniqueness of individuals', due to the fact that the Greek philosopher functioned in a very undemocratic society. By the same token, this situation also put limitations on what education could achieve.

Nonetheless, a critical look at Dewey's defence of Plato's views on democracy and justice points to Dewey's failure to see idealism as the major reason why some of his (Plato's) ideas could not be realised, rather than solely the historical and social conditions of Ancient Greece.

Dewey's view of democracy deprecates the widely accepted view that democracy is merely a form of government. Instead, he sees the term as a social and political ideal (Festenstein, 2014). As such, he advocates for some form of participatory democratic system in which individual members of society have a say. He does this by emphasising the role of the individual as a member of community in the process of democratisation. Hence, he advocates for a type of society where the well-being of the individual is tied to that of the community. As he puts it in his 'Ethics of Democracy':

> Freedom in a 'positive' sense consisted not merely in the absence of external constraints but the positive fact of participation in such an ethically desirable social order … 'men are not isolated non-social atoms, but are men only when in intrinsic relations' to one another, and the state in turn only represents them 'so far as they have become organically related to one another, or are possessed of unity of purpose and interest' (as cited in Festenstein, 2014). The above view of the individual and society has influenced Dewey's concepts of 'knowledge' and education. To him, true knowledge is 'the product of competent inquiries'; and such inquiry is social, as it needs to be exposed to examination, confirmation and/or rectification by other members of society – what he calls 'intelligent social control or social action' (as cited in Feinstein, 2014).

As a pragmatist, Dewey not only believed that philosophy essentially was 'the generalised theory of education', but also that education facilitated and guided the individual to become involved in 'a process of critical enquiry', with the aim of reaching real solutions. Teachers, he contends, are co-operative older and wiser learners whose role it is to assist pupils/students discover 'the values of democratic participation' through critically examining actual problem situations and thereby finding 'constructive solutions' to those setbacks. Part of the aim of education, therefore, is to instil democratic values, which to a degree are obtained within a social context through observing appropriate rules (Bowen & Hobson, 1974).

Plato's conception of democracy might come closer to what is known today as direct democracy, in which, according to the Collins Dictionary of Sociology's (Jary & Jary, 1995) delineation, all adult members of society can, theoretically, qualify to become part of a policy-making body. On the other hand, Dewey's conception of democracy goes far beyond Plato's. Dewey (1916/2010, p. 54) warns against grounding the concept of education on some distant, ideal society in favour of one that actually exists. This point marks the difference between Plato the idealist and Dewey the pragmatist. To Dewey (ibid, p. 57), democracy is about the:

> … widening of the area of shared concerns and the liberation of a greater diversity of personal capacities [through education].

According to Dewey, this means providing educational opportunities to the majority rather than to a select few. Plato's emphasis on knowledge as a virtue, together with his belief regarding the potential of the individual using his/her knowledge and skills to serve society, and Dewey's idea of education's capacity to unleash a great variety of individual capabilities with the aim of solving both the individual's as well as society's problems, provide useful lessons to the global community at large and to Africa in particular – provided that we do not merely reproduce these ideas, but also contextualise them in order to fit the reality of the society concerned.

The aims of education in a democratic society: Perspectives from the south

In *Education for Self-Reliance*, Julius Nyerere (1967) aspired to building a socialist society based on equality, respect for human dignity and the sharing of societal resources. In his view, the aim of education is to prepare and enable the young to play a dynamic and constructive role in the development of society and to make society self-reliant. His educational philosophy, 'education for self-reliance', was based on the above principles. He built his educational vision on a basic principle that the goals of education be guided by societal values and set objectives. Having lived at a time when Tanzania was predominantly a rural, under-developed society, Nyerere placed his faith in the country's natural resources (land), human resources and education as being the foremost enablers that would lead Tanzania out of poverty toward self-reliance and, eventually, industrialisation. Education for self-reliance, as he conceptualised it, would not only instil '... the social goals of living together, and working together, for the common good' (Nyerere, 1967), but also serve as a tool for critical consciousness by enabling people to think for themselves, take informed decisions on issues that affect their lives, and make independent judgements on decisions taken on their behalf, as opposed to being passive agricultural workers and implementers of directions from above. Thus, for education to serve its intended purpose, it must be extended to the rural populations as well, rather than being concentrated in urban areas. As such, democracy, to him, meant not only ensuring equality in all spheres of life – economic, political and social – but also utilising material and human resources in the spirit of self-reliance (Nyerere, 1967). Although, to a large extent, Nyerere's socialist ideas have been praised as being progressive, they have also been criticised in some quarters for being too idealistic, because he failed to curb poverty and under-development in Tanzania during his rule. As Samoff (as cited in the *Encyclopedia of Informal Education* [Infed], (2003), observed:

> Judged today, the educational reforms met with some success and some failure. The policies were never fully implemented and had to operate against a background of severe resource shortage and a world orientation to more individualistic and capitalist understandings of the relation of education to production. However, primary education became virtually universal; curriculum materials gained distinctively Tanzanian flavours; and schooling used local language forms.

Taking the above critique into consideration, one would conclude that Nyerere's view on society and education was not only idealistic, but broad-minded as well. Ibhawoh and Dibua (2003) saw the criticism of Nyerere as being a reflection of the west/south divide. Thus, while the *Newsweek* of 25 October 1999 (as cited in Ibhawoh and Dibua, 2003), posed the following question: 'How does a leader wreck a country's economy yet die a national hero?', *The Guardian* (Lagos, Nigeria) of 15 October 1999 (as cited in Ibhawoh and Dibua, 2003), pointed out that Nyerere's concept of *ujamaa* served '... as the basis for equitable economic production and distribution .... With the idea of *ujamaa*, he popularised the idiom of self-reliance and non-exploitive development'.

Be that as it may, Infed (2003) rightly noted:

> One of Africa's most respected figures, Julius Nyerere (1922–1999) was a politician
> of principle and intelligence. Known as Mwalimu (teacher) he had a vision of
> education and social action that was rich with possibility.

One can conclude nonetheless, that Nyerere's view of society and education was influenced by the materialist view which, according to Castles and Wüstenburg (1979), aims at producing '... "fully developed human beings"... who are capable not only of doing productive work, but also of controlling... [the economy] and running society' (Castles et al., 1979, p. 7). The materialist perspective views the purpose of education as being to develop and empower the individual through linking education with productive work as well as shaping people's consciousness. The fact that some of Nyerere's ideas were not realised seems to depend more on lack of implementation, which cannot entirely be blamed on him, but also on government as a collective.

In analysing the relationship between education and social development, Ishumi (1976, pp. 3–4) criticises the universal view. The conservative, for example, holds that the purpose of education is to conserve and recreate society; but to him, education is more than that, as it serves to create and recreate society. The latter purpose, which he terms the 'creative and conserving process', is what generates the link between education and social development. He was a firm believer in national planning and emphasised the necessity to interlink national planning, education and development, in order for education to make tangible contributions to social development. Besides, he observes that education also creates awareness of people's circumstances and thereby increases the quality of their participation in social development.

Thompson (1981), who goes to great lengths to critically analyse the concept of development, defines the term as what society should look like in its more advanced form. However, he makes it clear that:

> Development cannot be thought of simply as an accumulation of wealth but
> must be concerned with the distribution and use made of that wealth, with the
> impact both of the way in which it has been created and the way in which it is
> used upon the quality of the lives people lead (Thompson, 1981, p. 15).

In other words, social development induced, controlled and directed by central government, will have its real meaning only if it corresponds to the quality of life enjoyed by all citizens.

Thompson (1981) views education as a social institution that derives its focus from individuals and groups, whose perceptions coupled with the entire social context (including values and perceptions), serves to determine the direction and outcome of the education system. On the whole, he sees the aim of education as bringing about fundamental changes in people's lives and, by consequence, effecting change in the political, social and economic arenas. However, education in particular increases social tolerance for human diversity and can also raise the individual's awareness of different groups and, hopefully, their capacity to co-exist with such differences. Bangwato-Skeete and Zikhali (2011) in particular provide evidence that, for African countries, education enhances tolerance for neighbours of a different race, language, religion, immigrants and people living with AIDS.

It is clear from Thompson's expressed educational ideas that he not only sees education as a democratic imperative, but also as a means through which we can realise the goal of justice.

Like Thompson, Datta (1984) also sees education as being socially determined with both society and its various groups determining the direction that education takes. He argues from a standpoint that schooling strives to promote the interest of the dominant social group, and he defines education as not only a means to individual advancement, but also a social, innovative, political and economic function. This function partially comes to the fore through the utilisation of a pool of skills and capabilities of the learned within society.

Datta (1984, pp. 29–51) analyses at length the link between education and society in the African context, by outlining two major functions of education, namely:

The private function of education, which is largely about the benefits that an individual can accrue from formal education, such as economic benefits; and those one derives from knowledge, skills and the socialisation process, and:

The social function of education, in terms of which he differentiates between:

1. The conservative function, which is about the transmission and preservation of society's dominant culture, in terms of both its instrumental aspect (knowledge and skills), and the expressive aspect (values, norms, concepts and images of socially accepted behaviour).
2. The innovative function, which is about the production of new ideas and knowledge that contribute to social change.
3. The political function, which is about political socialisation which he defines as '... the transmission of values, beliefs, ideas and patterns of behaviour pertaining to the generation, distribution and exercise of power'.
4. The economic function, which refers to education's contribution to economic development. He pointed out, however, the difficulties in determining that relationship, and thus made a critical analysis of the issues at hand, while leaving readers to arrive at their own conclusions.
5. The selective and allocative function of education, which in his view refers to the way education serves as a 'filtering agency' by selecting and channelling people into 'different areas of specialisation and levels of operation. A 'pool of capabilities' is created if the educational system performs effectively.
6. The unintended consequences of education – the latent function of education – denotes to Datta educational outcomes that might not be anticipated, recognised or even welcomed by educational planners and implementers alike. These, he points out, can be both positive and negative. The negative spinoffs can be harmful to the social system, which he categorises in this case as 'dysfunctional'. He cites, among others, two examples: colonial education that unintentionally produced leaders of anti-colonial movements; and well-meant educational expansion that may lead to higher unemployment among the graduates.

Moyana (1988), who argues from a materialist perspective, describes how colonial education served to make the colonised reinterpret their history and outlook on life. He holds that the aim of post-colonial education should therefore be to alter the African peoples' outlook and help them 'develop a consciousness of themselves as an antithesis of the oppressor'. Moyana, whose ideas bear some similarity to Paulo Freire's (1968/1996), believes that the best way to achieve that type of consciousness among students is through creative writing. He also allocates considerable importance to the role of language in the development of 'conscientisation'. As he suggests in his book: 'The linguistic activity that involves the act of naming and the use of the word thus focuses upon the world. All this is directed toward the humanization of the individual' (ibid., p. 27).

At the same time he adds that the role language can play in this regard would be incomplete without changing perceptions, what Karl Marx called 'humanising the object of the senses'. Hence Moyana (1988) observes:

> The emancipation of the senses actually means a complete redefinition of a person's outlook on the world and a new language through which to express that outlook.
> The growth of a new idiom, a new critical awareness constitutes a rediscovery of a familiar. A new idiom, a new vocabulary ... (Moyana, 1988, p. 31).

A former teacher of history, English and drama in colonial Zimbabwe, Moyana used students' creative writing examples, coupled with an overview of African literature by Wole Soyinka, Chinua Achebe and others, to prove his point.

CONCLUSION

The overt aims of education differ depending on the historical period, the form of political governance and the peculiar needs of a particular society. Staying true to his famous dictum, 'knowledge is virtue and ignorance is vice', Plato concluded that rulers need to reach the level of philosopher kings to be able to govern competently. Having lived in an undemocratic society, Plato envisioned an ideal state that took the responsibility to fund education. It also took charge of the division of labour and ensured that each person performed his duties according to individual talent.

Subject specialisation, as we know it today, has some similarities with Plato's concept of 'division of labour'. Dewey, a pragmatist, negated the idea that democracy is simply a form of government. To the contrary, he conceptualised this term as a social and political ideal. He argues from a standpoint that an individual is not an isolated being but his existence is intrinsically tied in with the community. Therefore, the individual's satisfaction and achievement can only be realised within the context of social habits and institutions that promote it. Against this view, Dewey concluded that true knowledge is a result of 'competent social inquiries'. In a democracy, therefore, knowledge needs to be subjected to social scrutiny, or what he calls 'intelligent social control'. At the personal level, the aim of education is to unleash the individual's different capacities in order to solve both individual and societal problems.

However, education should also promote individual, micro-level effects that challenge and change values and attitudes towards others (with regard to those who are marginalised, the poor, and those of another gender, ethnicity, religion or sexuality etc.). Education in particular should aim at increasing social tolerance for human diversity and raising the individuals' awareness of different groups and hopefully their capacity to co-exist with such differences. In particular Bangwato-Skeete and Zikhali find that for African countries, there is stark evidence that education enhances tolerance for neighbours of a different race, language and religion, immigrants and people living with AIDS. This supposition relates to Dewey's claim that an educated populace secures the necessary freedoms upon which a democratic society is built.

Dewey sees education as the process of living through a continuous reconstruction of experiences. Such experiences can be conservative, retrogressive or progressive. Education can only end up cultivating skills and capacities, qualities of character, and habits of mind that enable members of a society to live and work in a manner that maintains its definitive economic, political and cultural features. Education, however, can also be a transformative social force, as suggested by Freire, Nyerere, Datta, Ishumi, Thompson and Moyana. It is up to societies to create schools that are innovative – and that make education a force for liberation and democratisation; a force that cuts across the barriers of ethnicity, race and class and overrides inequalities from birth and other social circumstances. In this sense the 'object and reward of learning is the continued capacity for growth' (Dewey, 2010/1916).

In the African context, this continued capacity for growth requires democratic practices that allow for the interests of citizens to dominate the process rather than education to be subjected to interests of special groups. Above all, education should be a tool for achieving social justice through its transformative purpose and by ensuring that issues of educational access, equity and quality are concurrently addressed.

References

Akinpelu, J. A. (1981). *An introduction to philosophy of education*. London: Macmillan Publishers.

Bangwayo-Skeete, P. F. & Zikhali, P. (2011). Social tolerance for human diversity in sub-Saharan Africa. *International Journal of Social Economics*. 38(6), 516–536.

Birch, A. H. (2007). *The concepts and theories of modern democracy* (3rd ed.). London: Routledge.

Bloom, A. (1991). *The republic of Plato* (2nd ed.). New York: Basic Books.

Bowen, J. (2003). *A history of western education*, (vols 1–3). London: Routledge.

Bowen, J. & Hobson, P. R. (1974). *Theories of education*. New York: John Wiley & Sons.

Castles, S. & Wüstenburg, W. (1979). *The education of the future: An introduction to the theory and practice of socialist education*. London: Pluto Press.

Datta, A. (1984). *Education and society: A sociology of African education*. London: Macmillan Publishers.

Dewey, J. (2010). *Democracy and education: An introduction to the philosophy of education*. Lexington, KY: BLN Publishing. (Original work published 1916).

Encyclopaedia of Informal Education (Infed). (2003). *Julius Nyerere, lifelong learning and education*. Retrieved from http://infed.org/mobi/julius-nyerere-lifelong-learning-and-education//

Festenstein, M. (2014). Dewey's Political Philosophy, In E. N. Zalta (Ed.). *The Stanford Encyclopedia of Philosophy* (Spring 2014 Edition). Retrieved from https://plato.stanford.edu/archives/spr2014/entries/dewey-political/

Fotopoulos, T. (2005). The multidimensional crisis and inclusive democracy. *The International Journal of Inclusive Democracy* (special issue, August 2005). Retrieved from http://www.inclusivedemocracy.org/journal/ss/ss.htm

Freire, P. (1996). *Pedagogy of the oppressed*. London: Penguin. (Original work published 1968).

Ibhawoh, B. & Dibua, J. I. (2003). Deconstructing Ujamaa: The legacy of Julius Nyerere in the quest for social and economic development in Africa. *African Journal of Political Science*, 8(1).

Ishumi, A. G. M. (1976). *Education and development*. Dar es Salaam: East Africa Literature Bureau.

Jary, D. & Jary, J. (1995). *Collins dictionary of sociology* (2nd ed.). Glasgow: Harper Collins Publishers.

Moyana, T. T. (1988). *Education, liberation and the creative act*. Harare: Zimbabwe Publishing House.

Nyerere, J. (1967). *Education for self-reliance*. Retrieved from http://www.swaraj.org/shikshantar/resources_nyerere.html

Plato. (1991). *The republic of Plato*. (A. Bloom, Trans.). New York: Basic Books. (Original work published 360 BCE)

Popper, K. (n.d.). *The open society and its enemies*. Retrieved from https://monoskop.org/images/6/6d/Popper_Karl_The_Open_Society_and_its_Enemies_The_High_Tide_of_Prophecy_Vol_2_1st_ed.pdf

Rusk, R. R. & Scotland, J. (1979). *Doctrines of the great educators* (5th ed.). (Original work published 1918). New York: St. Martin's Press.

Takala, T. (1998). Plato on Leadership. *Journal of Business Ethics*, *17*(7), 785–798.

Thompson, A. R. (1981). *Education and development in Africa*. London: The Macmillan Press.

5

Democratic values, norms and education in post-colonial societies

Tangeni C. K. Iijambo

You are encouraged to look for the author's opinions on the following issues as you read this chapter. Then decide, do you agree, or do you have additional/alternative ideas?

1. If education does not exist simply to serve the needs of the economic market, what else does it exist for?

2. What are five core values or principles of democracy essential for an African state, and how would an ideal education system promote these values or principles?

3. What constraints or challenges make it difficult for your country's education system to achieve these ideal values or principles?

4. Would a curriculum based on African cultural values be possible, and if so, what would it look like?

INTRODUCTION

Democratisation has been a trend that most developing countries have adopted or intend to adopt to steer their socioeconomic and political values, norms and overall development. Any deliberation on democracy may arouse lively debate among educators and those who exercise political power in various systems. Scrutiny of democratic processes shows these critical impulses to be timely and of utmost importance, which no one can ignore, especially educators. This chapter seeks to determine why countries evolve and consolidate democratic systems of government. It also attempts to explain that for democracy to succeed, we must value it and make it part of culture.

It is unfortunate, however, that political liberation on the continent did not always translate into socioeconomic and cultural independence. The powers that be and the elites in African societies often contribute negatively to the continent's development by under-valuing knowledge norms and languages of their own continent.

In this chapter, I first explore the historical background to democracy in Africa, and then I scrutinise democratic values, education and norms in post-colonial African states. After establishing what people consider normal and how they can enhance their livelihood in a democratic society, the chapter analyses some of the obstacles to democratic advancement in Namibia and on the African continent.

Freedom and democracy, although apparently holding a good deal in common, did not develop simultaneously. Critical social theorists argue that dominant ideologies and knowledge are built into social institutions that both privilege and exclude particular perspectives, voices, authorities and representations. Leistyna, Woodrum and Sherblom (1996, p. 24) eloquently state that 'within theories of cultural reproduction, schools, educators, and curricula are generally viewed as mechanisms of ideological control that work to reproduce and maintain dominant beliefs, values, norms and oppressive practices'. In Africa, the colonised areas obtained independence only during the late 1950s, through the 1960s, 1970s and 1980s until the last colonies on the continent (Namibia and South Africa) achieved independence at the beginning of the nineties.

Against this background, one cannot assume that concerns about freedom, equality and various rights in these territories are synonymous with the concept of democracy. Nor can we argue legitimately that each and any form of democratic education would fulfil post-colonial educational ideals. Clearly, much depends on how we define, conceptualise and express democratic education and questions of equality, in relation to country-specific politics and the authentic concerns of the citizenry.

Indeed, we need to pay far more attention to a consideration of how, theoretically, we might unravel the contradictions which currently manifest in the education and democracy of various cultures. An important contextual question to ask is: what about the social context when the national ideology is anti-democratic, or where democracy is on a long wish-list that includes providing the basic necessities of life? Proponents of democracy whose daily lives are a struggle to nurture democratic behaviours are constrained by a background of political and economic poverty.

The act of imagining the possible leads us to an understanding that there are many 'democracies' in today's pluralistic world. Just as we encourage the students in our classrooms to achieve their individual potentials, so the world's societies are moving along many paths to different ends. Howard (1997) argues that the uneven trajectory towards democracy in Africa, Asia, and Latin America emerges from the experiences of colonialism, which is a western concept and definitely an expression of non-democratic behaviour. The colonised person knows that s/he is inferior and has no right to participate in civil society.

The irony of modern history, however, is that the seeds of democracy were sown during the colonial era, and most often it was the schoolteacher, the imposed leader and the priest casting the seeds. If the process of transforming much of the harm done by colonial entities, particularly in rural communities, materialises, teachers and educators should experiment with country-specific geopolitical, economic, environmental and cultural values. New teaching strategies, that would involve students thinking about their threatened flora and fauna, should be enhanced and involve their families in the process. Students should preferably make presentations to community members about research they have done on the local environment. This would increase community awareness of animals, dunes and forest preservation issues and promote the development potential of young people taking more responsibility in their communities.

In Namibia, for example, where the vast majority of the population was prohibited from participating in the 'democracy' run by apartheid South Africa until independence, teachers should initiate dialogue in various exciting ways. This would help them keep up with trends and new methods across a large country that is sparsely populated.

Developing countries' support for democratic practices in the world's classrooms can come from listening, finding out what is going on and seeking to join the global dialogue. Teacher to teacher relationships across the globe are particularly important as the world faces so many current and future challenges that are fundamentally similar. Consequently, developing countries can also raise their voices before western governments, especially the United States of America, about such matters as their tendencies to support the rhetoric of democratic reforms while overtly or covertly assisting repressive regimes. Finally, raising the consciousness of educators across the global spectrum, as members of an international profession, and turning that into a conscious movement where societies share interests, values, democratic norms and goals, will support an increasingly informed global democratic future.

According to a report from the United Nations (UN), this 'brings home the fact that democracy is one of the universal and indivisible core values and principles of the United Nations; it is based on the freely expressed will of people and closely linked to the rule of law and exercise of human rights and fundamental freedoms' (United Nations, 2016).

Brief background to democratic values, education and norms in post-colonial states

Prior to colonisation, some African and other developing countries experienced a type of communal living dominated by kings, chiefs, headmen and headwomen as well as the aristocracy and the landed elite. These feudal and repressive systems stifled almost any realm of development, as the majority of people were poor and owed allegiance to the rulers of the time. We should note at the same time, however, that there were also pre-colonial African societies that were not hierarchical or repressive, e.g. San communities in southern Africa. Numerous African societies had traditions of participation, consensus and communal effort as aspects of their cultures. The cultures of these societies are still rich and valuable, and it is worth borrowing from them. However, colonial notions of hierarchy and patriarchy have replaced most of these traditions and cultures. In ancient Greece, Aristotle, cited in Diamond, Linz, and Lipset (1988, p. xi) lamented: 'Democracy is more likely to occur where the middle strata are large; oligarchy and tyranny where the population is overwhelmingly poor'. Diamond et al. continue to point out that the renaissance political theorist, Machiavelli, also placed an emphasis on class distribution in specifying the sources of political systems.

The advent of colonialism and slavery further diffused and confused inhabitants of these formerly colonised countries to the extent that long after their political independence, pockets of suspicion, disillusionment, chaos, anarchy and suppression were, and continue to be, prevalent.

Beginning with India in 1947, a host of new nations in Asia, Africa, and the Middle East, that had been colonies of the western democracies, were granted independence under constitutions following election procedures modelled on those of their former colonial rulers. In the initial years of post-independence eras in Latin America, Asia and Africa, the early political leaders were teachers. Teaching, like nursing, policing and preaching, all fields with strong religious emphasis, was one of the few professions open to colonial subjects, and teachers were the only educated or literate members, particularly of rural communities. Possessors of 'the word', as Freire (1995, p. 54) so simply and powerfully puts it, teachers used their literacy to transform their societies. In many cases the first steps on the path to democracy and empowerment were taken from illiteracy to literacy, the fundamental product of a teacher's craft. Schools in many communities are the only buildings that are both accessible and public in nature. They become centres for conversation and gathering, polling places if elections are held, and health centres or food distribution centres in times of emergency, showing the seamlessness of education and community development.

Often schools are the product of communal labour and usually are cared for with pride. However, as centres of knowledge – actually as 'satellites' rather than centres, because knowledge is not well distributed – schools can also represent oppressive government policies and irrelevant curricula, taking students from agricultural work to urban employment, with the relative exclusion of girls and women. In comparative education, the notion of privilege is referred to as 'cultural reproduction', where the children of the elite and well-to-do receive better education and have superior facilities, to the extent that they eventually replace their parents as successive leaders of their respective communities.

Constructing democracy in developing societies means first increasing participation and expanding access to education. That being the case, it is necessary to reconstruct democracy because of the disruption caused by the colonial era. As mentioned earlier in this chapter, there were also various pre-colonial societies in Africa that had traditions of participation, consensus, and communal effort as aspects of their culture, and these were replaced by colonial establishments. The Ovankhumbi in southern Angola and north-western Namibia, and the Lunda-Luba in Congo are examples. The Ovankhumbi, Aawambo and many others have traditional courts similar to the *khotla* in Botswana, and these institutions have survived to this era.

Today the colonial past is part of the seamless present, and countries join the world system knowing its rules and its possibilities. People are finding ways to teach the building blocks of democracy in the most daunting of circumstances. Provision of education as a right, and educating global citizens, are challenges for today's educators. The failure of past practices and legal documents to recognise education as a basic right that should be universal and implemented as vigorously as any other has not prevented education from emerging as a right. Halim (1997, p. 9) insists that: 'It remains for the UN and its member states to officially recognise this status and thus, further the provision of quality education to all children, regardless of gender, income level, ethnicity, race, or religion'. Could it be that to understand and realise that we are all on the same fragile planet, which we keep destroying with irresponsible policies and practices, might reverse this destruction in the interests of life on earth? The challenge lies squarely with us all, wherever we find ourselves on the globe. The ideal circumstances for our diverse planet earth and its inhabitants would be to mould people from diverse origins, cultural practices and languages into one, within a framework which is democratic in character, and which can absorb, accommodate and mediate conflicts and adversarial interests without oppression and injustice.

Brief definitions and various approaches

As the arguments in Chapters 2 and 3 above present, the term democracy is defined differently according to the society and or people who aspire to the policies and practices of democracy. There is hence no single overarching or dominant definition of democracy, as people vary according to cultures, norms, values, traditions and aspirations. Diamond et al. (1988, p. xvi) rightly argue that:

> Depending on the individual, ideology, paradigm, culture, or context, the term 'democracy' may mean many different things. In fact, it is reflective of the political climate of our time that the word is used to signify the desirable end state of so many social, economic, and political pursuits or else to self-designate and thus presumably legitimate so many existing structures.

Nevertheless, democracy or democratic practices indeed have certain principles that feature prominently whenever we pursue their definition. Included among many of the prominent terms that feature in the democratisation of a society or community are participation, transparency, flexibility and tolerance. These four concepts are pivotal to democracy and more so in the deliberations of this chapter, as there are obvious difficulties with many societies when we put these terms in perspective. If, for example, society established that 'all citizens are equal', yet the controversy of unequal policies and practices haunts the citizens, then that democracy requires revision or proper definition to clarify or untangle the confusion. Does a king, headman or chief have the right, for example, to remove an errant citizen's eyes? The above example is testimony to an absolutely different type of democracy than the one which says that the person who errs has the right to be tried by an established, competent institution in a country.

In this chapter, the term democracy is used to signify a political system, separate and apart from the economic and social system to which it is joined. Indeed, a distinctive aspect of this approach is to insist that issues of so-called economic and social democracies be separated from the question of governmental structure. Otherwise, the definitional criteria of democracy is broadened and the empirical reality narrowed, so much so that the study of democracy becomes very difficult. Democracy, then, as Dahl (1971) propounds it, is a system of government that meets three essential conditions:

1. Meaningful and extensive competition among individuals and organised groups (especially political parties) for all effective positions of government power, at regular intervals and excluding the use of force;
2. A highly inclusive level of political participation in the selection of leaders and policies, at least through regular and fair elections, such that no major (adult) social group is excluded; and
3. A level of civil and political liberties – freedom of expression, freedom of the press, freedom to form and join organisations – sufficient to ensure the integrity of political competition and participation.

While this definition is, in itself, relatively straightforward, it presents a number of challenges in application. For one, countries that broadly satisfy these criteria nevertheless do so to different degrees. The factors that explain this variation at the democratic end of the spectrum in degrees of popular control and freedom present an important intellectual problem. Even this limited focus on issues of democratic values, norms and education, leaves us with the challenge of conceptual problems. The boundary between democratic and non-democratic is sometimes a blurred and imperfect one, and beyond it lies a much broader range of variation in political systems. Diamond et al. (1988, p. xvii) stress that: 'The ambiguity is further complicated by the constraints on free political activity, organisation, and expressions that may often in practice make the system much less democratic than it appears on paper'.

Hence, some countries like Namibia are often classified as semi-democratic. These are countries where the effective power of elected officials is so limited, or political party competition is so restricted, or the freedom and fairness of elections so compromised, that electoral outcomes, while competitive, still deviate significantly from popular preferences; or where civil and political liberties are so limited that some political orientations and interests are unable to organise and express themselves.

An important variable to consider is stability. A stable regime is one that is deeply institutionalised and consolidated, making it likely therefore to enjoy a high level of legitimacy. The relationship between stability and legitimacy is an intimate one. Partially stable regimes are neither fully secure nor in imminent danger of collapse. Their institutions have perhaps acquired some measure of depth, flexibility, and value, but not enough to ensure that they can withstand serious challenges (Diamond et al., 1988). Unstable regimes are those which are more susceptible to breakdown or overthrow under pressure.

Democracy being one of the fundamental values, there should be no imposition of values, but rather the generation of discussion and debate, and acknowledgement that discussion and debate are values in themselves. Asmal's (2001) definition of democracy is convincing, stating:

> Democracy is the first of the ten fundamental values ... having relevance in education. More than merely adult enfranchisement, or an expression of popular sentiment, democracy is a society's means to engage critically with itself. Education is indispensable in equipping citizens with the abilities and skills to engage critically, and act responsibly.

Values, which transcend language and culture, are the common currency that makes life meaningful, and normative principles ensure ease of life lived in common. Inculcating or passing on values, the purpose of school is to help young people achieve higher levels of moral judgement. This involves an understanding that education does not exist simply to serve the needs of the economic market, but also is important to serve society, and that means instilling in pupils and students a broad sense of values that can emerge only from a balanced exposure to the humanities as well as the sciences. Enriching the individual in this way is, by extension, enriching society as a whole.

The Michigan Department of Education in the United States of America (2001) lists the core democratic values as: life, the pursuit of happiness, justice, common good, equality, diversity, popular sovereignty, patriotism and rule of law.

It may be appropriate to conclude this section with Okiror's (2011, p. 4) principles of modern democratic rule, which he stipulates are as follows: citizen participation, equality, political tolerance, accountability, transparency, regular, free and fair elections, economic freedom, control of the abuse of power, separation of powers, a bill of rights, a culture of accepting the results of elections, human rights, multi-party system, neutrality of state institutions and the rule of law.

Considering the above core values and principles of a democracy, achieving true democracy, good governance and accountability requires high levels of citizen participation, improved civic education and promoting more awareness and appreciation of democratic principles by the leaders and citizens, especially at the local level.

CULTURAL REQUISITES AND VALUES FOR DEMOCRACY

This section strives to determine the degree to which the cultural requisites of democracy are present in the contemporary political and educational culture of the formerly colonised countries. Namibia is not exempt from the query, although we must be cognisant of the differences in specific countries' socio-political and cultural developments. Similarities in some instances may be apparent. However, due to various pre-colonial, colonial and post-colonial developments in specific countries, coupled with their economic, geophysical features and available resources, each country does indeed have unique qualities. In this section we place focus on support for core democratic rights, liberties and institutions. Gibson, Duch and Tedin (1992, p. 329) lamented that: 'The best predictors of attitudes towards general democratic values were education, gender and age. The better-educated and the young tended to be more supportive of democratic institutions and processes'.

Socio-political, and consequently educational, change has occurred at a dizzying pace throughout the African continent since the advent of decolonisation. Nearly every country has witnessed new alterations in their respective status quo. The socio-political and educational worlds of many countries have been restructured, mostly along a more democratic mould. As discussed in more detail in Chapter 6, Namibia, for example, after dismantling the apartheid education system, hinged transformation on four major educational goals, namely:

1. 'Access' for all potential learners. Government's first commitment is to provide universal basic education.
2. 'Equity' among all social groups. The government's second commitment is to provide equitable access to schooling and to its benefits, even though unfortunately disparities persist.
3. 'Quality' education for all citizens throughout the country. The third commitment of the government is to make our schools good schools and to offer high quality, non-formal alternatives to formal schools.
4. 'Democracy' for all to tolerate and participate in the country's transformation. The fourth government goal of democracy is to develop democratic education (Ministry of Education and Culture, Namibia, 1993, p. 32).

It is by no means clear, however, that the changes currently occurring on the African continent will continue along a more democratic path. There is always the possibility of autocratically based counteractions to the inspired reforms. Ancient ethnic hatreds may consume even the most reform-minded movements within a given socio-economic context. Perhaps more importantly, structural transformations, imposed from the top down in African societies, may meet resistance from the more democratic political culture of countries on the continent. The beliefs, values, and actions of ordinary country-specific citizens certainly play a role in the processes of change. After all, democracy is more than a set of political institutions. As Gibson et al. (1992, p. 340) insist: 'It requires sustenance from a myriad of political, social, legal and economic values resident in the hearts and minds of ordinary members of the polity'. Certainly change in the political culture of African countries will pave the way for other changes, institutional as well as cultural.

This chapter is grounded in the basic assumption that processes of change are dependent upon the political culture and education of the polity. The beliefs, values and attitudes of ordinary citizens should structure and perhaps set limits on both the pace of and possibilities for change. Though cultural theory does not provide a complete explanation of political change, culture undoubtedly influences the process strongly. Nonetheless, it is necessary to determine whether the various attitudes in diverse African countries pertaining to democratic values are organised within a democratic belief system.

Political theorists have long attempted to identify the particular cultural values that are conducive to democratic polities (e.g. Almond & Verba, 1963, 1980; Dahl, 1971, 1989; Inglehart, 1990), and most would agree with the simple proposition that the building and development of a stable and effective democratic government depends on the people's political culture. One cannot fully explain the rejection of greater pluralism by the leadership without taking into account the weaknesses of democratic ideas, beliefs and traditions in Africa throughout its varied and divided history. Virtually every scholar who has thought about processes of democratisation has ascribed an important role to political culture (e.g. Almond & Verba, 1963; Di Palma, 1990; Huntington, 1984; Inglehart, 1990; Lijphart, 1990). At the same time, there is little agreement on a list of specific cultural attributes that are conducive to democratic development.

While nearly everyone recognises that interpersonal trust is important (because it facilitates coalition formation), and all believe that a healthy dose of political tolerance is essential, not everyone agrees that satisfaction with one's life, for instance, is crucial to democratic development. Perhaps more importantly, there have been only smatterings of attempts to test the hypothesis that culture influences democratisation (e.g. Almond & Verba, 1963; Inglehart, 1988, 1990), and many of these suffer from a host of methodological problems inherent in comparative research. Thus, at the general level, there is a broad consensus that democratisation is affected by culture, but there is much less agreement on the specifics.

One of the most persistent and insightful thinkers of this challenge is Dahl (1989). His conception of cultural values thought conducive to democratic development is of particular interest to this chapter. Dahl (1989) characterises a democratic citizen as one who believes in individual liberty and who is politically tolerant; who holds a certain amount of distrust of political authority but at the same time is trustful of fellow citizens; who is obedient but nonetheless willing to assert rights against the state; who views the state as constrained by legality and who supports basic democratic institutions and processes (as cited in Gibson, 1996, p. 957). Though there are undoubtedly those who would quibble with this list, it would be largely on the need to supplement it, rather than delete items from it.

To think about the cultural implications of national institutional guarantees, and the variety of cultural orientations, warrants a measure of reorganisation. A democratic political culture is a set of norms that (1) encourages the formation of individual and collective preferences; (2) submits those preferences to the political arena for satisfaction; and (3) provides a context of support for a set of institutional arrangements for political decision-making that is responsive to these preferences. At the stage of preferences formation and articulation, focus should be on democratic rights and liberties of the people; institutional arrangements are operationalised as support for democratic institutions. Each of these represents a sector of democratic political culture, and each will be the object of any serious inquiry.

This chapter focuses on support for basic democratic rights, liberties and institutions under the assumption that such beliefs can constrain structural processes of democratisation. For instance, competitive elections are difficult to implement in the context of widespread beliefs that diverse political parties exacerbate and create conflicts in societies. Similarly, to the extent that ordinary citizens are intolerant of political diversity, democratic openness and competition are impeded. Certainly, culture does not completely determine structure and practice, but it is difficult to understand the possibilities for reform without consideration of the beliefs, values and attitudes of ordinary citizens.

Values are something people cherish and will protect to ensure their survival. Culture, which is simply defined as a way of life of a given people, is a good example of an embodiment of values. Democracy as a value, then, means that people will do anything to protect it as it is part of their culture, thus a way of life of a given people. Okiror (2011, p. 11) insists that 'for democratic values to be passed on to the members of a given society, formally or informally, the political culture within a given country should be conducive to democratic ideals'. Consequently, Omilusi (2015, p. 17) contends that:

> Understanding democracy as a value, therefore, should mean that it will be practised at all levels and in all spheres of life. It is not limited to areas of formal political leadership but instead forms a guiding principle, even in everyday life.

In most cases the acute lack of political will within the formerly colonised countries stalls or inhibits the healthy evolving of democratic values, norms and principles.

THE CHALLENGES OF INEQUALITIES THROUGH POLITICISED EDUCATIONAL POLICIES AND PRACTICES

In a democracy, the expectation is that all citizens enjoy the amenities available to everyone in a society. However, numerous states and states-within-states experience shortcomings among some sections of society, which triggers the question, whose democracy is it after all? Brock-Utne (2000) appropriately addresses a barrage of crucial issues that may not be left out by anyone accepting of the status quo, particularly in post-colonial Africa. At the outset, on the pretences of a-politicising education, Brock-Utne laments that education is not only constituted by and constitutive of struggles over the distribution of symbolic and material resources, but also implies and confers structural and ideological power used to control the means of producing, reproducing, consuming and accumulating symbolic and material resources (Ginsburg, 1995; Ginsburg & Lindsay, 1995).

Political struggles about and through education occur in all realms of educational stakeholders and entities. These worker-consumer-citizens participate actively and passively in a nation's political activity. Brock-Utne (2000, p. xvii) convincingly states: 'These struggles not only shape educational policy and practice; they also are dialectically related to more general relations of power among social classes, racial/ethnic groups, gender groups, and nations.' Ginsburg and Gorostiaga (2003, p. viii) support this statement, stating that: 'the politics of education and the political work accomplished through education are ways in which existing social relations are reproduced, legitimated, challenged or transformed'. Information about education and politics deserves to be made readily available to students and the populations of nations, particularly in the rural areas of nation states. This will enhance the scrutiny of how in different historical periods and in various local and national contexts, education is highly political. Twenty-seven years after Namibia's independence, for example, some sectors of society are still being taught under trees and in tents without the necessary facilities, while schools in urban areas and private entities enjoy most of the benefits of contemporary schools anywhere in the world.

Despite government policies aimed at alleviating past inequalities and rampant inequities, facilitating access to education poses enormous challenges. Most learners in the country do have access to schools, as the new reformist government built schools countrywide to enable access to education as one of its prime goals to be accomplished for over 70% of the population. Nonetheless, wide access to schools, lack of facilities, under- and unqualified teachers with high learner ratios, and in some instances, no electricity, potable water or ablution facilities, are some of the major challenges still facing the Namibian Government in the execution of educational policies and practices. In spite of the good intentions, there are questions regarding implementation which remain a challenge for Namibia.

Inequalities, be they in education or other realms of this nation state, manifest in various capacities of respective social relations of the citizenry. Therefore, it is necessary for the Namibian population, or any other African population, to understand the nexus of education and politics, and to become actively involved in the democratic transformations of their development. Thus, the issue is not whether education should be taken out of politics, nor whether politics should be kept out of schools, nor whether educators should be apolitical. Rather the questions are toward what ends, by what means, and in whose interests educators and other worker-consumer-citizens should engage in political work in and about education (Ginsburg, 1995).

In most developing nations, those in Africa being prime examples, unequal educational opportunities are perpetrated by the terms of conditions imposed by donor countries and agencies which guide, limit and stifle national policies and practices. Brock-Utne (2000) documents how the structural adjustment programmes required by the World Bank and the International Monetary Fund (IMF) during the 1990s actually made it more difficult for African nation-states to provide education for all its citizens. Such programmes, which are included as conditions for obtaining loans, limited the amount of government expenditure on human services, such as education and health. The retrogressive consequence was the introduction of user fees and other forms of privatising versus nationalising the cost of education, which means that the poor, if they can gain access to schooling at all, pay a disproportionate share of their material resources for it. It is also worth noting the role that multinational (and bilateral) agencies play in reproducing inequalities of wealth within and among nations. (For more information see also Braun, 1997; Cavanagh, Anderson, & Pike, 1996). To evidence these superficial demands that polarised inequalities, Brock-Utne (2000) supplements and complements the structural analysis with cultural analysis, focusing on curriculum knowledge and the language of instruction. As a case in point, however, Namibia never accepted structural adjustment programmes, which saved the country from some of these difficulties.

If language, culture and development are linked, then inequalities are fundamentally ingrained, not only in the medium of communication and instruction but also in the dependency of African nation-states on former colonisers. African knowledge and languages do not occupy the core curriculum and instruction in many schools in African countries. Just as was the case under most forms of colonialism (Ginsburg & Clayton, 2001), elites within African societies have also contributed negatively during the post-colonial or neo-colonial period. Many of them were educated in European and North American institutions of higher education, and they not only learned non-African languages and knowledge, but often came to value these more than the languages and knowledge of their own continents.

Given European and North American hegemony within the world economic and cultural systems, the preference by the elites for other nations' languages and knowledge has a political and economic as well as psychological identity basis. As Brock-Utne (2000, p. xx) explains: 'It is not only their familiarity and comfort with non-African languages and knowledge, but also their perception of its utility for their countries' "development" that leads African elites to prize that which is foreign'.

To conclude this section, perhaps the pertinent question to ask is whether globalisation of the economy and culture can occur without 'excessive Euro-centrism or any mono-culturist form' coming to dominance. The pluralist nature of Namibia with a multiplicity of ethical values or a variety of cultural norms dictates that government incorporate this rich diversity in forging appropriate democratic measures. The inclusive element deserves to play a magnificent role where nationals from different orientations have their voices recognised.

GLOBAL CONSCIOUSNESS AND THE DEMOCRATISATION OF A LEARNER CITIZEN

Traditional knowledge and indigenous cultural heritage have value and validity in their own right and a capacity both to define and promote individual and community, as well as national, development (Amukugo, 1995; Sifuna & Otiende, 1992). As Bangura, Harber and Leon (as cited in Amukugo, 2013) stated, military and other forms of authoritarian rule were applied by some African countries in the early post-colonial period. Hence, it is not surprising that since the 1980s, there has been unprecedented growth of international concern for human rights, including, prominently, the right to choose democratically the government under which one lives, and to express and organise around one's political principles and views. Diamond et al. (1989, p. 20) lament that: 'Democratic government in Africa has been victimized by political violence and intolerance, intense ethnic conflict, poor economic performance and extensive corruption'. While the former coloniser is most often the focus of accusations for all these violations, the local elites, having acquired western ways of living, and thus continuing the dependency syndrome, are equally if not more destructive to the progress of their respective countries. A crucial question to ask, perhaps, concurring with Brock-Utne (2000), is what are the possibilities of building a university curriculum based on African culture and using African values, norms and languages?

The possibility of developing an African counter-expertise without strengthening the African universities is miniscule, or as per the current status-quo, non-existent. Brock-Utne's question (2000, p. 213) is thus very relevant to the prevailing circumstances. She asks: 'How is it possible to prevent the globalization of learning from meaning the integration of the African elites into the culture of the former colonial masters?' Strengthening African universities would have as an aim the restoration of African languages and culture, and lessen the south's curriculum dependency on the north. Such strengthening would eliminate the flow from global producers to local consumers and would ensure a more multidirectional flow, such as flows going south to south or south to north.

If, for instance, we refer to the issue of languages of instruction in Sub-Saharan African universities, such as the use of Kiswahili in Tanzania (Gran, 2007), the possibility is there for a programme to be conducted in any of the diverse indigenous languages. The languages of instruction at most universities in Africa are the European languages. Mazrui (1994, 1996) argues that the choice of European languages as mediums of instruction in African universities has had profound cultural consequences for the societies served by those universities. What implications does it have for the continent if African intellectuals conduct all their most sophisticated conversations in European languages? 'It is, therefore, because of these discrepancies that intellectual and scientific dependency in Africa is inseparable from linguistic dependency' (Mazrui, 1994, p. 121).

The worsening gaps between the rich and the poor within and among nations lead to differences in their capacities to generate and utilise knowledge, which creates new global 'apartheid' and increasing inequalities. It is generally recognised that traditional knowledge and indigenous cultural heritage have a value and validity in their own right and a capacity both to define and promote development. The follow-up question, however, is how can one reconstruct the curriculum of African education, to root it in African culture, with a great emphasis on indigenous research, preferably done by African scholars who clearly should also be African-based in their outlook? One cannot agree more with Mazrui (1978, p. 317) who notes that: 'The full maturity of African education will come only when Africa develops a capacity to innovate independently'. This independent innovation may incorporate elements from the west but must have African roots. Independent innovation might also help to strengthen the linkage between democracy, education and social justice on the African continent.

The widening gap between the rich and the poor, to the detriment of Africa, occurred in part because of an unequal flow of international assistance. For example, of all World Bank projects in support of science and technology in higher education and industry since 1970, no less than two-thirds were executed in the Asia/Pacific region. More than 75% of the value of all science and technology projects went elsewhere, while glaring inequalities are demonstrated in the opportunities for higher education. In only 15 years, the differences in university enrolment levels doubled in favour of the developed world (United Nations Development Programme, 1992). Democratic values and norms, desirable as they may be, and country-specific according to various dynamics in countries, are further jeopardised by the looming inequalities in developing countries years after they have received their independence. In an ideal democracy based on the principles, characteristic values and norms of the citizenry, we cannot disregard an individual or group's opinion simply because it contradicts the view of the government or party in power; democratically, we have to listen to and respect all views. As has been the practice in many countries, state agencies should not interfere when citizens exercise their freedoms as long as the freedoms are being exercised within the law.

CONCLUSIONS: REFLECTIONS, CONCEPTUALISATION AND RECOMMENDATIONS FOR DEMOCRATIC EDUCATIONAL VALUES AND NORMS

Having looked at various forms that democracy has taken on the African continent and in other parts of the world, particularly in developing countries, we must raise and revisit some pertinent questions addressing particularly crucial issues in education. The concern is more with the content of education, the attempts at curriculum reconstruction, the question of language of instruction, and the question of relevance. How relevant is the western schooling that pupils in Africa receive today in contrast to what they need? Perhaps the drop in enrolment rate, for example, in the Kunene region of Namibia both before and after independence, is a clear indication that parents and children do not find western schooling relevant. Perhaps they find that the education they get outside of school is more worthwhile.

Some scholars may ask if Africa was ever intellectually decolonised. The sobering response is probably 'no'. Attempts have been made at independence in one country after the other to build education in Africa on African roots. Brock-Utne (2000), for instance, claimed that those attempts had been constrained over the past 10 to 15 years, and considered that during the years since 2000, the trends of dependency, lack of originality and inequalities in various countries have continued unabated. Some educators in the west see that westerners have much to learn from other continents. Euro-centric curricula need to be changed to incorporate non-western understanding, not only to do justice to oppressed groups but also because this change will make for a fruitful cross-fertilisation of ideas. In these volatile times of conflicts, climate change, regime change, information explosion (due to the internet) and inevitable migration, it is important that as great a conglomerate of people as possible, and especially educationists, develop cross-cultural perspectives. The sensitisation and eventual education of global citizens to inevitable future challenges that demand coexistence and a collective pool of world resources for the common good are essential. As Okiror (2011, p. 15) reasons:

> A lack of people's participation in free associations bears the risk that since it is difficult for an individual to pressurise the government into meeting people's needs, the failure of individual efforts leads to individual despair and frustration, which may in turn lead to withdrawal from the campaign for democracy.

The west certainly has much to learn from Africa if the continent is allowed to develop from her own roots. The same applies to other formerly colonised territories that have abundant information from which westerners may learn. These should include, for instance, researching indigenous knowledge and mathematics that may lead to penetrating knowledge, which could potentially change conceptions, values and norms in the west. In the words of a mathematician from the west: 'Research on mathematics in non-western societies is changing our understanding of this fundamental human activity and helping educators develop more effective teaching strategies as well' (Struik, 1995, p. 36). Expressed crudely, there can be no 'global village' without the knowledge found in the villages of Africa or any other part of the planet.

If global citizens and students are to fulfil their obligations and rights as 'global' citizens, they must develop the ability to make careful judgements, based on a reasoned historical perspective and a meaningful conception of the basic democratic values underlying citizenship in our world, and guided by constitutional consciousness. To this end, according to Butts (1988), an agenda of 12 core civic values that are fundamental to the theory and practice of democratic citizenship in the United States has been devised. Termed 'The 12 Tables of Civism', this agenda includes six obligations of citizenship (justice, equality, authority, participation, truth and patriotism) and six rights of citizenship (freedom, diversity, privacy, due process, property and human rights). An in-depth discussion of each of these values, their place in the US political system, and the nature of both their true and corrupted forms is given. Schools in their respective countries have an unparalleled opportunity to influence entire generations of high school youth during the coming years, especially since currently, democratisation has become a desired trend for many countries all over the world.

For countries like Namibia, which was inundated by colonialism and apartheid policies and practices, a concept such as reconciliation, in its real terms, can be a core value. Healing and reconciling past differences remains a difficult challenge. More than merely being a question of saying sorry, it requires redress in other, even material, ways too. Putting the right history back into the curriculum is a means of nurturing critical inquiry and forming a historical consciousness. A critical knowledge of these issues without the imposed fear of asserting themselves as citizens, is essential in building the dignity of human values within an informed awareness of the past, preventing amnesia, checking triumphalism, opposing a manipulative or instrumental use of the past, and providing a buffer against the 'dumbing down' or abject ignorance of the citizenry. In this way, a tolerant, open and dynamic society can reaffirm the values of diversity, tolerance, respect, justice, compassion and commitment in young Namibians, Africans and ultimately the global citizenry.

It is also the duty of the powers that be through coherent and patriotic political will, to mould a safe and secure school system, which is essential to teaching and learning. For too many educators and learners, making schools a safe place in which to teach and learn, and ensuring the rule of law in schools or the entire education system, is a desperate yet necessary challenge.

Asmal (2001) reiterates that:

> The truth is, no matter how high the fences are or how sophisticated the security system, a school and its community are indivisible, and unless a school sees itself as part of its community and engages in the broader fight against crime it will not be safe itself.

Equally, reinstituting authoritarian structures does not restore the rule of law; this is achieved by building a system owned by all, where lines of accountability and authority are clear, where discipline is fair, just and proportionate, and where there is a sense of common purpose. Grounded ethics and the nurturing of the environment is about valuing our natural resources, assets and heritage in a manner that democratically sustains lives and makes it possible for us all to live decently now and in the future.

Institutions in their respective countries are a set of formal rules and informal norms, which together with their enforcement mechanisms structure human interaction. Historically, in Africa and many other formerly colonised territories, successive authoritarian and military regimes were able, blatantly, to violate their respective constitutions because the underlying democratic values and norms had not permeated popular consciousness sufficiently to constitute credible threats to the various dictatorships. Hussain (2011) succinctly pronounces that: 'Research on the subject over the last two decades, shows that the formal rules of a democratic institutional structure can be actualised in practice only when they are underpinned by norms and values conducive to its functioning'. Ultimately, then, it is of vital importance for governing institutions and the citizenry at large to recognise that the relationship between education, political participation and support for the norms and institutions of democracy is a central question to democratic theory and practice.

Finally, the value of social honour is a key element of citizenship in the making of, not a jingoistic patriotism, nor a slavish subservience, but a sense of honour and identity for any country where individuals are comfortable with a local, national, global awareness and acceptance of the fascinating infinite universe. The lack of or absence of well-informed, dignified citizens is tantamount to democratic processes continuing to be undermined by the positions of privilege that constitute and sustain existing and unjust institutions. As things are, post-colonial societies will continue to be the most affected.

References

Almond, G. A. & Verba, S. (1963). *The civic culture: Political attitudes and democracy in five nations*. Princeton: Princeton University Press.

Amukugo, E. M. (1995). *Education & politics in Namibia: Past trends and future prospects*. Windhoek: Gamsberg Macmillan.

Amukugo, E. M. (2013). Liberal democracy, education and social justice in Africa. *Journal for Studies in Humanities and Social Sciences*, 2(1), 144–157.

Asmal, K. (2001). *Manifesto on values, education and democracy*. Pretoria: Ministry of Education, RSA. Retrieved from http://www.dhet.gov.za/Reports Doc Library/Manifesto on Values, Education and Democracy.pdf

Braun, D. (1997). *The rich get richer: The rise of income inequality in the United States and the world* (2nd ed.). Chicago: Nelson-Hall.

Brock-Utne, B. (2000). *Whose education for all: The recolonization of the African mind*. New York: Falmer Press.

Butts, F. (1988). The morality of democratic citizenship: Goals for civic education in the republic's third century. Retrieved from http://www.civiced.org/papers/morality/morality_ch4a.html

Cavanagh, J., Anderson, S., & Pike, J. (1996). Behind the cloak of benevolence: World Bank and IMF policies hurt workers at home and abroad. In K. Danaher (Ed.) *Corporations are gonna get your mama: Globalization and the downsizing of the American dream*, pp. 97–104. Monroe, ME: Common Courage Press.

Dahl, R. A. (1971). *Polyarchy. Participation and opposition*. New Haven: Yale University Press.

Dahl, R. A. (1989). *Democracy and its critics*. New Haven: Yale University Press.

Diamond, L., Linz, J. J., & Lipset, S. M. (Eds.) (1989). *Democracy in developing countries: Africa*. (Vol.2). Boulder, Col: Lynne Rienner Publishers, Inc.

Di Palma, G. (1990). *To craft democracies: An essay on democratic transitions*. Berkeley, CA: University of California Press.

Freire, P. (1995). *Pedagogy of the oppressed*. New York: Continuum Press.

Gibson, J. L. (1996). Political and economic markets: Changes in the connections between attitudes toward political democracy and a market economy within the mass culture of Russia and the Ukraine. *The Journal of Politics, 58*(4), 954–984.

Gibson, J. L., Duch, R. M., & Tedin, K. L. (1992). Democratic values and the transformation of the Soviet Union. *The Journal of Politics, 54*(2), 329–371.

Ginsburg, M. (Ed.). (1995). *The politics of educators' work and lives*. New York: Garland.

Ginsburg, M. & Clayton, T. (1999). Imperialism and colonialism. In D. Levinson, A. Sadovnik, and P. Cookson (Eds.), *Education and sociology: An encyclopaedia*. New York: Taylor and Francis.

Ginsburg, M. & Lindsay, B. (Eds.). (1995). *The political dimension in teacher education: Comparative perspectives in policy formation, socialization and society*. New York: Falmer Press.

Gran, L. K. (2007). Language of instruction in Tanzanian higher education: A particular focus on the University of Dar es Salaam. (Master's thesis, University of Oslo, Oslo, Norway). Retrieved from https://www.duo.uio.no/handle/10852/30959

Halim, A. A. (1997). Education as a basic human right. *Democracy and education: The magazine for classroom teachers, 11*(2).

Howard, S. (1997). Knowing democracy: Teachers, schools, and global transformation. In *Democracy and education: The magazine for classroom teachers, 11*(2).

Huntington, S. P. (1984). Will more countries become democratic? *Political Science Quarterly, 99*, 193–218.

Hussain A. (2011, September 12). Norms, values and democracy. *The Express Tribune*. Retrieved from http://tribune.com.pk/story/250793/norms-values-and-democracy/

Inglehart, R. (1988). The renaissance of political culture. *American Political Science Review, 82*(4), 1203–1230.

Inglehart, R. (1990). *Culture shift in advanced industrial societies*. Princeton, NJ: Princeton University Press.

Leistyna, P., Woodrum, A., & Sherblom, S. A. (1996). *Breaking free: The transformative power of critical pedagogy*. Cambridge, MA: Harvard Educational Review.

Lijphart, A. (1990). The southern European examples of democratization: Six lessons for Latin America. *Government and Opposition, 25*, 68–84.

Mazrui, A. (1978). *Political values and the educated class in Africa*. Berkley: University of California Press.

Mazrui, A. (1994). The impact of global changes on academic freedom in Africa: A preliminary assessment. In M. Mamdani & M. Diouf (Eds.). *Academic freedom in Africa*. Dakar, Senegal: Codesria.

Mazrui, A. (1996). Perspective: The muse of modernity and the quest for development. In P. Altbach & S. M. Hassan (Eds.). *The muse of modernity: Essays on culture as development in Africa*. Trenton, NJ: Africa World Press.

Michigan Department of Education, USA. (2001). *Helping teachers teach and children learn*. Retrieved from http://educationextras.com/LOC%20pdfs%202012/Wayne%20County/KHribar%20core%20 democratic%20values%20for%20both%20lessons.pdf

Ministry of Education and Culture, Namibia. (1993). *Toward education for all: A development brief for education, culture, and training*. Windhoek: Gamsberg Macmillan Publishers.

Okiror, G. (2011). *Concepts and principles of democratic governance and accountability: A guide for peer educators*. Kampala: Konrad Adenauer-Stiftung.

Omilusi, M. (2015). From civil rule to militarized democracy: emerging template for governance in Nigeria. *International Journal of Politics and Good Governance, V1*(6.2), 17.

Sifuna, D. N. & Otiende, J. E. (1992). *An introductory history of education*. Nairobi: University of Nairobi Press.

Struik, J. D. (1995). Everybody counts: Towards a broader history of mathematics. *Technology Review, 98*(6), 36–44.

United Nations Development Programme. (1992). *Human development report*. New York: Retrieved from http://hdr.undp.org/sites/default/files/reports/221/hdr_1992_en_complete_nostats.pdf

United Nations. (2016). *Democracy*. Retrieved from http://www.un.org/en/sections/issues-depth/democracy/ index.html

6

Education in the Namibian context

Elizabeth Magano Amukugo

Before reading this chapter, and as you are reading it, bear the following questions in mind.

1. Do you think the traditional cultural background and the historic struggle for democracy in your country have had an effect on the educational needs of your country today? If so, in what way?

2. If you were designing an educational system aimed at producing a nation of non-critical, subservient workers, what would your aims be? How would these aims be different if you were designing an education system to produce participants in a successful democracy? How would your educational system be different if your main goal were your nation's economic prosperity?

3. What are the aims of the Namibian educational system and how well are these aims being achieved?

INTRODUCTION

Education does not operate in a vacuum but functions within a given society. As the authors of this book live and work in Namibia, it is necessary to place issues of democracy, education and social justice within the Namibian context as well. Namibia (formerly South West Africa) has been under the yoke of colonialism, first as a German protectorate from 1884–1915 and later on as a Class C Mandate under the South African regime from 1915–1990. The country gained political independence in 1990, after many years of struggle for liberation. Its population is only 2.4 million (2016) within a total geographical area of 824,292 square km. This chapter will critically examine the aims of education in Namibia during pre-colonial and colonial times, and in independent Namibia.

EDUCATION IN PRE-COLONIAL AFRICA

In pre-colonial Africa, traditional African education passed on to the young societal values, norms and beliefs, in addition to knowledge and skills necessary for the development of the society (Kibera & Kimokoti, 2007; Sifuna & Otiende, 1994). Education was then regarded as a common good. Formal education in pre-colonial times ranged from primary and secondary to university levels in some parts of Africa. Universities existed, for example, in certain North African countries (Egypt, Mali and Morocco), the Horn of Africa (Ethiopia) and along the East African coast long before Europeans set foot on African soil. These include the University of Fez (established in 859 CE) in Morocco and listed in the Guinness Book of Records as the world's oldest university; the University of Al Azher (970 CE) in Cairo, Egypt, recognised as the world's second oldest university, and the University of Timbuktu (982 CE) in Mali, the world's third oldest University (Amukugo, 1995; 'Oldest University', n.d.; 'Top 10 oldest universities in the world: Ancient colleges', 2009). In comparison, Europe's oldest university, the University of Bologna in Italy, dates back to 1088, followed by the universities of Paris and Oxford, that were both founded in 1096 ('Top 10 oldest universities in the world: Ancient colleges', 2009). America's oldest university, Harvard, was established as late as 1636 in Massachusetts ('25 of the oldest American colleges and universities', n.d.). We can hence safely conclude that Africa is historically the mother of formal education up to the university level. Therefore, contrary to a widely accepted view that Europeans introduced formal education on the African continent, Amukugo (1995, pp. 32–33), and Kibera and Kimokoti (2007, pp. 69–70), are right in advancing the view that systems of education in pre-colonial Africa existed before Europeans arrived.

Missionaries introduced western education in Africa, with the ambition of spreading the gospel of Christianity. Amukugo (1995, pp. 40–42) expounded the view that early missionaries in Namibia assisted both the German and South African colonial powers in their quest to create a submissive black labour force by means of religious indoctrination. A similar view has been voiced by the former SWAPO Secretary for Education in Exile, Nahas Angula, in his introduction to SWAPO (1984, p. 6):

> [i]n missionaries, the imperial order found an ally ready to teach, preach and pacify. Through the combined efforts of the colonial agents, the missionaries, and the imperial machinery of coercion, the subject people were expected to be awestruck at the might and mettle of the white man.

Referring to the situation in colonial South Africa, Molteno (1984) argued that missionaries generally were not eager to provide an academic education to the black population. On the contrary, they were content as long as they could offer an education which met their main objective: evangelisation. Molteno suggested further that since missionaries did not always share the interests of the colonialists, they avoided having their educational aims altered to suit colonial ideas. This conclusion is, however, contrary to a piece cited by him from the *Christian Express*, which points to missionaries' pacification efforts as follows:

> Missionaries are in no sense political agitators. They desire nothing so much as that the relations of the natives toward the Government should be those of perfect loyalty, and they invariably counsel the natives to be law-abiding and peaceful … (Molteno, 1984, p. 54).

Notwithstanding the missionaries' real intentions (good or bad), therefore, the fact that they taught the black population to obey colonial laws and be peaceful within the framework of colonial oppression, boiled down to pacification of the black people, which worked in the interest of the oppressors (colonialists). Contrary to the broader picture above nonetheless, clergymen such as Bishop Colin O'Brien Winter (1928–1981), Rev. Michael Scott (1907–1983) and others took the side of the oppressed Namibians and South Africans during colonialism.

THE AIMS OF EDUCATION IN COLONIAL NAMIBIA

The German and South African colonial powers designed an educational system that prepared Africans for subordinate positions within the labour market, encouraged submissiveness to the colonial social order and promoted rote learning, as opposed to critical analysis and understanding of what is being taught (Amukugo, 1995). In addition, education was elitist as it was available only to a few (Ministry of Education and Culture [MEC], 1993). The words of a German colonial administrator, Rohrbach, justify the above claim:

> White settlers require native servants; they can only ensure continuous supply by seeing to it that the servants are kept in a state of educational inferiority. To educate them … [would] inculcate such mischievous and intolerable ideas as democracy, the brotherhood of men … human freedom and the like. (Noble, 1977, p. 29)

Thus, apart from ideological indoctrination, the German colonialists were more interested in establishing a colony and opening up trade routes than educating the colonised. Consequently, education for the colonised remained largely under various missionary societies. Moreover, the apartheid ideology of separateness served to justify undemocratic practices within the white South African colonial socio-economic system and to ensure that these were in turn perceived as normal and hence acceptable. Describing this ideological function as 'social engineering', Morrow (2007, p. 141) agrees with the above view by suggesting that:

> Successful social engineering, particularly that kind which is widely regarded as unjust, needs to hide its mechanisms from public view. One way in which this can be done is to appeal to a plausible theoretical story. In the case of apartheid this story is constructed on the theme of 'cultural' (and moral) relativism. That different 'population groups' have different, and incompatible, 'cultures' is a convenient myth, and one which occludes the thought that the artificial separation of 'population groups' might itself spawn separate 'cultures'. This myth underpins the theory of education, called Fundamental Pedagogics, which the overwhelming majority of education students in South Africa are taught.

Whilst agreeing with the 'social engineering' concept above, this author hastens to point out that Dr Verwoerd, the architect of Bantu Education exclusively for the black population, did not hide its aims and objectives in accordance with the 'social engineering' concept described above. To the contrary, he stated in no uncertain terms that:

> When I have control of Native education I will reform it so that Natives will be taught from childhood to realise that equality with Europeans is not for them. People who believe in equality are not desirable teachers for the natives. Education must train and teach people in accordance with their opportunities in life, according to the sphere in which they live. (Tabata, 1980, p. 6).

With the words above, Dr Verwoerd echoed earlier views on the aims of the so called 'Native Education', as outlined in the Welsh Report of the Interdepartmental Committee on Native Education, 1935–1936, years before apartheid was legalised in South Africa in 1948 and in Namibia in 1962. The report stated that:

> From evidence before the Committee it seems clear that there still exists opposition to the education of the Native on the grounds that (a) it makes him lazy and unfit for manual work; (b) it makes him 'cheeky' and less docile as a servant; and (c) it estranges him from his own people and often leads him to despise his own culture. (Welsh Report 1936, as cited in Morrow, 1990, p. 172).

We can thus conclude that Bantu Education and its forerunner, Native Education, served to dehumanise the colonised and as such focused on achieving the purpose of 'banking education' as described by Freire (1970/1996, pp. 53–67).

THE AIMS OF EDUCATION IN INDEPENDENT NAMIBIA

The newly independent government and its Ministry of Education and Culture (MEC), being cognisant of glaring inequities that were reflected in the colonial policies of racial discrimination, moved to change the situation through, among other things, an alternative educational philosophy. Hence the MEC (1993, p. 19) stated that:

> Education also improves the quality of our lives, by helping us develop our abilities. As we learn more about our environment and the threats to it, we become better able to protect and preserve it. As we become better at identifying and solving problems, we also become better at creating jobs and increasing our income. As we develop our own new ideas and technologies, we become less dependent on imported innovations and the conditions that often accompany them. As it helps us become more successful in setting and pursuing our own goals, education is liberating, both individually and socially.

The above educational philosophy denotes an educational viewpoint that not only aims at developing problem-solving skills in students, but also innovation for socio-economic development. These are much broader educational aims if compared to the current technocratic view of education. However, the set educational objectives are not always in line with educational practice. This is partly because of the fact that education has its own internal contradictions, to such an extent that its aims do not necessarily lead to desired results at all times. One contributing factor to this phenomenon is, as Freire (1970/1996) suggests, that human beings are not passive but creative beings. This basically talks to people's capacity for critically evaluating both content and experience instead of passively reproducing facts.

The aims of education in post-colonial Namibia were primarily defined by the anti-colonial struggle for freedom, justice and socio-economic emancipation. As Amukugo (cited in New Era 20th Independence Anniversary Special Edition, 2010) illustrated, the philosophical base of an education system in post-colonial Namibia was laid down by SWAPO in exile as reverberated in among others, SWAPO's draft of *Education for all. National integrated educational system for emergent Namibia*, in which the liberation movement dedicated itself to '... [l]aying the foundation of a free and universal education system for all Namibians from primary through secondary to university level...' (SWAPO, 1984, p. 10).

Developed in the context of a view of a future society that is 'one and indivisible', SWAPO's educational philosophy not only recognised man [the human being] as a producer, thinker and creative being, but also intended to mould a specific Namibian personality, in addition to providing the knowledge and skills necessary for building a new Namibia, by creating a balance between theory and practice, study and production (SWAPO of Namibia, 1984, p. 6). In this respect SWAPO in exile developed a more progressive vision of educational purpose that encouraged people to ask 'why' rather than only 'how', and envisioned the type of students it wanted to produce and what kind of society students as future citizens of an independent Namibia would wish to build.

Part of the above vision has been carried over into independent Namibia through government's first major educational policy (MEC, 1993), which advanced the view that:

> Our commitment to education for all supports, and in turn is supported by, our commitment to building a democratic society. Literate citizens are better able to understand the issues that confront us and the alternatives that we must consider. We can consider different points of view and make educated decisions. Education for all will make it possible for all citizens to be active participants, not just voters, in governing our country.
>
> If we are successful in fostering a culture of lifelong learning, our education institutions will no longer be regarded primarily as places to get certificates and degrees. Instead, they will have become centres for popular mobilisation, empowerment and development. (MEC, 1993, p. 15).

The above passage reflects a vision of education that not only recognises human capacities and divergent views, but also promotes the democratic ethos of active participation, and firmly places learning within a social, political and economic context, rather than looking at knowledge and skills in a fragmented manner. As such, the educational vision above creates a clear linkage between education, democracy and social justice.

The MEC outlines four major goals of education in independent Namibia, namely: access, equity, quality and democracy (MEC, 1993, pp. 33–44). These goals were devised not only to make education widely accessible to all Namibians, young and old, across socio-economic barriers, but also aimed to provide educational resources more equitably and to increase participation through 'democracy'. Most of all, the new government undertook to unify the education system, as opposed to the eleven colonial educational administrations that existed at independence in 1990.

In contrast to colonial educational goals, independent Namibia introduced the concept 'Education for All', with the aim of addressing issues of access and inequities within colonial education. However, the process of decolonisation has not been without difficulties and controversies. In the context of libertarian education[1] as discussed in Chapter 2, Namibia forged ahead by developing the international idea of 'Education for All' into its own concept that spoke to the country's social realities and demands. Thus, the four major educational goals of access, equity, quality and democracy were developed to mean the following:

Access meant not only doing away with racial segregation and providing access to education for all, but also expanding capacity by increasing the number of schools and classrooms across the country, and addressing barriers to education.

Equity implied developing 'an egalitarian educational system' that takes into consideration the existing differences in school facilities, equipment, teachers' competence and other forms of inequities, and counteracts barriers to realising the equity objectives.

Quality referred to improving the value of education by first and foremost improving the quality of teachers, and by introducing a philosophy whereby assessment through examination does not exclusively represent educational quality. The concept of quality was defined in a broader sense, through incorporating issues of access and equity, as well as ensuring that educational programmes help learners to integrate knowledge and information into a coherent whole. This becomes possible if firstly, educational content is placed within the broader socio-economic context and/or global framework. Secondly, as Freire (1970/1996, 1998) suggests, teaching and learning, rather than representing a mechanical transfer of knowledge, should take place in a transformative manner that enables students to develop a capacity to critically evaluate both the content and the world (their environment). These understandings of the world in turn equip students with the capacity to actively participate and contribute meaningfully to social change. Freire's concept of 'education for critical consciousness', as outlined in Freire (1970/1996, 1974) clarify the above assertion more succinctly.

Through adopting democracy as an educational goal, the Ministry of Education (MoE) intends to develop a democratic education and ensure broad participation in decision-making, assisting learners to understand that democracy entails more than voting, as inequities at the socio-economic level can thwart democracy. As members of society it is incumbent upon learners to know their rights and responsibilities as well as to shape, cherish and defend achieved democracy (MEC, 1993, pp. 32–44).

The Namibian 'Education for All' goals reflect a much broader educational ideal as opposed to the narrow apartheid philosophy of education in pre-independent Namibia. Unfortunately, however, the more progressive educational ideals of newly independent Namibia were quickly eroded, partially by the introduction of the International General Certificate of Secondary

---

[1] A strong proponent of libertarian education, Paulo Freire views the concept liberation as praxis to mean '… the action and reflection of men upon their world in order to transform it'. Consequently, he sees the role of problem-posing education as not only encouraging the students' creative powers, but also as a persistent exposé of reality. (Freire, as cited in Darder, Baltodano, & Torres, 2009, p. 56).

Education and the Higher International General Certificate of Secondary Education (IGCSE/HIGCSE) in 1994 (described in more detail below), concomitant with liberal democratic[2] policies. Subsequently, SWAPO's educational goals as outlined in SWAPO of Namibia (1984) were revised to suit the new changes brought about by Namibia's political independence. These changes are described in SWAPO of Namibia (1990). The issue of free and compulsory education was revisited and confined to primary education only – a principle that was upheld in the new Constitution of the Republic of Namibia (Government of the Republic of Namibia [GRN], 1990). Paradoxically, free and compulsory primary education remained only on paper after independence, as it was only formally introduced in 2013, twenty-three years after independence. The current government, however, committed itself to extending free education to secondary schooling in 2016, which was accomplished on time, and to higher education levels at a later stage.

Lack of attentiveness to the educational philosophy contained in SWAPO (1984) and the MEC (1993) did not come as a surprise. In the context of this book, one can argue that the concepts of democracy, education and social justice should be at the core of any government that aspires to changing the socio-economic conditions of its citizens. As Nyerere (1967) rightly observed, we must first be clear on what type of society we wish to establish before we can develop an educational system that will serve our intended aims. In its quest to define what type of society independent Namibia should be, upon independence from the white South African colonial regime in 1990, the country joined the many African states that embraced liberal democracy as a system of governance. Consequently, educational practice was not always in line with some of the more libertarian post-colonial educational policies.

Thus, whilst SWAPO's educational philosophy was founded upon an idea of society where the ethos of equality, equity and justice were at the centre of social change (SWAPO of Namibia, 1984), only some of these ideals resonated in the government's first major policy (MEC, 1993). The country's adoption of a mixed economy based on capitalist ideals and liberal democracy as a form of political governance put limitations on the above initial educational ideals. But as Ngwane (2006) points out, '[while] few countries have thrived through liberal democracy, several have ended up either as failed states [or] rogue states'.[3] Furthermore he observed that; '(t)he African technocratic elites have been evasive of a democratic substance (economic development, social security, etc.) in favour of a democratic form that emphasises mainly party formation, elections and constitutional engineering ...' (ibid.)

So, the question is, in what way has liberal democracy impacted on educational theory and practice in independent Namibia?

We could argue that the aims and practices of education can be influenced by the political and socio-economic reality of a particular country. From this viewpoint, it is not unexpected that the past two decades have seen Namibian education developing towards a positivist technical rationality outlook that serves to fragment educational content into unrelated sub-sections, as discussed in more details further into this chapter. Over this time, the purpose of education gradually changed from developing a fully rounded human being through the cultivation of intellectual, aesthetic, and technical skills, to fragmenting knowledge into unrelated pieces,

---

[2] The concept of 'liberal democracy' has been described in more detail in Chapter 2.

[3] Blau, Brunsma, Moncada and Zimmer (2008) describe a rogue state as one that dehumanises its citizens by depriving them of their civil and human rights.

emphasising knowledge measurement through a focus on exams and tests, and thereby causing teachers and students alike to delink the aims of education from their social, political and economic context. In recent years, some influential figures in Namibia have been calling for an emphasis on the more positivist-based and narrowly focused natural sciences[4] at the expense of the broad-based humanities and the social sciences. The latter contribute more to the function of education as a tool for developing critical consciousness of the socio-economic reality, while at the same time providing tools for action (knowledge and skills) aimed at bringing about socio-economic change – a democratic imperative. Hence we need to create a balance between the natural sciences and the social sciences and humanities at a societal level.

The quotation below can serve as an example of the value given to mathematics and sciences:

> Despite the successes that we have made over the years, our country still faces many challenges. We still have a shortage of skilled and qualified human resources. We need engineers, medical doctors, geologists and quantity surveyors, amongst others. These are the people who will enable our country to achieve Vision 2030. However, we can only achieve Vision 2030, when we put emphasis on Mathematics and Science subjects. Mathematics and science are the backbone subjects to many of the professions. Without relegating the other professions to lower positions, our country needs engineers, medical experts, and agricultural experts. All these professions require mathematics and science. I would therefore like to encourage the learners to work harder and study science and Mathematics. (Nujoma, 2010, p. 1)

The above sentiments can be interpreted within the context of the National Curriculum for Basic Education (Ministry of Education [MoE], 2010). Referring to core skills, among which numeracy is one, it is stated that: 'With the increasing emphasis on science, technology and commerce learners must be fully numerate. ... Learners must come to understand and be able to use mathematical language confidently and effectively as a means of communication' (ibid., p. 11).

Surely, whilst one understands the possible rationale behind the above enunciation, which may be the nagging lack of science and mathematics teachers in many Namibian schools, it is not appropriate to expect most learners to have both the interests and necessary talents to pursue these subjects successfully. Because learners are differently gifted, they need to pursue specific study lines that correspond to their distinct gifts and interests. Leading most students towards similar professions irrespective of the difference in talent is a sure way of pushing them out of school through failure. Notwithstanding the 'balanced nature of the national curriculum across different subject areas',[5] the apparent bias towards mathematics and the natural science

---

[4] This is not to say, however, that the natural sciences are not important. As the Science in Society Programme under the EU's 7th framework rightly puts it, '... (s)cience is part of almost every aspect of our lives. Although we rarely think about it, science makes extraordinary things possible. At the flick of a switch, we have light and electricity. When we are ill, science helps us get better...' (as cited in Henriksen, Dillon, & Ryder, 2015, p. 8). Social Sciences and Humanities on the other hand, '... can provide a sound scientific framework for the analysis of and insight in the social, economic, political and cultural challenges facing us today.' (Verlaeckt & Vitorino, 2002, p. 9). As such the humanities can help us find solutions in sectors vital to socio-economic development.

[5] Key learning areas within which learners can acquire and develop essential knowledge include: languages, mathematics, natural sciences, social sciences, technology, commerce, arts and physical education. (ibid.)

areas will have negative implications for both the individual learner and society at large through increased unemployment and poverty among the youth.

The introduction of the Cambridge Education System (International General Certificate of Secondary Education–IGCSE and the Higher International General Certificate of International Education–HIGCSE) in post-colonial Namibia should be viewed in the context of positivist technical rationality, due to its strong focus on examinations. Originally developed by the University of Cambridge Local Examination Syndicate (UCLES), it is divided into Core and Extended levels. According to the UCLES, '(t)he Core curriculum is within the range of a large majority of students ... *and it is targeted at students expected to achieve grades (D-G)*' (as cited in UCLES, n.d.), and leads to (blue collar) employment and vocational training. On the other hand, '*(t)he Extended curriculum ... has been designed for the more academically able and leads naturally into higher education or professional training*' and white collar jobs. The IGCSE/HIGCSE assessment method includes short-answer questions, multiple-choice questions, structured questions, essays and practical tests (UCLES, n.d.).

A critical reflection on the IGCSE/HIGCSE model places it squarely within the Positivist Technical Rationality paradigm,[6] which Amukugo, Likando, Shakwa, & Nyambe (2010), though referring to teacher education, observed: '... is deeply rooted in the traditional positivist approach where teaching is viewed as an applied science, the teacher is viewed as a technician, and emphasis is on mastery of a repertoire of technical skills ... (to the neglect of) placing teaching in its social, political and economic context (ibid.). Based on an empiricist methodology, positivist technical rationality centres on measurement of knowledge in quantitative terms, which is why it applies the assessment techniques described above, with the exception of essays that draw on students' creative side.

Although referring mainly to research, an article by Steinberg (2015, p. 5) rightly observed that:

> ... educational issues in [the] positivistic framework are reduced to technical issues. Questions of ends or purposes are subservient to questions of means or techniques.

In this way, it is argued, teachers, students and educational leaders alike operate in a vacuum, unable to meaningfully answer questions such as: 'Why do we have to do this?' (ibid.). It is thus safe to conclude that the Positivist Technical Rationality model does not allow the full development and use of critical capacities of human beings due to its narrow scope.

The Namibian Government introduced the IGCSE/HIGCSE system in 1994, four years after independence, to replace the Cape Education Department system. But, as Amukugo (2005) states, 'the high failure rate at Grade 10 and 12 respectively (that characterised the entire IGCSE/HIGCSE period from 1994–2006) ... can partly be attributed to the government's instantaneous political decision to replace the Cape Education ..., without thorough consideration of educational

---

[6] The positivist technical rationality paradigm is bound to affect learners since teachers and learners co-exist in a teaching/learning environment, and learners receive the major part of content/knowledge through school. Over and above that, Amukugo (2005) points out that during 1999–2004, only 19% of the IGCSE students obtained a C grade; 80% of them left secondary school with a mere G grade, while only 12.8% of HIGCSE students graduated with Grade 1 (highest). About 80% left secondary school with a Grade 4 (lowest) (ibid., pp 11–13). This has negative consequences for youth unemployment.

implications' (ibid., p. 13). This resulted in teachers not being able to handle the new system with confidence as they were not adequately prepared for the new tasks, among other shortcomings.

Swarts (1995) outlines achievements and challenges in the process of implementing the IGCSE/HIGCSE system in Namibia during the early years. She observed the following problematic issues:

1. Out of 120 schools that were offering the Cape system, only 25 met the criteria for offering IGCSE;
2. Out of 42 IGCSE/HIGCSE subjects on the curriculum, only 17 were specially designed or modified for Namibia;
3. Most subjects were using text books mainly from the United Kingdom, which in her view had a negative impact on the issue of relevance in addition to being expensive;
4. The English text books were written for students for whom English is their first language. 80% of the Namibian learners who participated in the monitoring exercise stated clearly that they experienced problems understanding the English language;
5. There was a lack of text books in almost all the regions of Namibia; and
6. A brief survey conducted by the National Institute for Educational Development (NIED) in mid-1994 suggested that about 50% of the teaching force, mostly from the least affluent regions, did not have the necessary qualifications for the task at hand.

The last point can be linked to the fact that '… only 49.6 % of the teachers in service are well qualified' (as cited in National Planning Commission (NPC), 2004, p. 88), which implied that fourteen years after independence, Namibia had not made much progress in terms of improving the quality of teachers, on whom the quality of education mainly rests. These factors, along with the automatic promotion policy,[7] that allowed Grade 10 students at the end of IGCSE to be automatically promoted to Grade 11, the beginning of HIGCSE, irrespective of their performance, have contributed greatly to the constant high failure in the IGCSE/HIGCSE system, and have in turn contributed to rising youth unemployment. In fact, the 2005[8] IGCSE results show that while only 1.3% obtained an A symbol, a staggering 89.4% left school with a G symbol (Ministry of Education, 2006, January); less than 20 percent of Namibian learners reach senior secondary (NPC, 2004, p. 90), and to cite the Namibia Ministry of Labour and Social Welfare (2008, p. 65), '(t)he most affected group by unemployment is that of 15–34 years. This group is referred to as unemployed youth, with an average unemployment rate of 59.9 percent'.

---

[7] Automatic promotion can be defined as the act of allowing '… children to continue to the next year of study with the rest of their peer group despite not having met the minimum required standards' (Ndaruhutse, as cited in Sichombe, Nambira, Tjipueja, & Kapenda, 2011).

[8] As mentioned herein, the IGCSE and HIGCSE were replaced with the Junior Secondary Certificate (JSC, Grade 10) and the National Senior Secondary Certificate (NSSC, Grade 12) in 2006. Currently, however, Grade 10 students who do not meet the requirements to enter Grade 11 (points 0–22), and who are 17 years or younger are allowed to repeat Grade 10. Thus in 2016 a total of 2501 such candidates who did not make it in 2015 were permitted to repeat. The figure for those who were permitted to repeat Grade 10 in 2015 stood at 3286. Learners older than 17 who do not meet the requirements for Grade 11 are advised to enroll with Namibia College of Open Learning (NAMCOL) part-time institutions, in order to improve their grades (Ministry of Education, Arts and Culture (MEAC), 2016).

It goes without saying therefore, that the introduction of the IGCSE/HIGCSE system not only reflected the negative impact of political expediency, but it also demonstrates the limits of a positivist based educational philosophy.

In placing education within a socio-economic context, it is crucial to note that Namibia is known to be a land of contrasts in terms of both its landscape and social organisation. Thus, while the country has been applauded for having an enabling environment for development, it has also simultaneously been singled out as one of the most unequal societies in the world (Marope, 2005, p. xiii; NPC, 2008, p. 39). According to the Namibia Statistics Agency (2012b, p. 10), 29% of the Namibian population lived below the poverty line in 2009/2010, as compared to 38% in 1993/1994. This shows only a slight improvement in seventeen years for those living in abject poverty (destitute). According to the State of the Nation Address (GRN, 2015), the national poverty rate for 2010 stood at 28.9%, compared to 69.3% in 1994. These statistics suggest that whilst the living conditions of the destitute change slowly, the national poverty rate reduces a little faster.

When one takes a look at the regional situation, a different picture emerges. The Namibian Statistics Agency (2012a, p. 153) suggests that the poor are 'disproportionally located in rural areas' in comparison with the urban population. By 2012, the levels of poverty differed according to regions, with Kavango having the highest level of poverty (55.2 percent), followed by Caprivi (50%) and Oshikoto (44%). In comparison, the more affluent regions of Khomas and Erongo show a poverty level of 10.7% and 7.1% respectively, which is considerably below the national poverty level of 28.7% (Namibia Statistics Agency, 2012b, pp. 12–13).

Makuwa (2005) compared the socio-economic status and educational achievement of learners in the 13 regions of Namibia. He found that learners in the three most affluent regions of Khomas, Erongo and Hardap achieved higher educational results than the poverty-stricken regions of Caprivi, Kavango, Ohangwena, Oshana, Oshikoto and Kunene. Amukugo (2002, pp. 243–244) arrived at a similar conclusion. Namibia has been struggling with issues of educational quality (Amukugo, Likando, & Mushaandja, 2010; Marope, 2005) which cannot be resolved successfully without addressing the issue of social inequities. Therefore, although Namibia achieved a 92.3% net primary school enrolment rate in 2007, a primary school completion rate of more than 80% and a secondary school net enrolment of 49% (Van Der Berg & Moses, 2011); according to UNESCO (as cited in World Bank, 2016), recent figures show a 110 and 111% primary school enrolment in 2012 and 2013 respectively. It can be underscored that access without equity would be futile since issues of socio-economic inequities can erode the gains achieved through the educational goal of access.

A related question is why a country like Namibia, which is endowed with vast natural resources, can display such a high level of socio-economic inequities. Jauch, Edwards and Cupido (2009) assert that there has been no serious attempt (in post-colonial Namibia) to develop and implement a systematic programme of (resource) redistribution. Yet, in order to curb socio-economic inequalities, systematic structural changes are required (Jauch et al., 2009). This means that a social structure that makes it possible for the rich to amass wealth at the expense of the poor needs to be subjected to a systematic structural change in order to close the ever widening gap between the haves and have nots, since periodic reforms have so far not resolved the nagging problem of poverty. Such action would change Namibia's international reputation as one of the most unequal societies in the world. As the United Nations Development Program (UNDP, Namibia, 2016) pointed out in relation to poverty reduction:

> Namibia has one of the least equal distribution[s] of income and wealth and increasingly, access to productive resources and basic services, in the world. While this structural inequality has its origin in colonialism and apartheid rule, it has also been sustained by policy and programme implementation constraints over the post-independent era.

It is therefore not surprising that while Namibia's economic growth has averaged five percent during the period between 2002–2012, this positive development has, according to the United Nations Partnership Framework (UNPAF) (2013, p. xiv), '... not translated into substantial employment creation, reduced rates of poverty or equitable distribution of income and productive resources'.

The Namibia Household Income and Expenditure Survey 2009/10 (Namibia Statistics Agency, 2012a) re-emphasises the point that inequality in Namibia remains high. Thus, whilst the poorest ten percent of Namibian households share a mere one percent of the country's total income, the wealthiest ten percent control more than fifty percent (ibid.). It is encouraging to note, however, that according to the National Planning Commission (2015), at the national level, poverty had declined by 11% during the period 2001–2011. The report also identified lack of education as being among the major root causes of poverty (p. 11).

The Namibian Government has nonetheless not been sitting with folded hands in the face of educational challenges. Efforts have been made over the years to address glitches facing the educational system. Two important documents in Namibia have helped steer the educational reform process during the twenty first century. These are: Vision 2030 and the Education and Training Sector Improvement Programme (ETSIP).

Vision 2030 is a long-term national plan, which aims at transforming Namibia into an industrialised society by 2030. The vision is anchored in principles of good governance; partnership between government, individuals, communities and civil society; and by addressing issues of equity; capacity enhancement through investing in people and institutions; comparative advantage by utilising the country's natural resources appropriately and efficiently; and promoting people-centred economic development (NPC, 2004, pp. 33–35). Through Vision 2030, the government further undertakes to ensure a high standard of living, good quality of life, access to quality of education and safeguarding justice, equity and equality (ibid., pp. 41–42). Education has been accorded a central place so as to guarantee that, among other objectives, Namibian society will be made up of 'literate, skilled, articulate, innovative, informed and proactive' persons, (NPC, 2004, p. 95), through the addressing of shortcomings within the educational sector.

In its quest to transform Namibia into a knowledge-based society, the government, through Vision 2030, aims at turning Namibia into a healthy and food secure nation in which people enjoy 'high standards of living, a good quality life and have access to quality education. ... There will be equal access to excellent educational and vocational training institutions' (ibid., p. 8). The Vision is also meant to minimise the disparity between rural and urban living, through provision of essential social services, education and training, health and security (ibid., p. 21).

Vision 2030 has, over time, been implemented through the various National Development Plans. The latest, Namibia's Fourth National Development Plan (NDP 4) 2012/13 to 2016/17

(NPC, 2012), points to various challenges faced so far in achieving equal access to education. Government also admits that while investments in education are high, quality outcomes are problematic. The challenges associated with quality education include limited access to early childhood development (ECD),[9] an insufficient number of learners reaching grade 12 due to limited spaces and non-achievement of a grade 10 pass, and an insufficient number of vocational and technical schools. The quality of skills of some teachers is also suspect. As late as 2013 for example, the Ministry of Education, Arts and Culture (MEAC) (2013) acknowledged that Namibia was experiencing a shortage of qualified teachers throughout the country. In fact the Ministry was, in the same year, faced with 2227 vacant teaching posts in 14 regions countrywide, and had to employ teachers from neighbouring SADC countries to teach in priority fields of specialisation: mathematics, sciences and English for grades 5–12.

This problem is accompanied by low teacher quality in some schools and/or regions, which was partly due to the 'Basic Education and Teaching Diploma' (BETD), that was previously offered by the former teacher training colleges, and which was widely criticised for lacking content. This problem has now been addressed by the merging of all teacher training colleges with the University of Namibia in 2011, with a view to improving teacher quality. Currently all teachers, from pre-primary school to secondary school levels, are trained through the University of Namibia's Faculty of Education.

Whilst Namibia succeeded in the educational goal of access, with 90% of school-going children being in school (NPC, 2004, p. 88), most research work on Namibian post-colonial education speaks volumes about the difficulties that the country experienced in realising the goals of equity and quality, which has direct implications for the relationship between education and social justice.

Taking the above into consideration, one wonders whether Vision 2030 can live up to the stated objectives, given the persistent gap between the haves and have nots within society. What is the implication for education? The Fourth National Development Plan, 2012/13–2016/17 (NDP 4), for example, echoes the above analysis by acknowledging that there are serious challenges to be faced by the education system, and states that:

> Since independence in 1990,[10] Namibia has invested significantly in the education sector. Education has, in fact, received the lion's share of the National Budget almost every year. Despite this, there is broad consensus in Namibia that the education system remains weak by international standards, and requires significant intervention for the future of the country. ... The problems associated with education are extensive, and range from a lack of quality to a lack of infrastructure and information and communication [and] technology (ICT). (NPC, 2012, p. 46)

---

[9] The ECD issue was addressed in 2013, with the inclusion of pre-primary education into the generic primary education system.

[10] As in previous years, the Namibian education sector has, during the Annual Budget 2015/16, received the largest share, with the Ministry of Basic Education, Arts and Culture receiving 73.7% of the total budget for education, and the remaining 26.3% going to Higher Education.

The above quotation suggests that there is a mismatch between educational goals and aspirations as expressed at policy level and impact of such policy in terms of results. Furthermore, as the NPC points out above, high investment in education has over the years not meant value for money.

Moreover, government also recognised through Vision 2030 that the education system is 'fragmented', '…with few opportunities for learners to pass from one provider to another' (NPC, 2004, p. 88). To this end, the government commits itself to resolving the fragmentation issue through legislative and policy interventions. Vision 2030 was meant to facilitate the transition to a knowledge-based society. Its main objectives with regards to education were to help achieve the following:

> A fully integrated, unified and flexible education and training system that prepares Namibian learners to take advantage of a rapidly changing environment and contributes to the economic, moral, cultural and social development of the citizens throughout their lives (NPC, 2004, p. 89).

The above statement, though suggesting a more integrated education system, would in this author's view, be difficult to realise within the framework of Namibia's liberal democratic system which, as discussed herein, not only breeds inequities but is also the very cause of 'fragmentation' problems within the education system. Therefore, Vision 2030 promises much without indicating in concrete terms how Namibia will become the Promised Land in 2030.

A World Bank (2005) study identified various shortcomings in education in Namibia, and established that weaknesses within the educational system included the following: poor quality, low efficiency, low capacity to create knowledge and initiate innovations, and more importantly, lack of economic relevance. On the basis of these findings and other factors, the government introduced the 15-year Education and Training Sector Improvement Programme (ETSIP) in 2006, to improve the situation. It was the World Bank study findings, other relevant research results, the government's own internal critique, and commitment to Vision 2030 which compelled the Namibian Government to undertake this major reform programme in the form of ETSIP in order to improve quality and efficiency in education.

ETSIP is a 15-year strategic framework (from 2006–2011; 2012–2016; and 2016–2020) aimed at comprehensively reforming the educational sector from pre-primary level to university education, and was originally supported financially by the European Union and the World Bank. ETSIP has nine components: Early Childhood and Development (ECD) and pre-primary education; General Education; Vocational Education and Training; Tertiary Education and Training; Knowledge Creation and Innovation; Adult and Lifelong Learning; Information Communication Technology (ICT); HIV and AIDS; and Capacity Development. Changes in education were to be achieved through comprehensively addressing weaknesses within the system, with the aim of contributing to economic growth in the long term. ETSIP '…represents the education and training sector's response to the call of Vision 2030' (GRN, 2007, p. 2). To address the short-term needs, it focused on substantially enhancing the education sector's contribution to the attainment of strategic national development goals and facilitating the transition to a knowledge-based economy. It hinges on a recognition that a weak educational system would be unable to contribute substantially to the attainment of complex developmental goals. To this end, ETSIP was also meant to address the perceived shortage of skilled labour in Namibia which was seen to impede economic growth (GRN, 2007). This ambitious programme thus focused on addressing shortcomings in the entire educational system from Early Childhood programmes to Higher Education.

Early Childhood Development and pre-primary education

At independence in 1990, only 10% of learners had access to government-funded pre-school education (PSE). However, instead of improving on that and increasing access, the government decided to eradicate the pre-school programme altogether. In its place, the Early Childhood Development (ECD) policy was developed and implemented in 1996, with the Ministry of Regional and Local Government and Housing being tasked to oversee the ECD programme management (GRN, 1999). But, as Amukugo (2010) pointed out:

> [W]hilst pre-primary education caters for the child's development needs, it also focuses on scholastic development of children between the ages of 3–5 years old; and thereby preparing the young for school life .... Thus, an emphasis on ECD while neglecting PSE not only denied a large number of Namibian children the pre-school grounding, it discriminated against children from poor socio-economic background who need such preparation most (p. 13).

In addition, the World Bank Report (2005) observed that 80% of Namibian children start primary school without the necessary learning readiness. To remedy the situation, ETSIP focused on enhancing early childhood education management systems, access and quality; and provided teacher support along with material development (GRN, 2007). Above all ETSIP's Phase I was meant to develop policy and institutional framework in the Ministry of Education, so as to improve management and provision of pre-primary education nationwide (ibid.).

Consequently, pre-school education was made part of the generic primary education in 2013. Given the fact that primary education is currently both free of charge and compulsory, the decision to incorporate pre-school education into the primary education system has the potential to assist greatly in improving the aspect of access, equity and democracy in education, especially for the disadvantaged communities.

General education (grades 1–12)

Nine years after independence, many children in rural areas were still walking 20 km or more in order to get to school. Shortage of classrooms, books, materials, equipment and transport, classrooms under trees, financing and management of education, and poorly trained teachers were some of the major problems identified by the Presidential Commission on Education, Culture and Training (GRN, 1999). Although access to general education was achieved in a short period of time, as testified by an instant increase in enrolment rates after independence and some improvement in teacher qualifications, the quality of general education was less impressive and was bound to threaten the country's transition to the envisioned knowledge-based society. Moreover, whilst the educational goal of access was achieved, inequities in terms of resource distribution and access to conducive learning environments in rural areas, secondary education's incapacity to produce the quantity and quality of output required to feed higher education, and inefficient use of resources were among the shortcomings that haunted general education (GRN, 2007, pp. 17–18) and threatened to arrest the educational vision as visualised by Vision 2030.

Government's continued inputs (as outlined in this chapter) notwithstanding, challenges within disadvantaged regions still persist. It is somewhat disturbing that more than 25 years after independence, there are still primary school learners who are taught under trees due to classroom shortages, and a number of secondary school learners who have to endure lack of basic necessities (Tjihenuna, 2014).

Moreover, lack of hostels force some underprivileged secondary school learners to live under harsh conditions. As late as 2015, for example, some 167 long distance learners from the impoverished region of Kunene were forced to sleep under trees at Omuhonga. The school, which lacks a hostel, is situated about 120 km from Opuwo on the way to Epupa Falls. Its learners sleep in the open even during winter time, and get soaked during the rainy season. Furthermore, shortage of linen forces them to share blankets. Also, they shower in self-made ablution amenities constructed from tree branches and leaves and utilise pit latrines ('167 Kunene learners sleep under trees', 2015). The evidence above indicates that quality and equity at the general education level are still outside the reach of some of the underprivileged learners.

Nonetheless, contrary to the above evidence and in contrast with the findings by Makuwa (2005) and Amukugo (2002) as described herein, recent secondary school performances at the national level give rise to a sigh of relief, at least for now. To start with, the Oshikoto region (the third poorest region in the country) has shown that with focus and hard work learners can perform wonders. Thus, between 2009 and 2013, Oshikoto ranked number one in Grade 10 results at the national level for five consecutive years (Ministry of Education, January 2010, 2011, 2012; Namwandi, 2014 December), and ranked second in Grade 12 results during both 2013 and 2014 (Namwandi, 2015 January). The region maintained its second position in Grade 12 results during 2015 (Windhoek Observer, 13 January 2016). During 2014, the Oshikoto region maintained its number one national ranking for Grade 10, with other poor rural regions of Oshana, Omusati and Ohangwena scooping the second, third and fourth places on the national scale, with Kavango East, Zambezi and Kavango West fifth, sixth and seventh respectively (Namwandi, December 2014, p. 7). Ironically, the more affluent regions of Khomas, Erongo and Hardap only managed the tenth, eighth and fourteenth spots on the national ranking respectively. The poorest region, Kavango, prides itself on having at least one secondary school, St Boniface,[11] which has been named the best performing school nationally from 2006 to 2015 (Ministry of Education, January 2007, 2008, 2009, 2010, 2011, 2012; Namwandi, 2014 December; Hanse-Himarwa, 2016). The underprivileged regions of Kavango East and Oshikoto respectively took the first and second overall best performing regions in 2015. The former struggling affluent regions of Erongo and Khomas made it to the top five overall best performing regions, at the third and fifth place separately (Hanse Himarwa, 2016). These figures indicate a persistent contradiction between poverty and educational attainment as observed earlier in this chapter. This demonstrates the human being's capacity to defeat adverse circumstances and perform well within the context of a conducive environment. The superior brain postulate is thus defeated by the power of environmental determination of educational performance.

These results, showing that poor learners are out-performing their more affluent counterparts, confirm the contradictions that are embedded in an education system which practically makes it

---

[11] St Boniface College is a Roman Catholic private secondary school, situated in the Kavango East region of Namibia.

difficult to draw a corresponding line between educational input and output. This is so mainly because the educational outcome is influenced by a combination of complex socio-economic and educational factors. Historical experience has taught us that planned educational inputs can produce unexpected educational outcomes. Besides, the above positive development may also be an indication that government's reformist approach, as exemplified by remedial programmes such as ETSIP, combined with bi-lateral development projects and multi-lateral co-operation projects, have started bearing fruit. These inputs have led to tangible results in the form of improved physical, material and human resources, especially in the rural areas, where new classrooms were built, more school books distributed and teacher quality somewhat[12] improved.

At the same time, the Namibian Government sees general education as being crucial in building the foundation for lifelong learning for most of the youth and as a vital base for developing the necessary human resources for a sustainable and competitive economy. In essence, '…general education is [regarded as] the key foundation for building the skills required for Namibia's accelerated development and for achieving vital social goals' (GRN, 2007, p. 17). To achieve the expected results, Phase I of ETSIP focused on (a) improving educational quality, (b) ensuring equality of opportunity, including equitable access to quality senior secondary education, and (c) improving system management and efficiency (ibid., p. 19), as well as on transforming curricula from being subject-based to being competence-based. The ETSIP programme also identifies general education as being crucial to achieving a knowledge-based society and to achieving Vision 2030, with secondary education (a) determining the quality of tertiary education, (b) providing human resources for a sustainable competitive economy, (c) enhancing capacity intake for Vocational Education and Training (VET), and (d) driving export-led growth through knowledge and skills building (GRN, 2007, p. 17).

It is, however, worth noting that such competencies are to be determined through setting 'quantifiable targets for learning'. Moreover, educational achievements will be decided upon on the basis of obtained 'measurable skills, knowledge and competencies' (GRN, 2007, p. 19), in a positivist technical rationality fashion as discussed herein. It will also be interesting to see the impact of ETSIP's phase I, more especially against the backdrop of continued underperformance at the critical secondary school levels, grades 10 and 12, which are supposed to direct the future of Namibian youth, and the limited access to higher education, partly due to weaknesses within the secondary school system on which higher education depends for the supply of quality students. The same can be said about its impact on the quality and equity goals of education.

Higher education[13]

It is generally an accepted view that higher education has both a 'utilitarian' and 'non-utilitarian'[14] function for both the individual and society. Its utilitarian purposes include: the creation

---

[12] The word 'somewhat' is used in recognition of the fact that the problem of unqualified teachers continues to haunt general education in Namibia.

[13] According to the Oxford Dictionary Thesaurus & Wordpower Guide (Soanes, Waite, & Hawker, 2001), higher education refers to 'education to degree level or equivalent, provided at universities or colleges'. In Namibia therefore, higher education includes the University of Namibia; the former Polytechnic of Namibia, which was transformed into the Namibia University of Science and Technology by Act No. 7 of 2015, and the International University of Management, which is a private institution.

[14] Knowledge created through 'basic research' or acquired for its own sake, without immediate benefit (utility).

and dissemination of knowledge produced through research, including generating new ideas through discoveries and inventions; producing of advanced skilled human resources for socio-economic development, thereby enhancing the quality of life of all citizens; instilling moral and aesthetic values into those who go through it; providing leadership by being exemplary, which includes setting standards for the national education system; and strengthening the country's foundation for democracy through interpretation of its conceptual framework, both in writing and through debates. It should be underscored though, that both the utilitarian and non-utilitarian functions of a university are necessary for socio-economic development in the short and long-term perspectives, and thus need to be recognised and encouraged.

Just as universities elsewhere were at one point or another regarded as exclusive ivory towers disconnected from the rest of society, higher education in Africa, too, was seen previously as an expensive endeavour that mostly served the interests of the privileged few within society. This perception has changed of late, and higher education is now being perceived as a key institution that propels 'productivity, competitiveness and economic growth' (Bloom, Canning, & Chan, 2006). The new baby on the block, Namibia, is no exception to this comprehension. It is therefore not by accident that the country's first university, the University of Namibia (UNAM), was established in 1992, only two years into political independence, by Act No. 18 of 1992 (GRN, 1992). The establishment of a university during the first two years of Namibia's independence was necessitated by the fact that at independence in 1990, no single university existed. Instead, the Academy for Tertiary Education had been established in 1980 as the first institution of higher learning during the colonial era. Lack of an apposite university in colonial Namibia was in line with the colonial government's intention to keep the black majority in a state of educational inferiority so as to meet the needs of manual labour for the colonial economy – a position that the independent Namibian government was determined to reverse. As the Founding President of the Republic of Namibia succinctly stated when he was installed as UNAM's Founding Chancellor in 1993:

> ... I see the University of Namibia as a centre of higher learning, served by dedicated men and women of quality, and producing graduates determined to uplift the standard of living of our people. I see the University of Namibia taking its rightful place in Southern Africa in particular, Africa in general, and the world at large, and making its contribution in every area of the world body of knowledge ... (University of Namibia, 1995, p. 5).

These visionary thoughts captured the mission and vision of the new university, or as UNAM itself says: The above words '... encapsulate the motto of UNAM: education, service and development' (ibid.). The founding Vice-Chancellor, Professor Peter Katjavivi, and his team enthusiastically built the university almost from scratch, separating its size, mission and vision from the erstwhile insufficient Academy.

From its inception in 1994, therefore, the University of Namibia increased the Academy's paltry student enrolment of 1,342 at independence (ibid., p. 2), to 3,212 students (ibid., p. 15). A year later, the number of faculties increased from five (plus two Centres) at the Academy (ibid., p. 2), to seven (plus five Academic Centres) (ibid., p. 16).

The new university also improved access to higher education, in contrast to the former Academy which was characterised by '... gross imbalances with respect to geographical origins, ethnic groups, and in some fields, also gender perspectives' (ibid., p. 3). By being inadequately accessible to disadvantaged communities, the Academy violated the ethos of democracy. As an individual who taught at the Academy for one year in 1990, this author observed that the quality of education was also at stake, since prior to independence, the Academy could show only a fraction of PhD holders amongst its lecturers, which in turn led to a very low research output. Even the library was very small, unable to support research activities. This view is supported by a report from the University of Namibia (1995) which pointed out that the library had only 40,000 books, journals and periodicals (ibid., p. 3).

Unlike the Academy, by 1994, UNAM boasted an academic staff complement of 200 (ibid., p. 15). Out of these, 12 were Full Professors, 21 were Associate Professors, and 33 were Senior Lecturers, while a number were Lecturers and Junior Lecturers (ibid., pp. 18–33). The newly formed institution also offered many more academic programmes.

Although UNAM achieved its goal of access in terms of gender representation during the first ten years, the aim of providing adequate geographical distribution was not that easy to achieve. Students from the more affluent regions of Khomas and Hardap accounted for a much higher student representation than students from other regions (Figure 1: UNAM, 2006, p. 16), the majority of whom were disadvantaged.

Today (2017), the university boasts 12 campuses, situated in different regions across Namibia, and a student enrolment of 25,267 (University of Namibia, 2016), which should improve the issue of access also across regions. Having established a Faculty of Medicine in 2010, UNAM graduated 35 medical doctors in 2016, thereby making history in Namibia. Mechanisms to check quality have been put in place by (a) establishing a Centre for Quality Assurance and Management (CEQUAM), (b) placing emphasis on self-evaluation, complemented and validated by external evaluation of academic functions, including internal and external moderation of academic programmes and examinations, (c) registration of all qualifications with the National Qualification Authority, and (d) ensuring appointment of qualified and experienced academic personnel to deliver those programmes and provide the necessary support staff and resources. The latter point has unfortunately not always worked in accordance with UNAM recruitment policy, as politics, nepotism, favouritism and sheer corruption sometimes creep in, thwarting democratic principles and fair labour practices, and gradually breeding inefficiency and discontent, especially among academic staff. Those who dare to speak out against injustices may even be made examples of in a bid to deter others from raising critical voices.

UNAM was followed by the establishment of the Polytechnic of Namibia by Act No. 33 of 1994 (GRN, 1994), (since 2015 known as the Namibia University of Science and Technology, [NUST]) . The two government-funded higher education institutions are complemented by a private university, the International University of Management (IUM). Founded by an indigenous Namibian, David Namwandi, in 1994, it started off as the Institute of Higher Education and was transformed into a university in 2002. Although IUM formally became a university 13 years before NUST, it remains third in the Namibian universities' list as shown, for example, by international universities' ranking (Ranking Web of Universities, 2017). Today, both NUST and IUM are offering degrees up to the PhD level.

In a further attempt to improve higher education in the country, the higher education sector was made part of the ETSIP strategic framework discussed earlier in this chapter. ETSIP's strategic objectives for Phase I include: to strengthen tertiary education's institutional capacity; to enhance its relevance and responsiveness; to augment its quality and training system; and to mobilise and ensure efficient utilisation of financial resources. The objectives of higher education as stipulated by the government above are to a larger extent in line with internationally accepted aims, and government has addressed many of these at the policy level. But whether they have been addressed at the implementation level remains to be seen, all the more so in the light of changes made to the ETSIP implementation process.

ETSIP's ambitious programme was never implemented in its entirety, raising questions about the extent to which its objectives were met. In 2011, the Ministry of Education organised a three-day ETSIP Review Meeting at Heja Lodge, outside Windhoek. The meeting dealt with issues related to policy, structure, monitoring and evaluation, and capacity building among others. One important outcome of this meeting was the Ministry's resolve to develop a 5-year Strategic Plan (2012–2017). As a result, instead of being implemented as separate entities in terms of the original course of action, phases II and III of ETSIP were incorporated into the ministries' programmes instead. Similarly, the European Union's funds were incorporated into the State Revenue Fund as a short-term measure. Presently, therefore, ETSIP is wholly funded through the Ministry's Annual Budget.

The reason behind the unexpected changes in the implementation strategy is not clear. Attempts to collect documentary evidence within the Ministry of Education were not successful, partly due to the departure of the erstwhile ETSIP Coordinator, although under normal circumstances, institutional memory could have provided the required information.

The Namibian Government's view as outlined in the ETSIP document, is that higher education '… informally sets quality standards for the entire education system … produces high level technical and managerial personnel required for economic growth and competitiveness … generates knowledge workers and researchers essential to knowledge-driven development … provides enterprises with technical support and partnership to spur knowledge-based innovation … [and] delivers policy analysts and managers to the public and private sector' (GRN, 2007, p. 37).

The key question, however, is to what extent have the set aims been realised? During the first 15 years of Namibian independence, higher education was criticised for high cost, lack of coordination which led to duplication of efforts between UNAM and the Polytechnic of Namibia (GRN, 1999, p. 150), and a weak linkage between the university's and the polytechnic's programme content and national human resources needs, to mention but a few examples. The coordination issue was addressed by establishing an umbrella Act covering the UNAM and Polytechnic Acts, namely, the Higher Education Act No. 26 of 2003. This Act establishes the National Council for Higher Education (NCHE), whose major objectives are to promote:

1. A co-ordinated higher education system;
2. Better access for students to higher education;
3. Ensured quality in higher education; and
4. Advice with regards to apportionment of funds to public higher education
(GRN, 2003)

To strengthen and ascertain quality in higher education, the NCHE has recently developed an institutional audit, which apart from having been piloted at NUST, has not yet been implemented.

The linking of higher education content to socio-economic needs is always problematic, partially due to the 'utilitarian' versus non-utilitarian functions of such institutions as discussed above. This difficulty is supported by research in higher education productivity measurement. Relevant argument points to various factors that make the evaluation of higher education achievements cumbersome, partially for the following reasons:

1. Institutions of higher education are multi-product firms (that is, they produce multiple kinds of services);
2. Inputs and outputs of the productive process are heterogeneous, involve[ing] nonmarket variables, and are subject to quality variation and temporal change; and
3. Measurements are impeded by gaps in needed data [and distinct research methodology].

('Why measurement of higher education productivity is difficult', 2012)

The quality of output between institutions also differs depending on the quality of academic personnel and level of programmes offered. Thus, a university with more PhD holders, professors and skilled researchers is more likely to produce competitive high level graduates than a higher education institution that possesses fewer of those attributes. Some years ago, for example, UNAM produced 700 degree holders (including PhDs) per year. The Polytechnic (now NUST) had a total annual output of 1,000 at national diploma and certificate levels (GRN, 2007, p. 37). In this context, the three above-mentioned Namibian higher education institutions are bound to create different levels of productivity. That notwithstanding, the three institutions have, over the years, allotted human resources to both private and public institutions.

At the same time, they have also produced multi-skilled individuals, some of whom create their own employment and even provide employment to others. Experience shows that currently, more young people fall into this category, although lack of start-up capital impedes this development, which in turn contributes to increased youth unemployment. According to the World Bank, youth unemployment in Namibia (15–24 years old) stood at 38.7% in 2014 (Trading Economics, n.d. a). This figure is higher than the country's unemployment rate in the same year, which stood at 28.10% (Trading Economics, n.d. b).

It is necessary at this juncture to give an indication of the quality and level of competitiveness of our higher education institutions. If the university rankings at both African and world levels are something to go by, these institutions' appearances on the ranking list should be applauded, considering their comparatively short existence. Namibia's oldest and major university, UNAM, made it onto the 2016 Ranking Web of Universities in Africa and the World, as number 67 out of 200 African universities, beating much older institutions such as the University of Fort Hare. At the time of writing, NUST was placed in 124th place. On the world stage, UNAM took 2759th place, whilst NUST was at 3911th place (Consejo Superior de Investigaciones Científicas (CSIC), 2017).

CSIC rankings reflect both the scholars' and institutions' global quality, mainly by appraising professors' and other researchers' activities, plus electronic access to scholarly publications. Criteria such as educational quality, internationalisation, size of institution, research output, impact and prestige form the basis upon which the institutional quality is assessed (ibid.). The resultant evaluation of the level of regional and global competitiveness may serve as an impetus for both the institution's internal critique and its further development. It can be said therefore that both UNAM and NUST are internationally competitive, albeit with a sizable difference between them.

In terms of institutional relevance to socio-economic development, there have been complaints about a mismatch between the industry and university graduates. From this author's perspective the expressed dissatisfaction is not entirely correct, in that a university's mission goes beyond provision of skills for the industry. As the University of Namibia (1995) eloquently expounds:

> University institutions are oases of knowledge and interaction. They are fountains out of which spring teachers to develop the inquisitive minds of our children and our youth. They are gardens out of which spring the seed of future academics, who constitute the cutting edge of creativity, future industrial and technological innovators, whose creations will enable us to live in greater comfort, prosperity, and happiness, and future scientists and medical practitioners, who will discover antidotes for the many diseases afflicting us and our livestock, and who will invent control methods for the pests that destroy the various crops of our farmers (ibid., p. 2).

This initial university vision has to a greater extent guided UNAM's development as outlined above.

Government has, over the years, emphasised inadequately skilled human resources as being an impediment to socio-economic development. In spite of this, however, not much has been done to produce national human resources audits. Yet such audits are crucial both for planning and to create a connection between higher education output and socio-economic needs. A more comprehensive Human Resources Plan has been developed by the National Planning Commission with the support and participation of a broad range of national institutions, including higher educational institutions such as the University of Namibia, the Polytechnic of Namibia, the International University of Management and the National Council of Higher Education, among others. (GRN, 2012a)

The plan is meant to '… guide the government, private sector, civic organisations and training institutions on how to invest into industries with high growth and employment potential and into critical skills to meet the current and emerging developmental challenges' (ibid., p. iii). As such, the plan seeks to address the utilitarian function of higher education in Namibia, which is critical for socio-economic development.

EDUCATIONAL REFORM THROUGH PUBLIC DEBATE

In a further attempt to improve the educational system, The Ministry of Education organised a National Education Conference in 2011. The aim was to systematically interrogate the educational system, with a specific focus on identifying challenges and opportunity for change. In his closing remarks, the then Minister of Education, the late Dr Abraham Iyambo, observed that the conference met the intended purpose by exposing strengths and weaknesses within the system and offering renewed hope for a brighter future. Sounding a word of optimism, he held that '[w]e have shown … that with diligence we can turn the tide and shape an education system that meets the needs of our country and people' (Iyambo, 2011).

A closer look at the conference resolutions suggests that the conference recognised the importance of 'leadership' in the 'transformative role of education' and in the effectiveness of educational practice. As the leadership guru, John Maxwell, rightly asserts: '[E]verything rises and falls on leadership' (Maxwell, 1993, p. viii). The conference's focus on leadership thus places its objectives in a broader perspective. Likewise, the issue of accountability was seen as crucial in delivering the required effectiveness within the system. It was deemed necessary to emphasise both the recruitment and retention of quality teachers and lecturers on whom the desired educational quality depends. In addition, the teaching profession is to be accorded a higher status in line with the important role they play in education and society at large.

The conference further resolved that whilst academic skills should be emphasised in determining the quality of teachers, the aspect of 'values'[15] should not be overlooked. Mother tongue[16] as a medium of instruction during the first four years of schooling was re-emphasised, as it was seen to play an important role in building a strong foundation for future learning.

In order to improve quality in education, the conference called for continuous in-service training for school principals, specifically in the areas of leadership and management. To address the issue of equity, the conference suggested the promotion of equitable resource distribution in line with national priorities. Besides, wastage was to be identified and an effective auditing and reporting system introduced as a way to control how allocated resources were spent. Establishing a management information system (HEMIS) that informs funding, access and equity policies and planning in higher education was suggested, as well as the setting up of a procedural framework for budgeting in higher education, with the aim of prioritising funding programmes in accordance with the degree to which they address national social and economic needs (Namibian National Education Conference Resolutions, 2011).

The outcome of the 2011 Namibian National Education Conference points to the Namibian Government's willingness to learn from diverse experiences and face challenges. If implemented efficiently, these resolutions can help strengthen the national education objectives as outlined in this chapter. However, the success of the aspired education system overhaul will depend on a strong resolve to implement effectively these resolutions and lessons learned, coupled with a robust monitoring system that can identify challenges and suggest solutions. The Ministry started with implementation of the above resolutions in 2013. With time, monitoring and evaluation of their effectiveness will inform the nation of success and challenges.

THE ROLE OF EDUCATION IN THE 'HARAMBEE PROSPERITY PLAN' (HPP)

Government has often been criticised for coming up with lofty programmes and policies without concrete implementation plans. There may be a light at the end of the tunnel, given the recently launched 'Harambee Prosperity Plan (HPP) 2016/17 – 2019/20)' which is said to

---

[15] Core values, according to the Ministry, include: integrity, accountability, commitment, respect and empathy, teamwork and professionalism. (Ministry of Education, 2012, p. viii).

[16] English was introduced at independence as a language of instruction despite poor levels of English across the country. This policy especially affected teachers, the majority of whom functioned in Afrikaans, the lingua franca during South African colonial rule. However, as time went by, more teachers mastered the language skills, which benefited the teaching and learning process.

be '… a focused and targeted approach to achieve high impact in defined priority areas' (GRN, 2016, p. 6). The Plan was launched in April 2016 by Namibia's third President, Dr Hage G. Geingob, and builds on five pillars, namely: effective governance, economic advancement, social progression, infrastructure development, and international relations and cooperation. Its major focus is most importantly on reducing poverty and inequality through creating prosperity for all. As such, its core strategic objective points to addressing poverty effectively '… through wealth creation, which is done by growing the economy in a sustainable inclusive manner and through the creation of decent employment opportunities' (GRN, 2016, p. 7). At the end of the four year-implementation phase, the Plan is expected to achieve seven goals including the following:

1. A more transparent Namibia;
2. A culture of high performance and citizen-centred service delivery;
3. A significant reduction in poverty levels; and
4. A reputable and competitive vocational educational training system.
   (GRN, 2016, p. 5).

The Harambee Prosperity Plan is meant to complement various government initiatives including Vision 2030 and the various National Development Plans, especially the current NDP 4–2012/13 to 2016/17, (ibid., p. 6), that have been discussed herein.

Since our book is about the relationship between democracy, education and social justice, it is useful at this point to focus on Chapter 5 of the Harambee Prosperity Plan (HPP) which deals with 'Social Progression', a term dubbed the '… cornerstone of the HPP' (ibid., p. 38). To understand this better, consider how the Washington-based 'Social Progress Imperative' describes social progress as '… *the capacity of a society to meet the basic human needs of its citizens, establish the building blocks that allow citizens and communities to enhance and sustain the quality of their lives, and create the conditions for all individuals to reach their full potential'* *(Social Progress, n.d.).*

Tezanos (1992), however, defines this term from a socialist perspective. To understand the notion of 'social progress' he argues, presupposes an assessment of social relations through productive relations. To achieve social progress, therefore, requires that we confront social relations within society. This is necessary, since it is social relations that produce inequalities and alienation [exclusion], which in turn breed social unrest. To him socialism is the 'motivating force in social progress', since it rejects deprivation and exploitation, extends freedom, and promotes equality and equity.

Whilst the liberal definition of social progression as expressed by the Washington-based 'Social Progress Imperative' may be useful, especially by pointing to the society's [state's] responsibility to meet the basic human needs of its people, Tezanos's argument is more advantageous in that it redirects us to focus on the key socio-economic issues of inequality and exclusion, which if not addressed, he cautions, can breed social unrest. To alleviate poverty and achieve social progress, therefore, presupposes addressing first and foremost inequities and exclusion, which is also a precondition for creating social justice.

This is important to take note of in this discussion, given the fact that HPP chooses to focus on Vocational Education and Training (VET) as a separate entity divorced from the overall general education system, which is worrisome. From our point of view it would be more beneficial for Namibia to focus on creating VET opportunities and pathways/study lines within senior secondary schools so as to create a solid foundation on which VET Centres can build. This is so because not all secondary school students possess the theoretical acumen and interest to proceed to university level. There is hence a need to create chances for all through multiple pathways/study lines within the secondary education system. Such VET programmes can be implemented in conjunction with industries as one way to create the linkage between education and industry, which government has often emphasised. As the HPP points out:

> Vocational training is not meant for so called dropouts or those that fail to get admitted to universities. It is promoted because it is the backbone of our economic development. It is therefore, not an inferior skill but one highly rated under HPP. Vocational education [and] training will be prioritised in line with core skills needs identified as per National Skills Development Plan (GRN, 2016, pp. 44–45).

Whilst the rationale above sounds attractive as a policy statement, the HPP's proposed modus operandi (creating separate VET centres) will not only attract those who cannot make it elsewhere, including school drop-outs, but will also be counterproductive to the core and spirit of the government assertion in the quotation above. Therefore, an alternative, robust VET programme within the secondary education system would give real meaning to the needs of aspiring VET professionals, as it would encourage choice of VET pathways out of interest as opposed to their being the only opportunity for those who fail to make it elsewhere. Besides, this proposal would create a strong foundation for post-secondary VET education and training programmes. Students who successfully complete VET training at secondary level should receive appropriate certificates that they can use to continue with post-secondary VET studies.

The HPP's narrowly-focused VET programme, as opposed to the broad-based educational intervention suggested herein, has further led to a misplaced perception that '[d]eveloped economies were not built by PhD holders, but by craftsmen and artisans' (GRN, 2016, p. 44). VET training mainly pays attention to the 'how to do' aspect as opposed to the 'why' side of things. Stated differently, VET training emphasises practical skills at the expense of the theory that is supposed to inform practice. In this respect, what the VET graduates implement is mainly based on ideas developed by skilled researchers and theoreticians, including PhD holders. Since theory informs practice, PhD holders, craftsmen and artisans then contribute directly and/or indirectly to building economies and developing societies.

The argument that plays down the importance of theoretical knowledge to socio-economic development has often led to low utilisation of scholars in African countries. Many Africans who did their post-graduate studies in developed countries would agree that those countries recognise and make use of their knowledgeable and skilled PhD holders much more than some African countries who prefer to engage first world consultants or political appointees. This causes the nagging brain drain from this continent, as lamented by both the African Union and The Foundation for Democracy in Africa (2002) as well as the New Partnership for Africa's Development (NEPAD) (African Union, 2001, Article 120). This phenomenon impedes the much needed development on the African continent.

CONCLUSION

Since education functions within the broader context of society, ideas about its role and place within it are influenced by the political, social, economic and cultural factors of a particular society at a given historical juncture. Consequently, the objectives of colonial education, for example, were inconsistent with the goals of post-colonial education. This holds true if one considers Freire's (1970/1996) 'banking education' concept which he says suppresses students' creative powers and instead encourages their naivety, in line with the oppressors' interests. In addition to the above, the aims of colonial education in South Africa and Namibia not only served to reproduce cheap black labour power for the colonial economy, they also utilised the ideology of apartheid to justify colonial injustices. Post-colonial education on the other hand was meant to mitigate the structure and aims of colonial education.

This chapter brings to the fore the fact that the aims of education during Namibia's liberation struggle took into consideration the importance of aesthetic aspects of 'values' in an education system, among other key goals as discussed herein. The post-colonial education system, on the other hand, focused mainly on knowledge and skills in line with the technical rationality viewpoint discussed earlier. It is therefore gratifying to note that of late, the issue of 'values' in education has been reflected in the 2011 National Educational Conference, which provides the basis for further articulation in the Ministry of Education's future Strategic Plan.

The educational values of the Strategic Plan include: integrity, accountability, commitment, respect and empathy, teamwork and professionalism. (MoE, 2012, p. viii). The issue of values in education is crucial for participation in a democratic process. As Carr and Hartnett (1996) point out, knowledge and skills combined with the necessary attitudes (values) are crucial not only for democratic participation, but the curriculum also needs to foster these values to enable learners and students to look critically at the dominant social, political and economic institutions of society. In other words, to take an interest in what goes on around them, learners and students need to be subjected to participatory rather than instructional teaching methods, since a participatory approach assists in inculcating a democratic ethos. The implementation of Education for All principles has made a difference in terms of increasing access to education at both primary and secondary levels.

As revealed in this chapter, we are currently still struggling with issues of inequities within the system which mirror inequities within the broader society. It is hoped though that the introduction of free secondary education in 2016 will lead to tangible results, that the quality of our education will improve further, and that the persistent nagging issue of high failure rates at secondary school level will become a thing of the past in the not too distant future.

Liberal democracy, which is a form of governance in Namibia, emphasises abstract political rights at the expense of concrete economic rights, and legalistic equal rights at the expense of social equity. As such, it consequently limits education's capacity to sustain democracy and social justice. To remedy the situation, there is a need to implement what Ake (2000) terms 'structural democratization' at the level of the state, in a way that guarantees concrete economic rights, addresses economic inequalities and increases democratic participation of the disadvantaged within society (ibid.). Such a move would address the key educational goals of quality and equity.

The Namibian Government's recently launched 'Harambee Prosperity Plan', with clearly pronounced objectives and an implementation strategy which aims at (amongst other goals) poverty eradication and combating socio-economic inequality, is a step in the right direction. Its suggestion for a rather narrowly focused VET education programme is, however, problematic and needs to be reviewed if it is to make a meaningful contribution to eradicating poverty and promoting socio-economic development. On the whole, the HPP's substantive impact will best be judged four years from now, pending a robust monitoring and evaluation system.

References

25 of the oldest American colleges and universities. (n.d.). Retrieved from http://affordableschools. net/25-oldest-american-colleges-universities

167 Kunene learners sleep under trees. (2015, July 1). *New Era*. Retrieved from https://www.newera.com. na/2015/07/01/167-kunene-learners-sleep-trees/

African Union. The Foundation for Democracy in Africa (2002, December). Report on the First African Union Western Diaspora Forum. Washington D. C: The Foundation for Democracy in Africa.

Ake, C. (2000). *The feasibility of democracy in Africa*. Dakar: Council for the Development of Social Science Research in Africa (CODESRIA).

Amukugo, E. M. (1995). *Education and politics in Namibia: Past trends and future perspectives*. (2nd Rev. ed.). Windhoek: Gamsberg Macmillan.

Amukugo, E. M. (2002). Education for all in independent Namibia: Reality or political ideal? In V. Winterfeldt, T. Fox & P. Mufune (Eds.). *Namibia society sociology*. Windhoek: University of Namibia.

Amukugo, E. M. (2005). Eighty% of youth leave school with only G Grade. In *15 Years of independence: Celebrating a legacy, continuing with nation-building*. Windhoek: New Era. pp. 9–14.

Amukugo, E. M., Likando, G. N., & Mushaandja, J. (2010). Access and quality dilemma in education: Implications for Namibia's Vision 2030. *Higher Education Forum*, 7, 101–111.

Amukugo, E. M., Likando, G. N., Shakwa, G. N., & Nyambe, J. (2010). A critical review of teacher education in Namibia. In K. G. Karras, & C. C. Wolhuter (Eds.), *International handbook on teacher education worldwide: Issues and challenges for teacher education* (pp. 805–822). Athens: Atrapos editions.

Blau, J. R., Brunsma, D. L, Moncada, A., & Zimmer, C. (Eds.). (2008). *The leading rogue state: The US and human rights*. Boulder. CO: Paradigm Publishers.

Bloom, D., Canning, D., & Chan, K. (2006). *Higher education and economic development in Africa*. Harvard University. Retrieved from http://www.uhasselt.be/Documents/UHasselt_EN/International/ Lezing%20N-Z%202013/Higher_Education_and_Economic_Development_in_Africa.pdf

Carr, W. & Hartnett, A. (1996). *Education and the struggle for democracy: The politics of educational ideas*. Buckingham: Open University Press.

Chimanikire, D. P. (2005, December). Brain Drain: Causes and economic consequences for Africa. Livingstone: AAPAM (African Association for Public Administration and Management).

Consejo Superior de Investigaciones Científicas (CSIC). (2017). *Ranking web of universities*. Retrieved from http://www.webometrics.info/en/Africa

Darder, A., Baltodano, M. P., & Torres, R. D. (Eds.). (2009). *The critical pedagogy reader.* (2nd ed.) London: Routledge.

The Foundation for Democracy in Africa. (2002). *The African Union. Report on the first Africa Union.* Western Diaspora Forum. Washington D. C. December 17–19. Retrieved from http://democracy-africa.org/articles/aurep02final.html

Freire, P. (1974). *Education for critical consciousness.* London: Sheed and Ward.

Freire, P. (1996). *Pedagogy of the oppressed.* London: Penguin. (Original work published in English 1970).

Freire, P. (1998). *Teachers as cultural workers: Letters to those who teach.* (Rev. ed.) Boulder: Westview Press.

Government of the Republic of Namibia (GRN). (1990). *The Namibian Constitution.* Retrieved from http://www.gov.na/documents/10181/14134/Namibia_Constitution.pdf/37b70b76-c15c-45d4-9095-b25d8b8aa0fb

Government of the Republic of Namibia (GRN). (1992). *University of Namibia Act.* (Government Gazette No. 460, Act No. 18). Windhoek: Government Printer.

Government of the Republic of Namibia (GRN). (1994). *Polytechnic of Namibia Act.* (Government Gazette No. 991, Act No. 33). Windhoek: Government Printer.

Government of the Republic of Namibia (GRN). (1999). *Presidential commission on education, culture and training, Vol. 1.* Windhoek: Gamsberg Macmillan.

Government of the Republic of Namibia (GRN). (2003). *University of Namibia Act.* (Government Gazette No. 3125, Act No. 26). Windhoek: Government Printer.

Government of the Republic of Namibia (GRN). (2007). *Education and training sector improvement programme (ETSIP) Phase I (2006–2011).* Windhoek: Ministry of Education.

Government of the Republic of Namibia (GRN). (2012a). *National human resources plan 2010–2025.* Windhoek: National Planning Commission.

Government of the Republic of Namibia (GRN). (2012b). *Strategic plan 2012–2017.* Windhoek: Ministry of Education.

Government of the Republic of Namibia (GRN). (2015). *State of the Nation address.* Retrieved from http://www.gov.na/documents/10181/22710/STATE+OF+THE+NATION+ADDRESS+2015+BY+HIS+EXCELLENCY+DR.+HAGE+G.+GEINGOB+PRESIDENT+OF+THE+REPUBLIC+OF+NAMIBIA/5d50418d-7b14-434c-9257-02db06945f58

Government of the Republic of Namibia (GRN). (2016). *Harambee prosperity plan 2016/17–2019/20: Namibian Government's action plan towards prosperity for all.* Windhoek: Office of the President.

Hanse-Himarwa, K. (2016, January 13). Grade 12 pass rate declines as St. Boniface remains top. *Windhoek Observer.*

Iyambo, A. (2011). Remarks by Hon. Dr. Abraham Iyambo, Minister of Education on the occasion of the closing ceremony of the National Education Conference. Windhoek: Republic of Namibia.

Henriksen, E. K., Dillon, J., & Ryder, J. (Eds.). (2015). *Understanding student participation and choice in science and technology education.* New York: Springer.

Jauch, H., Edwards, L., & Cupido, B. (2009). *Inequality in Namibia.* Retrieved from http://www.osisa.org/sites/default/files/sup_files/chapter_3_-_namibia.pdf

Kasanda, C. D. & Phiri, F. A. (Eds.). (1995). *Proceedings of The (H)IGCSE colloquium on teacher education.* University of Namibia, Windhoek, 27–29 March.

Kibera, L. W. & Kimokoti, A. C. (2007). *Fundamentals of sociology of education with reference to Africa.* Nairobi: University of Nairobi Press.

Makuwa, D. (2005). *The SACMEQ II Project in Namibia: A study of the condition of schooling and quality of education.* Harare: Southern and Eastern Africa Consortium for Monitoring Educational Quality.

Marope, M. T. (2005). *Namibia human capital and knowledge development for economic growth with equity.* (Africa Region Human Development, Working Paper Series – No. 84). Retrieved from http://documents.worldbank.org/curated/en/179781468774580944/pdf/327960NM0Human0capital0A RHD0No84.pdf

Maxwell, J. C. (1993). *Developing the leader within you.* Nashville: Thomas Nelson.

Ministry of Education, Namibia. (MoE). (2006, January). Press Statement. Release of the Oct/Nov 2005 IGCSE results for full-time and part-time candidates. Windhoek: Ministry of Education.

Ministry of Education, Namibia. (MoE). (January 2007, 2008, 2009). Press Releases: Results of the Junior Secondary Certificate (JSC) Examination for full-time candidates. Windhoek: Ministry of Education.

Ministry of Education (January 2010, 2011, 2012). Press Statements: Results of the Junior Secondary Certificate (JSC) Examination for full-time candidates. Windhoek: Ministry of Education.

Ministry of Education, Namibia. (MoE). (2010). *The national curriculum for basic education.* Retrieved from http://www.ibe.unesco.org/curricula/namibia/sx_befw_2009_eng.pdfhttp://www.moe.gov.na/news_article.php?id=133&title=%20Recruitment%20of%20Qualified%20Teachers%20From%20 SADC%20 countries

Ministry of Education and Culture, Namibia. (MEC). (1993). *Toward education for all: A development brief for education, culture and training.* Windhoek: Gamsberg Macmillan.

Ministry of Education, Arts and Culture, Namibia. (MEAC). (2013). *Recruitment of qualified teachers from SADC countries.* Retrieved from http://www.moe.gov.na/news_article.php?id=133&title=%20 Recruitment%20of%20Qualified%20Teachers%20From%20SADC%20%20countries

Ministry of Education, Arts and Culture, Namibia. (MEAC). (2016). *Media release: admission of grade 10 full-time repeaters in 2016.* Retrieved from http://www.moe.gov.na/news_article.php?type=pressrele ase&id=213&title=MEDIA RELEASE: ADMISSION OF GRADE 10 FULL-TIME REPEATERS IN 2016

Ministry of Labour and Social Welfare, Namibia. (2008). *Namibia labour force survey.* Retrieved from http://www.mol.gov.na/documents/432260/1697652/Namibia_Labour_Force_Survey_xNLFSx_2008_ Final_Report.pdf/a06418cc-4e52-4a44-b895-d71e004172a8

Molteno, F. (1984). The historical foundations of the schooling of black South Africans. In P. Kalleway, (Ed.). (1990). *Apartheid and education: The education of black South Africans.* Johannesburg: Ravan Press.

Morrow, W. E. (1990). Aims of education in South Africa. *International Review of Education, 36*(2), 171–181.

Morrow, W. E. (2007). *Learning to teach in South Africa.* Cape Town: HSRC Press. Retrieved from http://www.hsrcpress.ac.za/product.php?productid=2196

National Conference on Education (Namibia) Resolutions. 2011. Windhoek: Ministry of Education, Arts and Culture.

National Planning Commission (NPC). (2004). *Namibia Vision 2030*. Retrieved from http://www.npc. gov.na/?wpfb_dl=37

National Planning Commission. (2008). *A review of poverty and inequality in Namibia*. Windhoek: National Planning Commission. Retrieved from http://www.undp.org/content/dam/undp/documents/poverty/ docs/projects/Review_of_Poverty_and_Inequality_in_Namibia_2008.pdf

National Planning Commission. (2012). *Namibia's fourth national development plan (NDP4) 2012/2013 – 2016–2017*. Windhoek: National Planning Commission. Retrieved from http://www.npc.gov. na/?wpfb_dl=37

National Planning Commission. (2012). *National human resources plan 2010–2025*. Retrieved from http:// www.npc.gov.na/?wpfb_dl=203

National Planning Commission. (2015). *Namibia poverty mapping*. Retrieved from www.npc.gov. na/?wpfb_dl=225

Namibia Statistics Agency. (2012a). *Namibia household income & expenditure survey (NHIES) 2009/2010*. Retrieved from http://cms.my.na/assets/documents/p19dmrae8os57rbnfuvbrgoae1.pdf

Namibia Statistics Agency. (2012b). *Poverty dynamics in Namibia: A comparative study using the 1993/94, 2003/04 and the 2009/10NHIES surveys*. Retrieved from http://cms.my.na/assets/documents/ p19dnar71kanl1vfo14gu5rpbkq1.pdf

Namwandi, D. (2014). Press Release on the 2014 Results of grade 10 and 12 Namibia Senior Secondary Certificate (NSSC) higher level. Retrieved from www.moe.gov.na/files/downloads/611_Press Release for Grade 10 full-time and part-time and Grade 12 Higher Level 2014 17 December.pdf

Namwandi, D. (2015, January). Press Briefing: On the Release of the 2014 Results of Grade 12 Namibia Senior Secondary Certificate (NSSC) Ordinary Level for full-time and part-time candidates. Windhoek: Ministry of Education. Retrieved from https://www.moe.gov.na/files/downloads/b54_ Dr%20Namwandi%20Speech%20Grade%2012%20Results%2015%20January%202015%20%20 Examination.pdf

Ngwane, M. G. (2006). *Deconstructing liberal democracy in Africa*. Retrieved from http://www.gngwane. com/2006/01/deconstructing_.html; last accessed 19 October 2011.

Noble, J. (1977). *Education in Namibia*. (Master's thesis). University of Nairobi. Retrieved from http:// erepository.uonbi.ac.ke/bitstream/handle/11295/55399/Noble_Education%20In%20Namibia... pdf?sequence=3&isAllowed=y

Nujoma, S. (2010). *Statement made on the occasion of a fundraising gala dinner for the Sanjo Senior Secondary School, Katima Mulilo, 30 July*. Retrieved from: http://www.samnujomafoundation.org/zoomteg/html/ previous%20speeches/Statement%20%20AT%20SANJO%20SENIOR%20SECONDARY%20 SCHOOL.pdf

Nyerere, J. (1967). *Education for self-reliance*. (Policy Booklet). Dar Es Salaam: Government Printers.

Oldest university. (n.d.). In *The Guinness book of records*. Retrieved from http://www.guinnessworldrecords. com/world-records/oldest-university

Ranking Web of Universities. (2017). Retrieved from http://www.webometrics.info/en/search/Rankings/ namibia%20type%3Apais

Sichombe, B., Nambira, G., Tjipueja, G., & Kapenda, L. (2011). *Evaluation of promotion policy requirements in Namibian schools*. National Institute for Educational Development & Ministry of Education.

Retrieved from http://www.nied.edu.na/assets/documents/03Research/04PromotionPolicy/RE-PO_Evaluation-of-PromotionRequirements_2011.pdf

Sifuna, D. N. & Otiende, J. E. (1994). *An Introductory history of education*. (Rev. ed.). Nairobi: University of Nairobi Press.

Soanes, C., Waite, M., & Hawker, S. (2001). Higher education. In *The Oxford dictionary, thesaurus, and wordpower guide*. Oxford: Oxford University Press.

Social Progress. (n.d.). *Social progress imperative*. Retrieved from http://www.socialprogressimperative.org/custom-indexes-european-union-findings/

Steinberg, S. R. (2015). Employing the Bricolage as critical research in teaching English as a foreign language. In M. Vicars, S. R. Steinberg, T. McKenna, & M. Cacciattolo (Eds.). *The praxis of English language teaching and learning* (PELT): *Beyond the binaries: Researching critically in EFL classrooms*. Rotterdam: SensePublishers.

Sullivan, T. A., Mackie, C., Massy, W. F., & Sinha, E. (Eds.). (2012). *Improving measurement of productivity in higher education*. Washington: The National Academic Press.

SWAPO of Namibia. (1984). *Education for all. National integrated educational system for emergent Namibia*. Luanda: SWAPO Department of Education and Culture.

SWAPO of Namibia. (1990). *The national integrated education system for Namibia: Draft proposal for education reform and renewal*. Windhoek: SWAPO Department of Education and Culture.

Swarts, P. (1995). The new senior secondary system in Namibia: Achievements and challenges. In C. D. Kasanda & F. A. Phiri, (Eds.), *Proceedings of the (H)IGCSE colloquium on teacher education. University of Namibia, Windhoek, 27–29 March*.

Tabata, I. (1980). *Education for barbarism*. Lusaka: Unity Movement of South Africa.

Tebeje, A. (n.d.). Brain Drain and capacity building in Africa. Ottawa: International Research and Development Centre (IRDC). Retrieved from: https://www.idrc.ca/en/article/brain-drain-and-capacity-building-africa

Tezanos, F. T. (1992). *Socialism and social progress*. Retrieved from http://www.fundacionsistema.com/wp-content/uploads/2015/09/art-JF-Tezanos-Socialism-and-social-progress2.pdf

Tjihenuna, T. (2014, June 4). Open-air classrooms still order of the day. *The Namibian*. Retrieved from http://www.namibian.com.na/index.php?id=124014&page=archive-read

Top 10 oldest universities in the world: Ancient colleges. (2009). Retrieved from http://collegestats.org/2009/12/top-10-oldest-universities-in-the-world-ancient-colleges/

Trading economics. (n.d. a). *Unemployment; youth total (% of total labor force ages 15–24) in Namibia*. Retrieved from http://www.tradingeconomics.com/namibia/unemployment-youth-total-percent-of-total-labor-force-ages-15-24-wb-data.html

Trading economics. (n.d. b). *Namibia unemployment rate*. Retrieved from http://www.tradingeconomics.com/namibia/unemployment-rate

United Nations Development Programme (UNDP), Namibia. (2016). *Poverty reduction*. Retrieved from http://www.na.undp.org/content/namibia/en/home/ourwork/povertyreduction/overview.html

United Nations Partnership Framework (UNPAF) (2014–2018). (2013). Retrieved from http://www.na.undp.org/content/namibia/en/home/library/UNPAF20142018.html

University. (2016). In *Encyclopaedia Britannica*. Retrieved from http://www.britannica.com/topic/university

University of Cambridge Local Examination Syndicate (UCLES). (n.d). *International General Certificate of Secondary Education: An introduction*. Retrieved from http://www.cie.org.uk/ programmes-and-qualifications/cambridge-secondary-2/cambridge-igcse/curriculum/

University of Namibia. (1995). *First five year development plan 1995–1999*. (K. E. Mshigeni, A. du Pisani, & G. E. Kiangi, compilers). Windhoek: UNAM.

University of Namibia. (2015). *Quality Assurance and Management Policy*. Windhoek: UNAM. Retrieved from http://www.unam.edu.na/sites/default/files/content/quality_assurance_and_management_policy. pdf

University of Namibia (2016). Statistics 2016. Windhoek: UNAM.

Van Der Berg, S. & Moses, E. (2011). *Southern and Eastern Africa Consortium for Monitoring Educational Quality (SACMEQ 1995–2013)*. Retrieved from http://www.sacmeq.org/education-namibia.htm

Verlaeckt, K. & Vitorino, V. (Eds.). (2002). *Unity and diversity: the contribution of the social sciences and the humanities to the European research area. Proceedings of the 2001 Belgian EU Presidency research conference, Bruges, October 29–30, 2001*. Luxembourg: Office for Official Publications of the European Communities, 2002

Vicars, M., Steinberg, S. R., McKenna, T., & Cacciattolo, M. (Eds.). *The praxis of English language teaching and learning (PELT): Beyond the binaries: Researching critically in EFL classrooms*. Rotterdam: SensePublishers.

Why measurement of higher education productivity is difficult. (2012). In T. A. Sullivan, C. Mackie, W. F. Massy, & E. Sinha (Eds.), *Improving measurement of productivity in higher education*. Washington: The National Academic Press.

World Bank. (2005). *Namibia – Education and training sector improvement program (ETSIP)*. Washington D. C.; World Bank Group. http://documents.worldbank.org/curated/en/142631468062936389/ Namibia-Education-and-Training-Sector-Improvement-Program-ETSIP

World Bank. (2016). *Gross enrolment ratio, primary, both sexes (%)*. Retrieved from http://data.worldbank. org/indicator/SE.PRM.ENRR

7

Democracy, human rights and freedom in Namibian education

John Makala Lilemba

Before you read the opinions of this author, ask yourself the following questions:

1. How would you define 'human rights awareness'?

2. How important is it for education in a democracy to address human rights awareness? How could this be done creatively?

3. What do you think are the main challenges to building up human rights awareness through education? Are these challenges unique to Namibia (or your country)?

INTRODUCTION

This chapter addresses the importance of democracy, human rights and freedom in education world-wide, and in Namibia in particular, after independence in 1990. It details the subject and skills areas where democratic education would be most useful, and also the challenges to providing such an education.

Some former colonised countries (e.g. Namibia and South Africa) have undergone tremendous changes over the past few years in terms of democratising their education systems to reach every school-going child. Before attaining a new political dispensation (Namibia in 1990 and South Africa in 1994) these countries were denied the type of education which was centred on democracy, human rights and freedom. The Bantu Education system both in Namibia and South Africa was primarily for training black workers to understand and implement colonial masters' orders. By design, Bantu Education was low quality, poorly funded and restricted in scope to blacks.

Since 1990, Namibia has created a universal school system. The country has invested in school buildings, trained thousands of teachers and enhanced the skills of poorly trained teachers, integrated schools, designed a new curriculum and made English the language of instruction. The government also has spent a more reasonable amount of its budget on education, for example, as manifested in the national budget for 2015/2016 in Parliament, tabled by the then new Minister of Finance, Calle Schlettwein, April 1, 2015. The report on the 2015/2016 budget states, 'As has been the tradition, the largest share of the N$67.08 billion national total expenditure budget for this financial year, goes to the education sector with an allocation of N$11.32 billion (18% of the budget)' (Ministry of Finance, 2015).

To realise the importance of democracy, human rights and freedom, Namibia has, through its legal and constitutional organs, made education compulsory and free of any costs at both primary and secondary levels. These tremendous leaps in the education system have been brought about partly by the realisation that education is a right for every child and therefore a tool for economic and social development. It is in this regard that Namibia has followed the call to democratise education by liberating the minds of people (Freire & Ramos, 1972). Namibia has been determined to get ahead in the quest for an education system which is based on democracy, human rights and freedom.

The new Namibian government introduced a system of governance that guarantees and protects civil freedoms and rights such as freedom of speech, association, and participation and equity before the law. In this regard, democratic institutions such as schools are expected to produce outcomes that not only guarantee and protect the civil liberties of citizens, but also improve the quality of education in their communities (Ministry of Basic Education, Sport and Culture [MBESC], 2004). At school level, a body known as a School Board was created, composed of learners, teachers and parents. In addition, a booklet was published with the sole aim of guiding school board members. These guidelines explain that when school board members are actively involved, empowered and committed to reforming their own schools, they can develop and implement school policies to meet the challenges faced in schools. The emphasis is on the reorganisation of schools through their governing bodies to advance the efficient use of public resources, improve educational quality, and provide for democratic, school-based decision-making. It is one reason why, for example, government has been allocating a reasonable sum of money towards education to cater for democratic and quality education.

SYSTEMS OF DEMOCRACY, HUMAN RIGHTS AND FREEDOMS

There are many systems of democracy of which the main ones are direct and representative forms. A paternalistic form of democracy is used in cases where parents decide on behalf of their children, as the latter are not permitted to make their own decisions because they are considered not to be responsible enough (Moore, 1982). In education, a democratic culture implies that learners should be taught to adopt decisions arrived at by the majority of their peers and other stakeholders. Through this democratic process, learners should be taught to respect the freedoms of others and at the same time treat them equally.

Human rights are entitlements that enable people to fully develop and use their potential, qualities, intelligence and talents to satisfy their spiritual and other needs without infringing on the rights and freedoms of other people (Nangoloh, Mnakapa, & Ngaringombe, 1999). Human rights education involves examining issues such as the women's suffrage movement, civil rights, the issue of hunger and poverty in some communities and the right to schooling without bias (Flowers, 1998). Human rights are divided into three categories: first generation human rights are commonly known as blue rights and are civil and political rights. They include the right to life, freedom of expression, religion, political opinion, conscience and association. These rights are legally actionable if interfered with. Second generation human rights, known as red rights, are social, economic and cultural rights. They include the right to education, social security, housing, health and an adequate standard of living. These rights are only legally actionable depending on the availability of resources. Third generation human rights, also known as green rights, include the right to a clean environment, the right to peace, the right to self-determination, the right to development and people's rights. These rights are usually referred to as solidarity rights (UNESCO, 2001).

Freedom is defined as the absence of constraint and coercion imposed by another person, the state or any authority (UNESCO, 2001). This concept suggests that learners in schools can be allowed the freedom of electing their representatives in school organs and given opportunities to assist in drawing up school rules. Around the globe, many people aspire to democracy, human rights and freedoms.

DEMOCRACY, HUMAN RIGHTS, FREEDOM AND EDUCATION

Although the concepts of democracy, human rights and freedom involve various interpretations, they all promote an environment of participation, care and security of learners, with the goal of enabling them to be responsible citizens.

These concepts are not entirely new. During the fifteenth century, Comenius advocated the democratisation of education by arguing that teachers should respect children's human dignity rather than coerce them physically or psychologically (Akinpelu, 1981). Dewey (1916) on the other hand believed that a democratic state should have a democratic form of education. In this regard he advocated 'child centred' schools with curricula and instructions tailored to facilitate the development of the individual learner.

In 1948, the United Nations General Assembly adopted the Universal Declaration of Human Rights. Article 26 explicitly states that:

1. Everyone has the right to education and education shall be free and compulsory, at least in the elementary and fundamental stages.
2. Parents have the right to choose the kind of education that shall be given to their children.

The General Assembly of the United Nations came up with another Convention on the Rights of the Child which was adopted on 20 November 1989 by sixty-one countries. Namibia is signatory to this convention. Article 28 of this convention explicitly deals with the provision of education as a human right. Thus state parties recognise the right of the child to education, and with a view to achieving progressively and on the basis of equal opportunity, shall, in particular:

1. make primary education compulsory and available free to all;
2. encourage the development of different forms of secondary education, including general and vocational education, make them available and accessible to every child, and take appropriate measures such as the introduction of free education and offering financial assistance in case of need;
3. make higher education accessible to all on the basis of capacity by every appropriate means;
4. make educational and vocational information and guidance available and accessible to all children; and
5. take measures to encourage regular attendance at schools and the reduction of drop-out rates (United Nations, 1989).

UNICEF/UNESCO (2007) equally addressed the issue of education from a rights-based approach. Three interrelated rights are identified:

1. The right of access to education: With this right in mind, education must be available to all learners, irrespective of their social status. In the Namibian education system this right is the first of the major goals of education sometimes referred to as the Namibian philosophy of education. The other three goals of education are equity, quality and democracy (Ministry of Education and Culture [MEC], 1993). Although this right is usually stressed and emphasised by two conventions, the Convention on the Rights of the Child (United Nations, 1989) and the Universal Declaration of Human Rights (United Nations, 1948), very few countries completely achieve it.
2. The right to quality education: For this right to be realised, education needs to be child-centred and relevant, and needs to embrace a broad curriculum and be appropriately resourced and monitored. Many countries fail to realise the achievement of this right because of the scarcity and mismanagement of resources. There are, of course, a few exceptions, where countries commit more than a quarter of their national budgets to education with the main aim of achieving quality education. Although the Namibian Government arguably allocates a reasonable amount of money to education, as in the 2015/2016 financial year where N$11.32 billion (18% of the budget) went to education (Ministry of Finance, 2015), the performance and educational turnover remain poor (Government of the Republic of Namibia [GRN], 2007) compared to other countries, particularly in the SADC region, like South Africa, Zimbabwe, Zambia and Botswana.
3. The right to respect within the learning environment: Education must be provided in a way that is consistent with human rights, must show equal respect for culture, religion and language and above all, must be free from violence. For many years, in Namibia and many other countries, learners have been subjected to the use of corporal punishment, which can be considered a form of torture and terror. In the Namibian Constitution (1990), corporal punishment of both learners and adults is seen as inhumane and degrading, and hence in conflict with Article 8 which says that the dignity of all persons shall be inviolable. Although corporal punishment has been outlawed in Namibian schools, some teachers still use it on the basis that it instils order in the learners. During the constitutional debate prior to Namibian independence, some parents and politicians expressed the opinion that corporal

punishment is a biblical injunction as per Proverbs 13: 24, which states clearly that parents are not supposed to spare their children the rod when disciplining them.

THE PARADOX OF DEMOCRACY, HUMAN RIGHTS AND FREEDOM IN SCHOOLS

In terms of development and the distribution of resources, Namibia is one of the most unequal societies in the world (Nangoloh, Mnakapa, & Ngaringombe, 1999; World Bank Country Report, 2009). The majority of Namibians who were denied freedom and liberty during the long span of colonialism did not comprehend the demands and requirements of democracy, human rights and freedoms (Harber, 1997; MEC, 1993). This also applied to learners in schools. Although the situation has been changing gradually, many teachers still complain that since independence in 1990, which ushered in a period of democracy, human rights and freedom, learners have become even more unruly than before the 'dawn of self-determination' ('Education minister warns unruly learners', 2012).

Many parents too, question what is happening in schools, and some feel that school is no longer a safe place for their children (MEC, 1992, 1993). This scenario is further complicated by the role of the teacher during the years of apartheid. The role of the African teacher was contradictory in the colonial education system. On the one hand, teachers were employees of the South African Government which expected them to transmit apartheid ideology, and on the other hand they were also members of the oppressed and were expected to loathe the system of oppression (Harber, 1997). It should also be understood that Namibians, like many Africans, had their own democratic educational systems which worked before the advent of the colonisers (Amukugo, 1993; Chazan, Mortimer, Ravenhill, & Rothchild, 1992). Africans are by nature democratic, as can be seen in their traditional administrative structures where even the chief is to be elected, not imposed on them. Furthermore, the chief is expected to consult his council with regard to all matters of the community, including the education of the youth under his or her jurisdiction. Although the elders adhere to a strict code of conduct, the Africans want their children to grow and develop responsibly (Lilemba, 2009; Pretorius, 1975).

While many modern southern African states adhere to the principles of democracy, constitutionalism, freedom and human rights, which are seen as offering greater protection for the individual, some people might feel that this is an imposition of alien concepts and values that threaten their survival and identity both as individuals and as communities. The question is one that concerns the relationship between the traditional and the modern democratic constitutional process (D'Engelbronner-Kolff, Hinz, & Sindano, 1998). Even in really liberal democracies, particularly where learners are too young to know what is good for them, teachers can be seen to be undemocratic when they oppose the likes and desires of learners, and this may seem out of tune with democracy. In such situations some educators opt for a paternalistic type of democracy (Moore, 1982) where fellow colleagues are encouraged to cooperate with the head of the institution for the latter to take care of their interests. This leadership is not oppressive in any way because teachers are free to express their opinions, but they are expected nonetheless to toe the line of the school principal.

Despite some misgivings, democracy, human rights, freedom and related concepts have picked up momentum in Africa. The impact of these ideas is difficult to ignore (Grobler, Sasman, & Titus, 2000). In this regard, many countries have introduced human rights, freedom and democracy as separate subjects in schools (United Nations Educational, Scientific and Cultural Organization [UNESCO], 1999). Namibia, in particular, has made democracy its fourth goal of education (Ministry of Education [MoE], 1993). The paradoxical aspect of democracy in schools is that *while we expect learners to develop principles of democracy, human rights and freedom, education itself does not seem to be democratic* (Hamm, 1989).

The system of imposing undemocratic educational practices on learners may appear contradictory to the goals of democracy, human rights and freedom. In many cases education can be said to be undemocratic, but at the same time, parents and teachers cannot simply expect immature learners to participate in a decision making process which they do not understand.

In many countries, eighteen is the age at which young people are allowed to vote for the first time. In the voting process, people exercise their right to remove either the minister for education or any member of parliament who does not deliver adequate educational services. Biological age determines when human beings can be regarded as politically competent. Unfortunately most learners at school are usually below the age of eighteen; therefore, as the learner is still regarded as too young, he/she cannot make decisions at a political level. Thus children depend on their parents to make political decisions for them, including issues related to education. This in itself could be considered to constitute an undemocratic process, because the children are not allowed to participate in issues which affect them.

An education process involving teachers and learners usually cannot be conducted along the lines of equality between the two groups of participants, because the learners are not regarded as developed or rational enough to make the right decisions. Teachers and/or parents impose their wills on the learners, which is not purely democratic.

It is universally recognised that the main objective of any education system in a democratic society is to provide quality education for all learners so that they will be able to reach their full potential and will be able to meaningfully contribute to and participate in that society throughout their lives (MoE, 1997). Contrary to this belief is the notion that youth are prone to criticise anything and want to change everything, including our whole way of life (Becker, 1967). Limited participation of youth is also justified on the grounds that no community can exist unless the freedom of its members is enhanced by appropriate and acceptable means (Cohen & Travers, 1970).

The democratisation of education is fraught with challenges. In Namibia, the new government in 1990 introduced a democratic constitution amidst the forces of a colonial and apartheid legacy which did not respect the wishes of the citizens in every sphere of life, education included (Harber, 1997). The Namibian political system itself is not always democratic in nature; for example, it encourages party lists where the leader of the political party either nominates candidates or may even intimidate party members to vote for candidates of his/her choice. The difficulties posed by this scenario are that political leaders in particular and citizens in general tend to treat others who hold different views and opinions suspiciously and with hostility. People with critical views are often stigmatised and treated as social outcasts. (Nangoloh, Mnakapa, & Ngaringombe, 1999).

In such situations, citizens are typically expected to follow everything the political leaders say, whether right or wrong. In other words citizens can be treated like robots. This system can ultimately kill the reasoning capacity of both the citizens and their young ones, as they are discouraged from creativity and progression. In addition, people are often expected to treat their leaders as demigods and look to them for everything (Nangoloh, Mnakapa, & Ngaringombe, 1999). However, the new dispensation in education emphasises that students in all corners of the country should be consulted along with their communities, and the educational leaders should receive contributions from all parties, so that education can be more democratic in nature (Nkomo, 1990). Whereas it is democratic to include school learners on the school board, many of them are still considered too young to engage in the debates, which are sometimes intense. Some educators see school democracy as controversial, and feel that children's participation in school governance is neither desirable nor possible (Entwistle, 1970). This is despite the fact that the role of teachers is to instil democratic values and an understanding of the democratic process in their students.

Furthermore, for teachers to do this, they must be familiar with the principles of democracy themselves (Namibia Institute for Democracy, 2000). According to the Namibian Ministry of Education, Culture, Youth and Sport (MECYS) (1990), many teachers find themselves threatened by the new educational system. For instance, the learner-centred approach threatens the authority of many traditional teachers who do not understand what it really means.

The new education system introduced after independence in 1990 demands that each school should have a school board to run it (Government of the Republic of Namibia [GRN], 2001; MEC, 1990). The Namibian education policy also requires that schools advertise, recruit and appoint teachers in their schools according to the rules and regulations of labour laws. In reality, not every school understands this new system, let alone implements it.

Another problem of teaching democracy in Namibian schools concerns language. Although English was made the official language for Namibia, previously, the majority of Namibians were taught in the medium of Afrikaans. Literature on democracy is in the English language. This is not always comprehended by teachers, learners and community members alike (MEC, 1993). The situation with regard to English, however, has been improving over the years, and more and more people are able to read in English.

The new learner-centred approach is also a challenge, as many schools, particularly in the rural areas, lack libraries and other materials to assist them in the independent learning process. Many Namibian teachers were trained in pre-independence Namibia, and their culture is not to allow learners to express themselves critically in class. The majority of teachers went through the apartheid system of education and therefore find the new learner-centred approach and other democratic practices quite challenging and difficult to understand. The traditional approach to teacher education was to fill the learner with content (Van Harmelen, 1999) and yet in contrast, the requirements of democracy, human rights and freedom are critical thinking and the nurturing of diversity (Morin, 2001). In addition, the school curriculum is characterised by principles, rules of procedure and logically related concepts which necessarily impose upon human learning (Entwistle, 1970).

Because human nature is malleable and can be shaped and formed, it is therefore possible to shape and direct human society and institutions (Ozman & Craver, 1986). This is applicable to the teaching of democracy, human rights and freedom in schools especially at an early age of learners. On the other hand some educators claim that it is wrong to choose any objectives for a child in any form (Hamm, 1989; Rousseau, 1762).

WHY AND HOW WE CAN APPLY PRINCIPLES OF DEMOCRACY, HUMAN RIGHTS AND FREEDOM IN THE NAMIBIAN EDUCATION SYSTEM

For centuries, Western or European values were imposed on African students at educational institutions, through curricula, syllabi, training courses, educational programmes, cultural activities, books and other educational instruments (Ellis, 1984; Higgs, 1995). During this process there was little respect for the usefulness of African norms in maintaining democracy, human rights and freedoms.

Human rights in Namibian school subjects

Many teachers fail to relate the teaching of certain subjects to the issues of human rights, yet human rights can be covered easily in the following subjects (Starkey, 1991):

History
1. The origins and growth of democracy
2. Slavery, colonialism, imperialism and their effects in Africa
3. Revolutions, their ideals and their impact in the developing world
4. The United Nations and the International Conventions on Human Rights
5. The European Union and its campaign for good governance and human rights as a requirement for donor funding
6. The African Union and its stand on the issue of human rights

Geography
1. Apartheid in South Africa and Namibia
2. Migration to cities
3. Colonialism and neo-colonialism
4. Protection of the environment
5. Consequences of poverty and starvation

Social Studies
1. Political and legal systems and their role in human rights
2. The police and the treatment of offenders as per human rights requirements
3. Trade unions and their stance on human rights and labour relations
4. Education and the role played by teachers in terms of human rights
5. The mass media and the role of journalists in human rights

Life Skills
1. Civic education
2. Cultures and traditions of the country, including cultural festivals
3. Main human rights cases in the country and beyond

Skills Areas

There are many general skills areas in which human rights can be instilled. Starkey (1991) lists the following:

Intellectual skills

These are associated with written and oral expression, including the ability to listen and discuss, and to defend one's opinion. In addition, communication skills are very important as they enhance participation in debates and discussions, particularly where topics of discussion may be provocative. Listening carefully is equally a very important skill, as active listening conveys respect for the speaker. This skill is fundamental among teachers as they are required and expected to listen to learners most of the time. They should act as models by listening attentively to what learners tell them.

Skills involving judgment

It is often common for young people in particular to pass judgment or carry prejudiced perceptions about people they interact with on a daily basis. These distortions are likely to create and perpetuate racism and sexism, as well as discrimination and inequality, if portrayed, for example, in textbooks. Human rights education should counter these distortions.

Social skills

Social skills are paramount in recognising and accepting differences. Human rights differences, be they physical or cultural, should have no bearing on a person's entitlement to freedom, equality and dignity. It is society which often gives a negative or positive value to physical or cultural characteristics, and learners should be made aware of stereotyping. Teachers should encourage learners to know one another, and teachers, in the same vein, should know their learners and other teachers, and learn to treat one another with respect and dignity. It is equally important that learners are encouraged to share their cultural traditions with other learners and are led to believe that no culture is inferior to another one. This can be done by displaying in class items and photographs brought from home.

Knowledge acquisition in human rights studies

The study of human rights in schools can be approached in different ways according to the age and circumstances of the learner and the particular situations of schools and education systems. The topics which can be covered may include the main categories of human rights, duties, obligations and responsibilities. In this case, learners can study economic rights, social rights, cultural rights, civil rights, civil liberties, political rights, individual rights and collective rights. A distinction should be made between the main rights that are internationally recognised, such as those found in the International Bill of Human Rights which consists of the Universal Declaration of Human Rights of 1948 and the two United Nations Covenants on Human Rights of 1966 which came into force in 1976, and the United Nations Covenant on the Rights of the Child of 1989. In addition, learners should be exposed to the following:

1. General conventions, which concern all or a large portion of human rights adopted worldwide or at regional level.

2. Specific conventions, which are intended to protect particular human rights, such as asylum, freedom of information, private life and social security, preventing such social ills as genocide, war crimes and crimes against humanity, slavery, human trafficking, forced labour, and torture.

3. Conventions on group protection, which correspond to the special needs of distinct groups like refugees, stateless persons, migrants, workers, women, children, combatants, prisoners and civilians in times of armed conflicts or wars.

4. Conventions concerning discrimination, which seek to prevent discrimination on the basis of race or sex, and discrimination in education, employment and occupation.

5. Injustice, inequality, discrimination, sexism and racism. As educators, teachers should know that learners may not be familiar with or recognise these ills at first hand. They may not even understand the basics about them. Schools then need to provide space for learners to express and discuss particular experiences pertaining to relevant incidents of the above. This platform will assist learners in understanding injustice in the wider context.

TEACHER TRAINING IMPLICATIONS

Many countries try to insert certain aspects of human rights into their teacher training programmes. This is an important tool for 'conscientizing' and concretising efforts to drive home the values and culture of human rights. Including human rights in the teacher training curriculum prepares aspiring teachers for their future contributions to teaching about human rights in their schools. As Starkey (1991) says, teachers in training programmes and those currently in service should be encouraged:

1. to take an interest in national and world affairs;

2. to study or work in a foreign country or different environment from their own. Nigeria has a good example where learners who complete their final grades and enter national service are required to serve in two different states apart from their own. This system exposes citizens to fellow nationals from different states and cultures in an attempt to minimise tribal tension and conflicts;

3. to identify and combat all forms of discrimination in schools and society and be encouraged to confront and overcome their own prejudices;

4. to familiarise themselves with the international declarations and conventions on human rights; and

5. to form committees in their schools which deal with human rights issues.

In addition, all teachers should be given the opportunity to update their knowledge on human rights through in-service training, and should be involved in the drawing up of a curriculum on human rights.

In all the subjects and skill categories listed above, it is crucial to note that human rights are not employed in a vacuum but are implemented in a society where people are affected. It is therefore important that at an early age, learners are exposed to the concept of human rights (Starkey, 1991). For example, the moment a child can say a few words, he/she should be encouraged to confidently pronounce her or his name. If the child fails to do so, it is the duty and responsibility of the members of the family to assist the young child. At school, the child should be received and treated with respect and dignity. Teachers and learners should desist from bullying new arrivals, including the young ones, especially on their first day at school. Learners should not be sneered at when they have made a mistake. It is a counterproductive and disrespectful practice for teachers to humiliate learners, for example pinching the ears of learners for a minor misdemeanour. The first impression that learners get on their first day at school may have a lasting negative or positive effect for the rest of their lives. Respect for others should be instilled early in the minds of learners.

A school is a place of learning where teachers, learners and community members interact with the aim of moulding and shaping the characters of the young minds. It is at school where learners should be taught the principles of human rights and freedoms. No matter what a child does, he or she should be treated with dignity at all times. When schools formulate policies, rules and regulations, they must do so along the following lines:

1. Teachers should have an understanding of human rights and the way they can be applied to life and the curriculum of the school.
2. Human rights concepts should be taught systematically, devoid of any contradiction. For example, if the Namibian Constitution prohibits human degradation and humiliation by all means, corporal punishment should not be justified by the leaders of any institutions.
3. School rules and disciplinary procedures should be based on fair treatment and due process.
4. The school should have policies to promote equality and avoid unjust discrimination such as discrimination on the basis of gender, race or disability.
5. Teachers should be encouraged and enabled to develop a global perspective.

Non-violent resolution of conflict and respect for other people should be promoted in schools. Much of early childhood education is about socialisation and learning to live harmoniously in a community with other people. Children should be encouraged to interact with others, and to know other people by name and respect them. Above all, children should be discouraged from taking violent action when confronted by an ugly situation or circumstance. Teachers and parents should be exemplary in this case. It would serve no purpose to reprimand children and tell them not to insult other people if teachers do so in their presence. The concept of respect is universal, although the mode may differ from community to community. The bottom line is to accord dignity to other members of the community, training them to respect and tolerate one another and their elders. This creates an atmosphere of love and responsibility towards others. It encourages treating other people with dignity, no matter how low these people seem to appear in the community. It reduces the impact of class consciousness, and treats everyone on an equal basis. It also avoids the humiliation and degradation of members of the society.

POLICY-MAKING

Policy-makers and teachers should be made aware of the role of human rights in a school situation. Human rights should be included in school textbooks and should be taught to children. Publishing houses which print and publish school textbooks should equally be cautioned against producing textbooks which are not human rights oriented.

It is always possible to find a situation where parents and learners hold different views which they may feel are threatened when controversial issues are raised at school. In dealing with parents, politicians and the community, the following considerations may be helpful:

1. School policy statements should reflect human rights values. In drawing up school policies, rules and regulations, consideration of human rights values should be a pre-requisite.
2. Learners should be prepared to participate in political life in a democratic manner.
3. Use of various materials from different sources which demonstrate an attempt to deal objectively with complex issues should be encouraged.

THE CHALLENGES OF HUMAN RIGHTS EDUCATION

There are many examples of countries, corporations and institutions violating democracy, human rights and freedoms, and it is obvious that some of the rights being violated are education rights. There are enormous challenges facing democracy, human rights and freedom. They include:

Armed conflicts
According to the United Nations Children's Fund (UNICEF) (2015), there are armed conflicts around the world, mostly in countries like the Central African Republic, South Sudan and Syria, to mention a few. The UNICEF Report further cites some of today's major challenges such as global warming, malnutrition and unavailability or inaccessibility to information, especially in war-torn countries. In these countries, the majority of people who die or are injured in conflicts are civilians, mostly children and their mothers. In serious war scenarios such as these, surely no one would expect children to attend schools where the atmosphere is not conducive to quality learning.

Poverty
At the World Conference on Education for All organised by the United Nations Inter-Agency Commission (UNDP, UNESCO, UNICEF, World Bank) (1990) in Jomtien, Thailand, it was reported that the world faces mounting debt burdens, the threat of economic stagnation and decline, rapid population growth, widening economic disparities among and within nations, war, occupation, civil strife, violent crime, the preventable deaths of millions of children and widespread environmental degradation. These problems constrain efforts to meet basic learning needs. With the protracted liberation war of independence, Namibia's loss of resources put its education system into disarray, and rehabilitating its education system will take time.

Colonialism, social prejudice and discrimination
One impact of colonial education is that the implementation of a new education system can leave those who are colonised with a lack of identity and a limited sense of their past. The indigenous history and customs once practised and observed by the colonised people slowly slip away. The colonised may become hybrids of two vastly different cultural systems. Colonial education makes it difficult to differentiate between the new, enforced ideas of the colonisers and the formerly accepted indigenous practices. During the apartheid regime and its racist policies, many children were excluded from education in Namibia and South Africa. The black

population was often stigmatised as lazy and barbaric through the Bantu Education system that was enforced and imposed upon the black masses in Namibia. In addition to the brutal terror campaign against the civilian society, school children were often instructed to believe and learn stereotypes through indoctrination that black Namibians were warmongers while whites were peace-lovers (Amukugo 1993; Ellis, 1984). Distortions and attitudes that Africans are slow thinkers, less civilised, unintelligent, dangerous, and irresponsible were often imposed by colonial ideologies. Unfortunately, even after independence, many African children are still subjected to discrimination, social prejudice and colonisation of some sort.

Aggressive ethnocentrism

Human rights are violated on a large scale on the basis of origin, gender, language and religion. For example, the genocide which took place in Rwanda in the mid-1990s seriously curtailed an education based on democracy, human rights and freedoms as it left many school-going children homeless, separated from their families and uprooted from everything familiar. Many Africans do not enjoy the rights and freedom guaranteed by the African Charter of Human Rights and People's Rights as many countries which signed this charter and the Universal Declaration of Human Rights have not yet fully implemented them.

Cultural practices

Some of the African cultural practices like forcing young girls to marry at an early age for bride price (*lobola*) border on violating both human rights and the right to education. However, not all African cultural practices are detrimental to human rights issues. The African position on human rights education, for example, was side-lined, as the colonial education system emphasized humiliation of the African learner by caning and other forms of degradation.

Lack of information and facilities

Many schools in many developing countries have a shortage of human rights education textbooks and library staff. It is difficult for schools which have no such facilities or staff to provide learners with information on human rights education. Very few schools have access to computers and the internet, making accessibility of human rights education and information an almost impossible task.

Lack of political will

In many developing countries information on human rights education is not made available to the citizens. Some politicians are afraid that should the citizens know their rights, they will become ungovernable. In a situation like that, human rights education is affected.

CONCLUSION

This chapter focuses on the universal provision of democracy, human rights and freedoms in education. Many countries are signatories to the Universal Declaration of Human Rights of 1948 and the United Nations Convention of the Rights of the Child of 1989, of which Namibia is signatory. Like the other signatories, Namibia is duty bound to provide education on a democratic basis. This chapter details some subject and skills areas in which such education would be most fruitful. Although the country has made strides by offering subjects which centre on democracy, human rights and freedom, there remains a lot to be done in terms of implementation. This chapter further details the many challenges that countries like Namibia face in providing education on a democratic basis. The greatest challenge in this regard, however, comes from the inability of teachers and administrators of education to comprehend the basics of these concepts. It is recommended that states should ensure that democracy, human rights and freedom are not only incorporated in the syllabus, but are actually taught and embraced by the education system. Government organs should enhance and encourage a spirit of tolerance among learners. It should therefore be the duty of all stakeholders in education to inculcate these principles in the minds of the learners at an early stage so that they grow and mature with these concepts for their benefit and that of others.

References

Akinpelu, J. A. (1981). *An introduction to philosophy of education*. London: Macmillan.

Amukugo, E. M. (1993). *Education and politics in Namibia: Past and future prospects*. Windhoek: New Namibia Books.

Becker, E. (1967). *Beyond alienation: A philosophy of education for the crisis of democracy*. New York, N. Y.: George Braziller.

Chazan, N., Mortimer, R., Ravenhill, J., & Rothchild, D. (1992). *Politics and society in contemporary Africa*. Boulder, CO: Lynne Rienner Publishers.

Cohen I. J. & Travers, R. M. (1970). *Educating for democracy*. New York, N. Y.: Freeport.

D'Engelbronner-Kolff, F. M., Hinz, M. O., & Sindano, J. L. (Eds.). (1998). *Traditional authority and democracy in Southern Africa*. Windhoek: New Namibia Books.

Dewey, J. (1916). *Democracy and education*. Canada: Collier-MacMillan.

Education minister warns unruly learners. (2012, October 25). *The Namibian*. Retrieved from http://www.264news.com/stories.php?id=00000008

Ellis, J. (1984). *Education, repression and liberation: Namibia*. London: World University Service and The Catholic Institute for International Relations.

Entwistle, H. (1970). *Child-centred education*. London: Methuen & Co.

Flowers, N. (Ed.). (1998). *Human rights here and now: Celebrating the Universal Declaration of Human Rights*. Minneapolis, MN: Human Rights Educators' Network, Amnesty International, USA.

Freire, P. & Ramos, M. B. (1972). *Pedagogy of the oppressed*. London: Sheed and Ward.

Government of the Republic of Namibia (GRN). (2001). *Education Act*. (Government Gazette No. 2673, Act No. 16). Windhoek: Government Printer.

Government of the Republic of Namibia (GRN). (2007). *Education and training sector improvement programme (ETSIP) Phase I (2006–2011)*. Windhoek: Government Printer.

Grobler, J., Sasman, C, & Titus, Z. (Eds.). (2000). *So this is democracy? Report on the state of the media in Southern Africa*. Windhoek: Solitaire Press.

Hamm, C. M. (1989) *Philosophical issues in education: An introduction*. New York, N. Y.: The Falmer Press.

Harber, C. (1997). *Education, democracy and political development in Africa*. Brighton: Sussex Academic Press.

Higgs, P. (1995). *Metatheories in philosophy of education*. Johannesburg: Heinemann.

Lilemba, J. M. (2009). *Indigenous Mafwe philosophy of education: Impact of western education from 1860 until 1990*. (Doctoral dissertation, University of Namibia, Windhoek, Namibia).

Ministry of Basic Education, Sport and Culture, Namibia (MBESC). (2004). *The work of the school board. Guidelines for Namibian School Board members*. Windhoek: MBESC.

Ministry of Education and Culture, Namibia [MEC]. (1992). *Discipline from within: Alternatives to corporal punishment – A guide for principals, teachers, learners, parents and communities*. Windhoek: Gamsberg Macmillan.

Ministry of Education and Culture, Namibia (MEC). (1993). *Toward education for all: A development brief for education, culture and training*. Windhoek: Gamsberg Macmillan.

Ministry of Education, Culture, Youth and Sport, Namibia (MECYS). (1990). *Namibian educational code of conduct for schools*. Windhoek: Ministry of Education, Culture, Youth and Sport.

Ministry of Finance. (2015). *Budget statement for the 2015/2016 financial year*. Windhoek: Ministry of Finance.

Moore, T. W. (1982). *Philosophy of education. An introduction*. London: Routledge & K. Paul.

Morin, E. (2001). *Seven complex lessons in education for the future*. Paris: UNESCO Publishing.

Namibia Institute for Democracy. (2000). *Democracy and you: A guide to better understanding*. Retrieved from http://www.nid.org.na/images/pdf/human-rights/Democracy_and_You.pdf

Nangoloh, P., Mnakapa, Z.-A., & Ngaringombe, T. (1999). *Choose your own representatives*. Windhoek, Namibia: National Society for Human Rights.

Nkomo, M. (1990). *Pedagogy of domination. Toward a democratic education in South Africa*. Trenton, New Jersey: Africa World Press.

Ozman, A. H. & Craver, S. M. (1986). *Philosophical foundations of education*. London: Merrill Publishing Company.

Pretorius, J. L. (1975). *The Fwe of the Eastern Caprivi Zipfel. A study of their historical and geographical background, tribal structure and legal system with special reference to Fwe family law and succession*. (Master's thesis, University of Stellenbosch, Stellenbosch, South Africa).

Rousseau, J. J. (1762). *Emile or education*. London & Toronto: J. M. Dent & Sons.

Starkey, H. (1991). *The challenge of human rights education*. London: Cassell Council Limited.

United Nations. (1948). *Universal declaration of human rights*. Retrieved from http://www.un.org/en/udhrbook/pdf/udhr_booklet_en_web.pdf

United Nations. (1989). *Convention on the rights of the child*. Retrieved from http://www.ohchr.org/Documents/ProfessionalInterest/crc.pdf

United Nations Children's Fund (UNICEF). (2016). *The state of the world's children*. New York, N. Y.: UNICEF.

United Nations Children's Fund /United Nations Educational, Scientific and Cultural Organization (UNESCO). (2007). *A human rights-based approach to education for all*. New York, N. Y.: UNICEF.

United Nations Educational, Scientific and Cultural Organization (UNESCO). (1990). *World declaration on education for all: Meeting basic learning needs.* Retrieved from http://www.unescobkk.org/fileadmin/ user_upload/efa/JomtienDeclaration.pdf

United Nations Educational, Scientific and Cultural Organization (UNESCO). (1999). *Education for human rights and democracy in Southern Africa: A teacher's resource manual.* Windhoek: Longman Namibia.

United Nations Educational, Scientific and Cultural Organization (UNESCO). (2001). *Education for human rights and democracy in Namibia: Teacher's guide.* Windhoek: Gamsberg Macmillan.

United Nations Inter-Agency Commission (UNDP, UNESCO, UNICEF, World Bank). (1990). *World Conference on Education for All.* New York, N. Y.: United Nations.

Van Harmelen, U. (1999). Is learner-centered education child-centered? In T. Sguazzin & M. Van Graan (Eds.) *Education reform and innovation in Namibia: How best can changes in classroom practice be implemented and supported?* (pp. 25–34). Namibia: Longman.

World Bank. (2009). *Namibia: Country brief.* Retrieved from https://openknowledge.worldbank.org/ handle/10986/2630

8

Inclusive education as a democratic imperative

Anthony Brown & Cynthy K. Haihambo

Before reading this chapter, check what you know about this topic:

1. What is inclusive education and what are the pro and con arguments for applying it in Namibia (or your country)?

2. Are there policies in place in Namibia which support a philosophy of inclusive education?

3. What is the relationship between human rights, social justice and the philosophy of inclusive education?

4. How do teachers' attitudes affect inclusive education?

INTRODUCTION

A review of democracy in education cannot be explored without the notion of inclusive education. Inclusion at root level is a matter of human rights, equality and opportunities, mainly advocated as an opportunity for a just education system (Thomas & Glenny, 2002). The history of all African countries, and more particularly that of Namibia, is written in the blood of those who struggled to achieve the right to equality. Moreover, Namibia is defined by features of its commitment to human rights and democracy, although more in theory than in practice. The authors of this chapter deem it necessary to provide a historical overview of the organisation and theoretical underpinnings of education for children with special needs in order to situate the current discussion on inclusive education as a democratic imperative.

A BRIEF HISTORICAL OVERVIEW OF SPECIAL EDUCATION IN NAMIBIA

As has been established earlier in Chapter 6, prior to independence in 1990, Namibia transitioned through four different education phases: traditional education; missionary education; education under German colonialism; and the ethnically disaggregated South African education system (see also Amukugo, 1995, pp. 32–102; Möwes 2002, p. 89). Education during the traditional and missionary phases, as well as during the German colonial rule, did not recognise diversity with respect to learning abilities, socio-cultural diversity or any other differences. With the exception of special schools created during the missionary period for children with severe sensory or physical disabilities, as well as those with emotional disturbances, no evidence of accommodation of diversity can be traced during these periods. What can be deduced about education during the German colonial rule is that blacks were presented an education aimed at preparing people to serve the masters, and keeping them inferior and without critical thinking skills. Although the missionaries provided education, the curriculum was prescribed by the German rulers and had to focus on biblical knowledge and basic German communication skills (Avoseh, 1999, p. 2; Katjavivi, 1988, p. 11).

The apartheid era from 1948 saw various commissions recommending segregated education for whites (superior) and blacks (inferior). It was an education system that was shaped by narrow vision, concerns and identities. Special education provisions for white children started in the form of opportunity classes at primary schools in 1950. Eros Primary School was the first school in the then South West Africa (now Namibia) to introduce opportunity classes. This practice was expanded to other white schools in the country. Later, remedial classes were introduced in almost all the white schools, and were later expanded to coloured schools. No specialised education was offered to children of the other ethnic groups (Möwes, 2002, p. 99).

During the 1970s and 1980s, more special schools started to open their doors to a very few black children who happened to be screened, mostly by chance. These special schools included the Engela Vocational Training Centre, the Ehafo Production Centre and the Jürgen Wahn Centre for people with severe mental disabilities (Möwes 2002, p. 101). It has to be acknowledged that stigma was attached to special schools, and not many parents wanted to be associated with them. Still, during this period, socio-cultural differences were used to divide rather than to unite people.

By the time of independence in 1990, pressure groups, including the Namibia National Students' Organisation (NANSO) and the Namibia National Teachers' Union (NANTU), had laid the foundation for ethnic integration in education (with regard only to the enrolment of black children into traditionally white-dominated schools). Parents of children with special needs of all racial groups started in large numbers to seek admission to special schools, but limited space was available. Up to this date, the few special schools had long waiting lists and could not accommodate all children who needed placement.

At the same time, history has instilled an expectation that the best placement for children presenting diverse learning skills is in special schools. It is this perception which is based on the Medical Model to diversity (Michigan Disability Rights Coalition, 2001), which continues to dictate to communities that any form of diversity can and should be fixed by specialised settings, with specialised services and resources. Inclusion, on the contrary, directs the opposite: that diversity should be embraced and dealt with using inner and exterior resources and the positive attitudes of the communities in which it occurs.

A DISCOURSE AND POLICY CHANGE FOR INCLUSIVE EDUCATION

As stated in earlier chapters, Namibia adopted the policy of Education for All, enshrined in the Namibian Constitution at independence in 1990 in Article 20, which states that 'All persons shall have the right to education' (Government of the Republic of Namibia [GRN], 1990).

This legal framework was established in consideration of the desire for a genuinely democratic society that recognises and respects diversity.

Furthermore, the Jomtien Conference, to which Namibia is signatory, states that:

'Every person, child, youth and adult, shall be able to benefit from educational opportunities designed to meet their basic needs', and that '[m]eeting basic learning needs constitutes a common and universal human responsibility'. The declaration further states: 'We, the participants in the World Conference on Education for All, reaffirm the right of all people to education' (United Nations [UN], 1990).

Mutorwa (2002, p. 11) states that independence in 1990 brought new hope to black Namibians, who were looking forward to the new political dispensation putting in place living conditions that were in line with universally accepted norms and human rights. In responding to this, the new government expanded access to education by elevating education to a basic fundamental human right.

According to Mutorwa (2002, p. 14), the new government has redefined access to education to mean:

1. bringing into the system learners who had been deprived of educational opportunities;
2. providing education for, and to, all;
3. creating more physical infrastructure and ensuring more places in educational settings;
4. eradicating physical and psychological barriers that hinder learners from attending school;
5. establishing adult literacy, distance and open learning programmes; and
6. convincing parents that education of their children is a future investment.

It is obvious that there has been great progress toward attaining most of these goals for the ordinary learner without major special needs. It is, however, clear that despite the commitment to 'Education for all', learners with additional diverse educational needs were not particularly targeted for this expanded access at the time of independence. Later efforts that led to the National Policy Guidelines for Educationally Marginalised Children (Mutorwa, 2002) and recently, the formulation of the Education Sector Policy on Inclusive Education (Ministry of Education, 2013) provide evidence of the prioritisation of the education of marginalised children and those with additional educational needs.

The policy guidelines for educationally marginalised children target, among other things, the inclusion of children of farm workers, those from ethnic minorities with distinct cultures, those with physical, sensory, learning and other challenges, street children, teen parents, orphans and other vulnerable children who are likely to be excluded or failed by the system if no particular attention is paid to their entry and retention in the education system. These policies encompass individuals at all levels of education, including those at the higher education level, general communities and larger society.

Since independence in 1990, the democratic Namibian Government has been in the process of developing an egalitarian and healthy society through various processes of social, political, economic and educational transformation. After decades of discriminatory legislation, the Namibian Government made education a right for all, with basic education being free and compulsory (GRN, 1990). The government also established access, quality, equality and democracy as educational goals (Ministry of Education [MoE], 1993, p. 32). These goals made it possible for all Namibians to have equal opportunities to access quality education within the newly established democracy. Furthermore, the Namibian Government implemented Universal Primary Education by declaring the payment of school fees for primary schools non-compulsory in 2013. All children now can attend primary and secondary school even if their parents do not have the money, as school fees are no longer compulsory, and in addition, the government pledged to provide the basic materials needed for children to benefit adequately from primary and secondary education in government schools. In addition, the school feeding programme that was introduced to many schools in poor communities has contributed to enabling environments for optimal learning in primary education.

While equality has been attained to a large extent, a lot more needs to be done to ensure equity, especially for those groups in our society for whom extra effort is needed in order for them to be included in education and learning for democracy. In our eyes, an inclusive society is one in which everyone has opportunities to live their lives to the fullest, and in which they have equitable access to resources and spaces that will allow them to play a meaningful role in society. Inclusion, therefore, entails embracing diversity and responding to diversity in meaningful ways. Teachers with an understanding of inclusive education should be able to teach for diversity, and learners should be allowed to learn, express themselves and be assessed through diversified methodologies. In democratic, inclusive settings, persons from indigenous communities would be embraced in mainstream society and not be forced to conform or adapt to fit in with the mainstream. Women and girls would not feel obliged to give up their career prospects in exchange for a family life. In terms of policies, guidelines and laws, the democratic Namibia has made remarkable strides in creating inclusive legal frameworks.

Among the laws in Namibia are the Orphans and Vulnerable Children Policy (MoE, 2008); the National Gender Policy (Ministry of Gender Equality and Child Welfare, 2010); HIV and AIDS Policy for the Education Sector (MoE, 2007); Education Sector Policy on Prevention and Management of Learner Pregnancy (MoE, 2010) and the Sector Policy for Inclusive Education (MoE, 2013). It is, however, worth mentioning that implementation of these policies lags far behind, resulting in many people still being excluded from democratic learning due to cultural and other unwritten but deeply-rooted expected codes of behaviour and socialisation. For example, many Namibian cultures describe a good woman as one who does not talk much, does not travel much, does not talk back, etc.

Being mindful of the fact that inclusiveness is not only an issue of disability, we would like to emphasise that we are using disability only as an example and focus of this chapter. The Namibian Government paid attention to persons with disabilities as one of the marginalised groups of the Namibian society. In 1997, the National Policy on Disability (Government of the

Republic of Namibia, 1997) was formulated and adopted by the Cabinet. This policy paved the way for the access and equity goals to be realised for all children, youths and adults, more specifically those with special educational needs and disabilities. This inclusion calls for a closer view of the journey that shaped the discourse and practice of inclusive education in Namibia as a democratic value.

It would be superficial to believe that persons with disabilities are fully included in and embraced by Namibian society. However, having a legal framework guaranteeing their right to inclusion has gone a long way towards securing their access to resources and provisions.

Similarly, the Constitution of the Republic of Namibia asserts the right to education (Article 20); the right to free movement, and many other rights (GRN, 1990). However, socio-economic, political, cultural and other eco-systemic barriers impede the citizen's utilisation of such democratic rights.

DEMOCRATIC EDUCATION: THE CASE FOR INCLUSIVE EDUCATION

Educational arenas can be viewed as platforms which provide an understanding of how diversity and democracy are operationalised because of the attention required for differing needs of students. The foregoing chapters in this book have illustrated that issues of diversity and democracy in Namibia have been on the forefront of academic and social discourses for a number of decades. In this section, the case for democratic education is discussed, and how its fundamentals have paved the way for inclusive education. For an education to be democratic, all students have to be prepared equally to be informed responsible citizens, and all have to be equally skilled in the participation process, regardless of individual differences (Osler & Starkey, 2001). It is therefore pivotal to organise schooling activities to create opportunities for all learners to develop a variety of citizenship skills. School should be a place where everyone is encouraged to reach his/her full potential. One of the major contributions to a democratic education is human rights, which are necessary to secure freedom and equality for all (Grover, 2007). Central to democratic education is the issue of how to maintain inclusiveness through polemic approaches by laying ground rules for debates and negotiations of tolerance and acceptance (Dewey, 1916). It is about how we learn to disagree without being disagreeable.

School is the environment where learners obtain knowledge and develop important skills. It is a place that prepares an informed and responsible citizen. If this is not the case, going to school is a waste of time. In this democratic environment, learners are to be prepared to respond to a range of perceptions. In turn, the classroom becomes the mirror image of the model of a democratic government. This platform hence proactively develops citizens who can use open debate and propose policy, practice and laws. Such schooling becomes a powerful process of empowerment because students experience imbalances throughout their lives, and knowing how to deal with them is crucial. It is through democratic balances that imbalances can be reduced.

In Namibia, at the dawn of independence, the goals of access, democracy, equity and quality became cornerstones upon which the new education system is based (MoE, 1993). Schools that were traditionally built around racial lines during the apartheid era were opened for all learners. Multi-cultural/multi-racial education became the order of the day. Although this process of integration created more imbalances than expected, black children were legally allowed to claim their places in learning spaces and in society. This process was not without challenges, but was obviously a democratic step in the right direction.

THE CONCEPT OF INCLUSIVE EDUCATION

Educational thinking in Namibia has been strongly shaped by international trends. It is imperative to highlight the blueprints that influenced the discourse on inclusive education in Namibia. Inclusive education in its wider context is based on a value system that recognises and celebrates diversity arising from gender, nationality, and language of origin, social background, and level of education achieved, functional disability, or any other forms that create barriers to learning and agency. The philosophy of inclusive education can be regarded as a moral issue of human rights and values and can be seen as part of the creation of an inclusive society (United Nations Educational, Scientific and Cultural Organization [UNESCO], 1994). An inclusive society is one where there is a positive appreciation of difference (Grover, 2007).

At school system levels, inclusive education is an approach that focuses on the provision of education for all children, youths and adults with various special and/or additional educational needs arising from various circumstances, and responses of communities and societies to those circumstances. It emphasises the shift from teaching learners with special needs in specially designed and isolated settings such as special schools to, as far as possible, teaching all children together while providing assistance and support to those who need it. Furthermore, inclusive education philosophy shifts the emphasis from children, youths and individuals and communities affected by 'traditional special needs', such as hearing impairment, blindness, cerebral palsy, intellectual impairments, to special needs arising from socio-economic, religious, and psycho-social factors. These, in a school setting, imply that schools should acknowledge and respond to the diverse needs of all learners, including those affected by abject poverty and living in difficult circumstances, victims of domestic and school-based violence, and those whose own sexual orientation, or that of their parents, is different from the norm. After acknowledging their needs, schools and communities should put systems in place to create an enabling environment for learners to access education, participate equitably, and achieve in all spheres of their lives (Humphrey, 2007). Consequently, inclusive education is parallel to Education for All, as described in the quote below:

> The key challenge is to ensure that the broad vision of Education for All as an inclusive concept is reflected in national government and funding agency policies. Education for All... must take account of the need of the poor and the most disadvantaged, including working children, remote rural dwellers and nomads, and ethnic and linguistic minorities, children, young people and adults affected by conflict, HIV/AIDS, hunger and poor health; and those with special learning needs (UNESCO, 2000, p. 14).

For Bevan-Brown (2006, p. 221), inclusion means that people from various backgrounds and diversity in terms of skin colour, gender, socio-economic status, religion, capability, sexual orientation, ethnicity, culture or physical appearance have the right to be treated with equality, respect and dignity and to be regarded as valued members of communities and society.

UNESCO (2005, p. 13) operationalises the concept of inclusion as '... a process of addressing and responding to the diversity of needs of all learners through increasing participation in learning, cultures and communities, and reducing exclusion within and from education. It involves changes and modifications in content, approaches, structures and strategies, with a common vision which covers all children of the appropriate age-range, and a conviction that it is the responsibility of the regular system to educate all children'. 'Rather than being a marginal issue on how some learners can be integrated in mainstream education, inclusive education is an approach that looks into how to transform education systems and other learning environments in order to respond to the diversity of learners' (ibid, p. 15). Environments in which ethos and culture are not responsive to the nature of the child and diversity do not auger well for the democratisation of education.

It is important to stress that the inclusive education approach reflects a move from a deficit model of adjustment of the individual towards a systemic change. It is for this reason that in its definition, UNESCO (2005, pp. 15–16) identifies four cornerstones of inclusion:

1. Inclusion should be a continuous activity of finding improved ways of responding to diverse needs of learners.
2. Efforts to reduce elements that may have negative impacts on learning should be a continuous process.
3. All learners should be given an opportunity to experience success in the learning milieu.
4. Inclusion targets learners who, for one reason or another, may fall in a risk category.

Naanda (2005, p. 16) reiterates that the success of inclusive education depends largely on a commitment to changing attitudes, policies and teaching approaches, while the needs of children enjoy priority in the planning and running of educational programmes. Some factors are necessary for successful inclusive education programmes, as per various scholars quoted by Naanda (2005, p. 17):

1. Effective leadership, not only by school principals, but by all role players in a school
2. Wider community involvement of all key players such as parents, teachers, learners and community members in school policies and decisions
3. A commitment to collaborative planning
4. Coordination strategies
5. Attention to potential benefits of enquiry and reflection
6. Staff development policy

These sentiments are shared by Ministry of Foreign Affairs of Denmark (2009) in pointing out that the most salient barriers to inclusive education are related to attitudes and power relations between role players in education. In contexts where children are looked upon as less human than adults, with limited rights to opinions, their democracy is inhibited. The same applies to various groups that are likely to be excluded in certain spheres and cultural contexts. These could be women, people from marginalised and or indigenous communities, persons with disabilities and many others. Other contextual factors that have a negative impact on inclusive education successes are macro-systemic factors such as political, economic, religious, and socio-cultural regulations and norms. These, in turn, have an impact on poverty, access to transport and access to basic needs by children, teachers and parents, which have direct or indirect bearing on teaching and learning. For example, when children and youths are poor, their participation in democratic processes is limited, and they start lagging behind their peers in almost all respects.

CHALLENGES WITH THE IMPLEMENTATION OF INCLUSIVE EDUCATION

For education systems to aspire to greater inclusivity there needs to be a serious approach to governance, and effective management. This section examines the educational changes in Namibia by critically considering the challenges in implementing inclusive education. Findings from research (Haihambo, 2010; Haihambo & Lightfoot, 2010; Möwes, 2002; Zimba, Haihambo & February, 2004) and evaluation studies (Haihambo, Brown & Tobias, 2011; Josua, 2012; UNESCO, 2007) have highlighted several challenges. These include societal and teacher attitudes, curriculum challenges, teacher education challenges and material and financial resource challenges as well as challenges emanating from lack of inter-agency collaboration.

Societal and teacher attitudes

The way in which we educate our learners is a reflection of our attitudes and beliefs. Segregating learners on the basis of disabling conditions reflects the belief that these learners are different in their needs and aspirations, and incapable of benefitting from that which is provided to the so-called 'normal' learners. It is therefore not surprising that children who attend special schools, as well as those with observable special needs who attend mainstream schools, are often subjects of ridicule and have their right to a democratic education compromised (Haihambo, 2010; Haihambo, Brown & Tobias, 2011). Desperate parents of children who are perceived to be 'different' from the majority of children continue requesting special schools irrespective of the degree of the special needs of their children. This reality shows how solid the belief has been, perpetuated by the history of special schools that best environment for addressing diversity is within special school settings. It underscores the need to extend inclusive education values not only to the school environment but to the broader society. Despite the fact that inclusive education approaches have not found prominence in the education sector and communities yet, parents have also not seen working models of inclusive schools. They thus fall back on what they know, whether what they know is good for their children or not. They keep demanding special school placements, even if children could function well in inclusive schools.

This call for inclusive schools does not only take into consideration the children with what we have traditionally called special needs. In the conference for indigenous minorities held in Windhoek in June, 2012, the call for secluded schools for San children to address issues of equity strongly reverberated, regardless of the adoption of an inclusive frame for education in Namibia. The call followed a discussion about factors such as stigmatization, bullying and poor understanding of the unique cultures of indigenous communities which leads to children from such communities running away from the schools they share with children from majority groups, i.e. non-San. In both cases, approaches such as segregation due to single-sex, single-race or any form of sameness are in total contrast with human rights and other principles of democratic inclusivity. Our laws are for inclusion, but we keep asking for separate schools for different groups. Broader value systems of difference and 'other' identities need to be explored from a holistic ecological approach. Schools are microcosms of society, and the scholastic practices and values should also transform the broader society from which they emanate.

Attitudes about learners with special needs vary from society to society in accordance with the particular socio-cultural, economic, political and religious dimensions. They also vary according to the different categories of disabling conditions, and in most societies it is possible to note a 'hierarchy of disabilities', where disabling conditions are ranked in terms of the public's degree of acceptance or dislike. There are many resilient forces against change within the established attitudes present in particular societies. Sometimes the change to include children with different needs is opposed by those who have a vested interest in segregated systems, and in other instances it may just be the general public who adhere to the 'It's ok – but not in my backyard' phenomenon (Miron, 1994). The latter group can be typified by parents of so-called 'normal' learners who fear that the quality of education will deteriorate when learners with special needs attend the local school with their children. In many traditional societies, the belief that spirits – good or bad – dwell within learners with disabilities greatly influences the treatment they receive and the educational provisions which they are given.

As stated earlier, the myths and negative perceptions towards disability should be examined from the broader epistemological understanding of diversity and 'othered' identities in Namibia. The historical inheritance of inequality and division has conditioned societies to constructs of 'us' and 'them'. Such binaries are used to justify marginalisation and exclusion and subsequently erode the possibilities of diverse and inclusive societies. For example, the Ministry of Education in Namibia has recently introduced a learner pregnancy prevention and management policy which allows girls who are pregnant to remain in school until they are close to their delivery dates, and then to re-access school as soon as the well-being of the new-born baby has been established (Ministry of Education, 2010). Critics from communities, schools and learners in schools seem to suggest that the visibility of girls who are pregnant in schools could serve as a 'popularisation' of pregnancy. What was intended as a democratic measure to expand access to education has now turned into a debate that seems to seek punishment for those who have become pregnant, irrespective of the eco-systemic factors that could have contributed to the pregnancies. Recently, a teacher in a secondary school inappropriately touched a learner who reported the case to her parents. The teacher was found guilty of indecent conduct and opted to resign from his post as a teacher. Reports following his resignation indicate criticism of this learner by her peers, teachers and community, blaming her for causing the teacher to lose his job! Similarly, orphans and vulnerable children, including street children and others affected by abject poverty, are clearly mocked by other learners and teachers (or with teachers' condoning the mocking), thus making it impossible for such learners to remain in an environment that clearly rejects them. These are clear indications of clashes between traditional norms (which do not always value the needs and individual rights) and the national legislative, inclusive and democratic rights. As highlighted by these examples, the role of attitudes, both collective and individual, is important and influential in the provision of services for learners with diverse needs and consequently can compromise their democratic inclusion.

It is argued that teachers' attitudes and beliefs are critical in ensuring the success of inclusive practices. Teachers' acceptance of the policy on inclusive education is likely to affect their commitment to implementing it.

A further complication regarding teachers' attitudes, specifically towards learners with special needs, is that these attitudes are not only reflected in their teaching methods and interaction with learners in their classes, but they also affect the way learners with special needs see themselves (Möwes, 2002). More often than not, learners with special needs are subjected to bullying and other forms of mockery or rejection in the education system. Many times, teachers and peers have low expectations of them. Subconsciously the rejected learners also start to develop low self-concepts and self-expectations, rendering them inferior despite a macro-system with a theoretically democratic legal framework.

To promote inclusive education in Namibia, teachers and other stakeholders in education should be encouraged to understand the inclusive education approach and change their attitudes and perceptions to children with special needs.

Curriculum challenges

The curriculum inherited from the previous government bore little relevance to the lives and experiences of most Namibians. Even though good instruction could remedy some of its defects, it was unsatisfactory in important respects. For example, the curriculum was fixed, allowed little room for creation of new knowledge and emphasised a passive process of learning. Learners were seen as receivers and not creators of knowledge (Möwes, 2002).

Teachers were expected to deliver prepared knowledge and skills. Also, the content of that curriculum was based on the realities of a minority group, thus decontextualizing it. In Namibia, educational reforms and policies that have been established since independence are aimed at broadening and diversifying the scope of education and enabling as many learners as possible to benefit from the system. Because Article 20 (a) of the Namibian Constitution guarantees the right to education for all, no Namibian can legitimately be barred from education because of contextual disadvantages, social problems or learning difficulties (GRN, 1990).

In the policy statement *Toward education for all,* which captures the educational goals of access, equity and quality, the Ministry of Education is mandated to provide education and training to learners with special needs and others with disabilities. Included in this group are learners with visual, hearing, physical, emotional and mental impairments. Also included are above average and gifted learners, as well as learners in regular classes who are seriously underachieving (Ministry of Education and Culture [MoE], 1993).

However, in studies conducted by Zimba et al. (2004) and Möwes (2002), school principals and teachers in special and mainstream schools reported that the curriculum:

1. did not make provision for children's different levels of ability, developmental and learning needs,
2. was not designed for learners with diverse needs,
3. did not take into account the different learning speeds of diverse learners, and
4. excluded content that was relevant for some learners with special needs and disabilities (e.g. orientation and mobility training for visually impaired learners).

Given this situation, it is imperative that the curriculum be reviewed to make it more responsive to diverse learning needs, thereby promoting inclusive education in the country.

The way forward should be to reform schools in ways that will encourage teachers to respond positively to learner diversity, seeing individual differences as something to be nurtured and celebrated. This kind of approach is only possible where there is respect for individuality and a culture of collaboration that encourages and supports problem solving. Such a culture is likely to facilitate the effective learning of all learners and the enhancement of the teacher's capacity to deliver appropriate inclusive education. Moreover, a departure from traditional instructional strategies towards a variety of strategies, such as peer-mediated learning and cooperative learning, can turn diversity into a tool for ensuring that different learner needs are met and learner initiative and social skills are promoted.

The Dakar Framework of Action (UNESCO, 2000) has focused on the strengthening and widening of strategies for addressing learners' needs, as discussed at Jomtien in 1990. These strategies include increasing access to early childhood education by developing equitable learning opportunities to facilitate good starts in life.

Teacher education challenges

Before independence, teacher education was fragmented and uneven. Teachers serving under the different administrations did not receive the same training. The various teacher education programmes had different entry requirements, scope, duration, organisation and focus. Some were very resource intensive, developed extended competencies, and provided relatively high level qualifications. Others were far more rudimentary, providing minimal qualifications. Some emphasised classroom study at the expense of professionalism (MoE, 1993).

As indicated in Chapter 6, teacher education is currently the responsibility of one main institution, the University of Namibia. With the exception of programmes offered by other universities and institutions, mainly from South Africa, the University of Namibia has been mandated by the Government of the Republic of Namibia to provide teacher education. Whereas the University of Namibia was historically responsible for teacher education for the secondary school phase and specialised postgraduate qualifications, it now offers teacher education for all levels, from pre-primary up to senior secondary phases. Postgraduate programmes of the University of Namibia provide students with skills to operate in higher education as well as other post-secondary environments.

Currently, all pre-service teacher education students in the University of Namibia take an introductory course to inclusive education, namely, Introduction to Inclusive Education, which is offered for one semester during the second year of study. The course covers, among other themes, definitions and scope of inclusive education, different models and approaches in the field of inclusive education, and international developments and legislation. The course further identifies and discusses various barriers to learning experienced by children in Namibia and on the continent as a whole. The same course is offered to students pursuing their training through distance or part-time modes. There are no pre-requisites for this course. This course is offered to all students across the levels (lower primary, upper primary and secondary phases). It is pitched at NQF level 7 and offers 8 credits. In addition to Introduction to Inclusive Education, other courses enhancing the inclusive education discourse include guidance and counselling, human learning and development theories, and practicals.

During the fourth year of study, students select a career specialisation from: Inclusive Education; School Leadership and Management; Life Skills; Curriculum Planning and

Development; Sport Organisation and Administration; Arts and Culture Development and Organisation and Advanced Sign Language (Faculty of Education, 2016, p. 128). The specialisation is a two-semester course but starts almost a month after the commencement of lectures for the academic year, as students first have to complete their school-based practice. For this course, the second year subject Introduction to Inclusive Education is a pre-requisite. The course is pitched at NQF level 8 and offers 12 credits. The Inclusive Education specialisation offers wide skill development and depth in content areas. An added requirement of this course is a one-hour practical session per week which is intended to give students an insight into the practical applications of inclusive education. These courses are offered as full-time as well as part-time and distance modes.

Besides these two courses, the University of Namibia offers a compulsory core module called Contemporary Social Issues. This course is offered to all students in the university and comprises HIV and AIDS, and Gender and Ethics sub-units. Although it does not directly address inclusive education, its underlying principle is that of enhancing tolerance and acceptance of all people irrespective of their differences (Haihambo, Brown, February & Hengari, 2009).

It is clear from the discussion on teacher education that the majority of Namibian teachers are not trained or oriented to teach learners with special educational needs. With the exception of the two courses mentioned, the majority of the courses on teacher education at the University of Namibia largely focus on preparation for the regular classroom context. The special needs content in the courses is very limited and in some cases non-existent. It is thus suggested that teacher education institutions should provide courses that will empower teachers with knowledge and skills to teach learners with and without special educational needs. To do this it is suggested that at pre-service level, education for diversity content should be integrated into all teacher education courses at the University of Namibia. It is furthermore suggested that educators at all levels who are already in the teaching and learning profession should be enabled to embrace the lifelong learning ethos with an inclination towards general inclusion and understanding of diversity, be it in terms of learning needs, socio-economic status, sexual orientation, religion, or whatever factor may introduce diversity and or pose barriers to learning in conventional learning environments. Both pre- and in-service teachers should be continuously provided with inclusive education in-service training in the form of workshops, seminars and short courses.

It is hoped that the Centre for Continuing Professional Development based at the University of Namibia, whose mandate it is to promote further and lifelong learning for educators, will take upon themselves the responsibility of developing teachers for the 21st Century and beyond who will have a sound understanding of democracy and how to realise its principles in school.

Teacher education can serve as a vehicle for inclusive education implementation by demystifying diversity and disabilities, while developing in teachers, attitudes and skills which are consistent with principles of inclusive education. Teachers following an inclusive education pedagogy should be able to balance cultural-social-centeredness with context-centeredness. Cultural-social-centeredness refers to 'the importance of teacher education to prepare teachers for the context in which they would teach – with all their uniqueness and peculiarities. This means that there is a need for a critical look at the universalized approach to 'Education for All' and inclusive education that is somewhat blind to context specificity by promoting the application of general principles' (Haipinge, 2012, p. 4). While teacher education prepares students for varying contexts, the context in which teachers are most likely to work in is crucial and teachers should be prepared for moving between their own belief systems and those of their learners and communities. Teachers who do not understand the culture, traditions and realities of the communities in which they work will create conflicts between the school and the community. Good teacher education preparation should enable teachers to apply inclusive education meaningfully and maintain cultural sensitivity (Haipinge, 2012).

Resource challenges

The different ways resources are allocated can either facilitate or obstruct the move towards inclusive education. If funds are not allocated in line with an explicit inclusionary policy, inclusion is unlikely to be realised in practice.

Namibia is one of the signatories to the Salamanca statement and framework for action on special needs education (UNESCO, 1994). Consistent with this, Namibia is committed to providing adequate human and financial resources when offering inclusive education services to all its children, including those with disabilities.

To live up to this commitment, Namibia gives the highest national budgetary allocation to education. Despite this, the education system is still faced with a lack of adequately trained teachers, classrooms and educational facilities. One explanation for this is that because most of the budgetary allocation is spent on salaries, a disproportionately small fraction is spent on addressing real education issues such as providing adequate school infrastructure and teaching and learning materials. This hinders the effective implementation of a coherent basic education programme in the country. The obstruction of a severe lack of human and material resources (Möwes, 2002) translates into a situation where many schools lack well-resourced classrooms to support the learning and teaching of learners from educationally-deprived backgrounds, effective nutritional programmes, and effective psycho-social support services, to engage in inclusive education practices.

CONCLUSION

Inclusive education means a continuous process of according full participation to everybody in all contexts, including teaching, socialising and creating peer communities that provide spontaneous support to their members. Social participation and the creation of caring cultures are dependent on resources, attitudes and structural and infrastructural adaptations (Janson, 2011). While inclusive education is considered to be the most appropriate strategy for addressing the diverse needs in Namibia, the implementation of this policy, and the adoption of inclusive principles in a diverse society, are the real challenge. Unlike other countries where policy formulation is a barrier, for Namibia, policy implementation, monitoring and evaluation remain huge challenges.

Inclusive practices have received support in many countries around the world, including Namibia. The next stage for inclusion, then, is to address on-going challenges to improve, legitimise and sustain current efforts. All these challenges appear surmountable, but require careful planning, dedicated effort, and internal and external financial assistance. Failing to do so simply fuels the fire for the suppression of minorities in the education system. Ending suppression and inequality is a human rights objective. The fundamental principle of inclusive education, at its root, is a matter of not only equality but also equity with a focus on rights and opportunities which advocates a fair and just education system (Kenworthy & Whittaker, 2000).

References

Amukugo, E. M. (1995). *Education and politics in Namibia: Past trends and future perspectives.* 2nd Revised Edition. Windhoek: Gamsberg Macmillan.

Avoseh, M. B. M. (1999). *Opening up adult education: women's empowerment in Namibia.* Pan Commonwealth Forum, proceedings of the Commonwealth Forum, (March 1–5, 1999).

Bevan-Brown, J. (2006) Beyond policy and good intentions. *International Journal of Inclusive Education, 10*(2–3) 221–234.

Dewey, J. (1916) *Democracy and education.* New York: Macmillan.

Faculty of Education, University of Namibia. (2016). *Prospectus 2016.* Windhoek: University of Namibia.

Government of the Republic of Namibia (GRN). (1990). *Constitution of the Republic of Namibia.* Windhoek: Ministry of Information and Broadcasting.

Government of the Republic of Namibia (GRN). (1997). *National policy on disability.* Windhoek: Ministry of Lands, Resettlement and Rehabilitation.

Grover, S. (2007). Children's rights to be educated for tolerance: minority rights and inclusion. *Education and the Law, 19*(1), 59–70.

Haihambo C. K. (2010). *Inclusive education: Challenges of students with disabilities in higher education institutions in Namibia.* Saarbrücken: Lambert Publishing.

Haihambo C. K., Brown, A., & Tobias E. N. (2011). *Responses, coping strategies and needs of caregivers of children with visual impairments in Namibia.* Saarbrücken: Lambert Publishing.

Haihambo C. K., Brown, A., February, P., & Hengari, J. U. (2009). *Responses of Namibian Vocational Training Institutions to Inclusive Education: Successes, Challenges and Future Prospects.* A Conference Paper presented at the SANORD Conference, Grahamstown.

Haihambo, C. K. & Lightfoot, E. (2010). Cultural beliefs regarding people with disabilities in Namibia. *International Journal of Special Education, 25*(3), 76–92.

Haipinge, E. (2012). *Reform of teacher-education to education for all.* Unpublished Concept Paper for the University of Oulu, Finland.

Humphrey, N. (2008). Including students with ADHD and ASD. In C. Forlin & J. Lian (Eds.). *Reform, Inclusion & Teacher Education.* University of Manchester.

Janson, U. (2011). *Concerns and challenges in developing inclusive preschool classrooms.* Conference Paper Presented at the University of Stockholm on 12 November.

Josua, L. M. (2012). *Challenges of inclusive education to school management: A case study of Gabriel Taapopi Secondary School in the Oshana Education Region in Namibia.* (Unpublished Masters' thesis). Windhoek: University of Namibia.

Katjavivi, P. H. (1988). *A history of resistance in Namibia.* Berlin: LIT Verlag.

Kenworthy, J. & Whittaker, J. (2000). Anything to declare? The struggle for inclusive education and children's rights. *Disability and Society, 15*(2), 219–231.

Michigan Disability Rights Coalition. (2001). *Models of disability*. Retrieved from http://www.copower. org/leadership/models-of-disability.

Ministry of Education, Namibia. (1993). *Toward education for all: A development brief for education, culture and training*. Windhoek: Gamsberg Macmillan.

Ministry of Education, Namibia. (2007). *Workplace HIV and AIDS policy for the education sector*. Windhoek: Ministry of Education.

Ministry of Education, Namibia. (2008). *Education sector policy for orphans and vulnerable children*. Windhoek: Ministry of Education.

Ministry of Education, Namibia. (2010). *Education sector policy for the prevention and management of learner pregnancy*. Windhoek: Ministry of Education.

Ministry of Education, Namibia. (2013). *Sector policy on inclusive education*. Windhoek. Ministry of Education.

Ministry of Foreign Affairs of Denmark. (2009). *Annual report 2009: Denmark's participation in international development cooperation*. Denmark: Ministry of Foreign Affairs.

Ministry of Gender Equality and Child Welfare, Namibia. (2010). *National gender policy*. Windhoek: Ministry of Gender Equality and Child Welfare.

Ministry of Information and Broadcasting, Namibia. (1990). *Constitution of the Republic of Namibia*. Windhoek. Ministry of Information and Broadcasting.

Miron, G. (1994). *Special needs education in Nicaragua. A study of the prevalence of children with disabilities in primary schools and factors affecting their successful participation*. Institute of International Education. Stockholm: Stockholm University.

Möwes, A. D. (2002). *Namibian teachers' views of inclusive education*. (Unpublished doctoral dissertation). Stellenbosch: University of Stellenbosch.

Mutorwa, J. (2002). *Access to education: 1990–2000. Reflections on the implementation of Namibia's policy of toward education for all*. Windhoek: Gamsberg Macmillan.

Naanda, A. N. (2005). *The development of an inclusive approach in early childhood education in Namibia*. (Unpublished doctoral dissertation). Stellenbosch: University of Stellenbosch.

Osler, A. & Starkey, H. (2001). Citizenship education and national identities in France and England: Inclusive or exclusive. *Oxford Review of Education, 27*(2), 287–305.

Thomas, G. & Glenny, G. (2002). Thinking about inclusion. Whose reason? What evidence? *International Journal of Inclusive Education, 6*(4), 345–369.

United Nations. (1990). *World declaration on education for all: Meeting basic learning needs*. World Conference on Education for All. Jomtein, Thailand, March 1990. Retrieved from http://www.un-documents. net/jomtien.htm

United Nations Educational, Scientific and Cultural Organization (UNESCO). (1994). *The Salamanca statement and framework for action on special needs education*. Paris, France: UNESCO.

United Nations Educational, Scientific and Cultural Organization (UNESCO). (2000). *The Dakar framework. Education for all: Meeting our collective commitments*. Paris, France: UNESCO.

United Nations Educational, Scientific and Cultural Organization (UNESCO). (2003). *Overcoming exclusion through inclusive approaches in education: a challenge and a vision-conceptual paper.* Paris: UNESCO.

United Nations Educational, Scientific and Cultural Organization (UNESCO). (2005). *Guidelines for inclusion: Ensuring access to education for all.* Paris: UNESCO.

Zimba, R. F., Haihambo, C. K., & February, P. J. (2004). *A situation analysis of special education provision in Namibia.* Windhoek: Ministry of Education.

9

Sexual harassment in institutions of higher learning: Breaking the silence

Lucy Edwards-Jauch and Ndeshi Namupala

Warm up your thinking on this topic with the following questions:

1. Does sexual harassment occur at your institution? How important is this issue to you?

2. Think of actual sexual harassment cases you know of and list the many forms it can take.

3. Why do you think sexual harassment occurs?

4. Can sexual harassment prevent some people from having equal opportunities in education, and if so, how does this happen?

5. How are power and sexual harassment linked?

INTRODUCTION

Since university curricula contain courses on gender, it is often assumed that there is no longer a need to reflect on gendered and patriarchal institutional practices. The action research on gender-based violence which forms the basis of this chapter provided an opportunity to reflect and act on young women's lack of control over their own bodies, and the institutional cultures and practices which impede such control. The aims of this Feminist Action Research were to enhance young women's research capacity and to identify and act on those factors which impede sexual and reproductive autonomy within the context of the university. Although the study revealed different forms of gender-based violence at the main campus of the University of Namibia, this chapter focuses on the broader concept of sexual harassment.

Feminist knowledge construction has democratic and egalitarian underpinnings, i.e. commitment to equality and democratic values like participation during the research process. This presupposes the conscious dismantling of a knowledge-power nexus that reflects and reinforces the broader structural levels of social inequalities. This research process was, therefore, a constant interplay between education, 'conscientisation' (an awareness of consciousness), skills training, information gathering, action and reflection. Multiple methods were employed to conduct these different activities in the research process. These methods included documentary research, semi-structured interviews, training and information gathering workshops, focus group discussions, mapping, campaign work, a demonstration, a petition, a survey on 'knowledge, attitudes and behaviour' (KAB), drama, poetry and a panel discussion.

Feminist Action Research tries to overcome the object–subject binary of traditional research, reflected in the relationship between researcher (expert) and the researched (provider of data). In Action Research, both contribute towards the process of knowledge construction. It is not only research for its own sake but research towards a social transformation. Research is seen as a process rather than just as an outcome. Action research is also not a linear process which starts and concludes at a certain point. Hence, our research is ongoing. Our findings may therefore be tentative. So far we have identified different forms of sexual harassment on the UNAM campus, which we have sought to bring into the public domain and to the attention of the university authorities. In the process we have enhanced research capacity and raised awareness about sexual harassment on campus.

Sexual harassment is a form of gender-based violence which reflects broader societal inequalities. It is an international phenomenon which pervades universities and educational institutions around the world. Despite its omnipresence, it is often denied or trivialised. Universities should be the vanguards of democracy. They should be open institutions which uphold democratic values of equality, non-discrimination, transparency, accountability and freedom of expression. There is, however, a deafening silence, fear, intimidation and repression around issues of gender-based violence and sexual harassment. These circumstances point to the undemocratic and patriarchal cultures which dominate many universities. Women who raise the issues of sexual harassment are often regarded as trouble makers. *Quid pro quo* sexual harassment in the form of sex in exchange for marks at tertiary institutions diminishes the fundamental rights of victims and impedes their educational achievement. Although our research revealed different forms of gender-based violence at the University, the focus here is on more general sexual harassment. While sexual harassment can affect all genders, women are the victims and men the perpetrators in the majority of cases of hetero-sexual harassment.

Sexual harassment is discriminatory because victims are targeted because of their sex. Despite its limitations, the Namibian Constitution and labour law ban discrimination on the basis of sex, and where sexual harassment occurs, victims have the right to redress. There are, however, a number of impediments to redressing, as victims often do not recognise the acts of sexual harassment. The power inequalities which give rise to sexual harassment in the first place may prevent victims from seeking redress as it is afforded by the law. Victims often fear further victimisation, and therefore the perpetrators are seldom held accountable for their actions. Lastly, patriarchal control and collusion often leads to a trivialisation of the issue and reluctance to act against the perpetrators.

Types of sexual harassment

The definition of sexual harassment was pioneered by MacKinnon in 1979 as the unwelcome imposition of sexual requirements in the context of a relationship of unequal power (Uggen & Blackstone, 2004). This includes unwelcome sexual advances, requests for sexual favours and/ or verbal, non-verbal or physical conduct of a sexual nature (Hall, Graham, & Hoover, 2004, p. 34). It can become part of an organisation's norms when professional relations become sexualised (Morely, 2011, p. 102). Legally, sexually inappropriate actions constitute harassment precisely because of the unsolicited, non-reciprocal, non-consensual and unwelcome nature of these acts from the side of the recipient or victim (Nwadigwe, 2007, p. 352). Sociologically, these acts of harassment take place in a broader social-cultural context steeped in power inequalities, social stratification and certain cultural expressions of sexuality and dominant masculinity (Uggen & Blackstone, 2004). While there is recognition that the gender system produces the unequal gender power relations implicated in sexual harassment, there is less recognition of how this gender system intersects other forms of social stratification like race, class and age (ibid.).

Age is an important social marker in African societies as the young are socialised into respecting and obeying their elders. In the university setting this is very relevant: younger students may find it difficult to transcend their own socialisation in order to resist or report elders who abuse their positions of power to commit acts of sexual harassment.

Sexual harassment can take the form of *quid pro quo* harassment where people in positions of power, like university lecturers, attempt to influence a process in exchange for sexual favours or to reward those who grant them sexual favours (Smit & Du Plessis, 2011, p. 189). The crucial aspect of *quid pro quo* sexual harassment is the exchange relationship between the perpetrator and victim.

Non-*quid pro quo* or hostile [environment] sexual harassment occurs when the sexual harassment is so persistent or severe that it creates an intimidating, abusive or threatening educational environment (Hall, Graham, & Hoover, 2004, p. 34). Hostile environment sexual harassment is generally unrelated to a particular 'reward' (Penrod & Fusilier, 2011, p. 154). The following are some sexually inappropriate acts that could be classified as sexual harassment:

1. Physical forms of sexual harassment include unwanted touching of a sexual nature, pinching, rubbing, sexual gestures and sexual assault (Hall, Graham, & Hoover, 2004, p. 34).
2. Verbal forms of sexual harassment include making jokes of an unwanted sexual nature, talking about one's sexual activities in front of others, spreading rumours about other people's sexual activity or performance, pressurising someone for sexual favours, using demeaning, offensive or crude language of a sexual nature, making offensive comments about someone's body or dress and name calling (Hall, Graham, & Hoover, 2004, p. 34).
3. Visual forms of sexual harassment include displaying unwanted visual material of a sexual nature. This could be with cartoons, drawings, posters, graffiti or calendars. It could also include the sending of sexually charged and offensive emails or text messages or posting them on social networking sites (Hall, Graham, & Hoover, 2004, p. 34)

SEXUAL HARASSMENT AND DEMOCRATIC VALUES

Sexual harassment is discriminatory, and is primarily against women. It undermines their rights to privacy, autonomy, equality, freedom and dignity (Kaplan, 2006; Penrod & Fusilier, 2011).

In addition, it raises serious questions of transparency and accountability inside institutions, if grades, jobs or promotions can be subject to individual whims or exchanged for sexual favours (Moreley, 2011). Generally, our view of democracy and citizenship is crafted through the prism of citizens' rights in relation to the state. Feminists, however, put forward the notion of citizenship from below. To be a full citizen, there should be no impediments to an individual's full participation in all aspects of human endeavour. What is critical to the feminist notion of citizenship is how women's bodies are used to assert power and control in public and private life. With sexual harassment, women's bodies are used to assert hegemonic masculinity, power differentials, or to humiliate (Schlyter, 2009). In the academic setting, this denies victims full and equal participation in academic life.

Sexual harassment is an abuse of power which can be exercised by both men and women in heterosexual or homosexual relations. International studies show, however, that women are overwhelmingly the victims of sexual harassment and men overwhelmingly the perpetrators. Shumba and Matina's (2002) study on sexual harassment at a university in Zimbabwe found that 66% of females experienced sexual harassment by males, while 95% of males did not experience it. Another study done at the University of Zambia about students' perceptions on sexual harassment found 71% of respondents felt that females were more likely to be sexually harassed than males (Menon et al., 2011). Eliason, Hall and Anderson (2012) cite research from the United States of America where 62% of victims of sexual harassment at university campuses are women. Moreley (2011) cites studies from the United Kingdom and sets the number of sexual harassment victims at 68%. Paludi, Nydegger, De Souza, Nydegger and Dicker (2006) reviewed studies from Brazil, Australia, Germany and North America. In one Australian study, 53% of women experienced harassment from lecturers and 88% from male peers. Nwandigwe (2007) found sexual harassment of women by men at Nigerian universities was so pervasive that he dubbed it the 'phallic attack'. In his own study, he found that 77% of women experienced sexual harassment. He argued that sexual harassment constituted a barrier to women's empowerment in higher education. Sexual harassment, therefore, is discrimination because women are treated differently from men who are less likely to experience sexual harassment (Siegel, 2003). Sexual harassment harms the individual's right to equality and strengthens discrimination against all women (Kaplan, 2006). Morely (2011, p. 104) argues that women's achievements will always be tainted with the suspicion that they were not based on real academic ability, but rather are because they have commodified their bodies, trading sex for marks. She therefore concurs that sexual harassment in academia is a form of sex discrimination that reinforces the social inequality of women and denigrates their academic achievements. Feminists extend notions of democracy and citizenship beyond the political and social realm to include sexuality. Increasingly, there has been an assertion of sexual citizenship and sexual democracy. Sexual citizenships denote a set of rights with regard to sexual practices and sexual identities (Robson & Kessler, 2008). At the International Conference on Population and Development in Cairo in 1994, the international body agreed that every person had sexual rights. This included the right to exercise sexual choices freely, autonomously and without coercion (International Community of Women Living with HIV/AIDS, 2005). Sexual harassment is coercive and therefore constitutes a form of gender-based violence. It is anti-democratic for it diminishes an individual's sexual rights.

METHODOLOGY

As mentioned above, this research followed the Feminist Action Research methodology. Feminist Action Research can be placed in a broader framework of social justice. It sees research as a collective exercise towards empowerment (Reid, 2004). It is a form of applied research which starts from a normative premise that knowledge should also be used to transform particular problems, particularly in the interests of socially marginalised groups (Fals-Borda, 2001). It normally follows a cyclical process of diagnosing problems, gaining knowledge, planning action and taking action towards change (Reid, 2004).

Our research was largely exploratory, but does provide some pointers on how action research can integrate education, skills building, data collection and action into an empowering process and lead subjects to recognise and assert their own agency. We adopted Fals-Borda's (2001) notion that knowledge construction should improve practice, and should therefore require the 'conscientisation' of educators. We thus combined the three sets of activities identified by Hall (cited in Reid, 2004), namely, research, education and action. The egalitarian underpinnings of feminist knowledge construction, and the aim to empower, presuppose the conscious dismantling of the knowledge-power nexus that reflects and reinforces broader inequalities.

This study sought to enable female students to tell their stories. This research process was a constant inter-play between education, 'conscientisation', skills training, information gathering, action and reflection. As introduced above, multiple methods were employed to conduct the various activities.

TYPES OF SEXUAL HARASSMENT ON UNIVERSITY OF NAMIBIA (UNAM) MAIN CAMPUS

While Namibia has a relatively high female participation in tertiary education, there has been a drop in female to male enrolment ratios. In 1992 it was 162 females for every 100 males. In 2011 it had gone down to 85,3 females for every 100 males (National Planning Commission [NPC], 2013). Curriculum choices reflect a gender bias with lower female enrolment in science, engineering, technology and agriculture (NPC, 2013). Women are still found in the stereotypical feminine fields of study like the humanities, social sciences, nursing and teaching, while men dominate engineering, agriculture and natural sciences (Xoagus-Eises, Brown, & Makaya, 2012).

Women are still subject to acts of sexual harassment despite constituting the majority of UNAM students. This is perhaps not surprising since Demographic and Health Surveys (DHS) over the last ten years show that the university is situated in a broader society which has a high level of tolerance of violence against women (Ministry of Health and Social Services, 2008, 2014).

The Action Research Team's (ART) (2010) study found a number of actions that could be classified as sexual harassment on UNAM campus. In most cases, these actions were perpetrated by male taxi drivers, security guards, lecturers and students. They included unwanted comments, jokes and gestures, emotional and verbal abuse. Female students were touched inappropriately, or physically pulled or dragged by taxi drivers to get them into their taxis. Female students were threatened and beaten up by taxi drivers at the main gate. Security guards insulted them in the corridors and at the hostels. The security guards also attempted to bribe students to cook for

Table 1. Female to male enrolment and literacy ratios

Ratios of female to males in education	Baseline: (year)	Latest status: (year)
Pre-primary education	88:100 (2008)	101:100 (2012)
Primary education	102:100 (1992)	96:100 (2012)
Secondary education	124:100 (1992)	112:100 (2012)
Tertiary education	162:100 (1992)	85:100 (2011)
Literate females (15–24 yrs)	110:100 (1991)	103:100 (2011)

Source: NPC (2013): *Millennium Development Goals Interim Progress Report No. 4*: Windhoek: National Planning Commission

Table 2. Ratio of female to male enrolment at selected tertiary institutions

Institution	Female to male enrolment
University of Namibia	153:100
Polytechnic of Namibia	127:100
International University for Management	114:100
Zambezi Vocational Training Centre	82:100
Valombola Vocational Training Centre	61:100
Windhoek Vocational Training Centre	61:100
Rundu Vocational Training Centre	45:100
Okakarara Vocational Training Centre	39:100

Source: NPC (2013): *Millennium Development Goals Interim Progress Report No. 4*: Windhoek: National Planning Commission.

them or buy them food. Guards at the main gates merely watched and failed to protect students from aggressive taxi drivers.

Some of the female students' experiences were captured by the following remarks:

'Boys tell you that they like your ass when you wear leggings.' Female Student

'Once a girl was late for a 7:30 class, the professor made sexual remarks about the skirt she was wearing. He abused her emotionally as the rest of the class was laughing and she was left embarrassed in front of the whole class of about 100 students. This particular lecturer insults the students, makes bad remarks about students' grades and performance in class'. Female Student

'Students who are pregnant are labelled and called names by friends and other students. In a recent case a pregnant student was absent from a test because she had to go for a check-up. Upon return the student went to the lecturer to explain why she missed the test. The following day the lecturer came back to class and asked the class who the pregnant women are. He then called the girl to the front of the class, so that the girl could ask "permission" from the rest of the class to allow her to write the test.' Female Student

CORRECTIVE SEXUAL HARASSMENT

Cases of sexual harassment as a 'corrective' form of punishment also emerged out of the study; assertive female students were often labelled 'opinionated' and stigmatised. Some students suffered corrective punishment in the form of rape, beating and other humiliations such as receiving pornographic materials of a sexual nature via cell phone, internet, Facebook and other social networks.

> *'This happened on the hostel premises where a girl was raped by an unknown man'.*
> Female Student

> *'Gang rape cases go unreported. Female students, mostly at the beginning of the year find themselves waking up around campus wondering how they ended up there (stadium, toilets).'* Female Student

Other common types of sexual harassment included sex for marks from lecturers, 'sexually transmitted marks' as students referred to it. Students reported that there were lecturers who exchanged marks for sexual favours although this is against the university's Sexual Harassment Policy (University of Namibia, n.d.).

> *'Some students have failed modules because they have refused to date the lecturer'.*
> Female Student

Other unwanted and unsolicited sexual advances include spreading sexual rumours about individuals, brushing up against someone in a sexual way and discrimination on the basis of appearance (inappropriate dress).

SEXUAL HARASSMENT, POWER AND HEGEMONIC MASCULINITIES

Gender-based violence is often an assertion of male power and control over women. Sexual harassment is a form of gender-based violence. It is often 'integral to the construction of hegemonic, hetero-sexual masculine identities' (Robinson, 2005, p. 22). Through sexual harassment, men may feel they can prove masculinity and superiority (ibid.). Moreley (2011) argues that sexual harassment is more about power than sex. She links acts of sexual harassment to hierarchical and gendered power relations in universities. The fact that men are overwhelmingly the perpetrators of sexual harassment and women overwhelmingly the victims reflects the patriarchal power structures and the masculine, androcentric (male-based) cultures within academia (ibid.). The majority of those who hold decision-making power in universities are men, and this contributes to an explanation of why the majority of perpetrators are male. The abusive nature of sexual harassment lies precisely in the power inequalities between victims and perpetrators. The power the perpetrator has within the institutional hierarchy grants him the ability to coerce. This can be the power to allocate grades, positions, promotions or scholarships.

Due to male dominance and androcentric cultures, sexual harassment often does not get the attention it deserves. Acts of harassment are often denied or trivialised. Shumba and Matina's (2002) study clearly shows the denial and trivialisation of sexual harassment by male students.

Table 3. Types of sexual harassment on main campus: Findings from ART study (2010)

Physical harassment	Verbal harassment	Visual harassment	Non-verbal harassment	Other
Grabbing; pushing, dragging	Lecturers who refer to female students as sweetheart.	Drawing naked women on toilet walls.	'Undressing looks'	Some male lecturers' probing female students' about their private lives.
Deliberately rubbing up against a woman's body.	Sexist jokes, particularly towards pregnant students.	Distribution of pornographic materials via social networking sites	Winking	Failed modules because women students refused to date the lecturer
Rape (this includes date and gang rape)	Asking a student to sleep with lecturer in exchange for marks (sexually transmitted marks).	Secret filming and distribution of sexual encounters as corrective punishment.	Whistling	
Touching, pinching	Spreading rumours	Text messages requesting sexual favours.		
Brushing up against someone in a sexual way.	Security guards insult students in the corridors.			
Dragging students around campus as a 'corrective' punishment.	Sexual remarks about women's clothes and body			
Males putting their legs between females' legs in the library cubicles.	Degrading remarks about grades and performance.			
Students beaten by boyfriends in the hostel.	Male students insult female students in the corridors.			

In their study, 72% of females against 14% of males agreed that sexual harassment was indeed taking place at the university, and 74% of females against 27% of males felt that it should be eliminated from the institution. Trivialisation and denial of sexual harassment in universities are often reflected in statements like 'It was only a joke', or 'What is the fuss all about? It is normal' (Keddie, 2009, p. 13; Robinson, 2005, pp. 25–26). The refusal to take sexual harassment seriously leads to organisational cultures in which predatory sexual behaviour is normalised and even seen as male entitlement (Bennet, 2009). Sexual harassment is multi-dimensional and can take many different forms and follow different directions. It can be perpetrated by male lecturers towards female students, male students towards female students, male lecturers towards female lecturers, as well as by and among non-academic staff (Imonike, Aluede, & Idogho, 2012). The study by Imonike et al. in Nigeria found that 80% of the sexual harassment experienced by female students was perpetrated by male students and 20% by male lecturers.

While perpetrators of sexual harassment are often males in positions of authority, who have the power to exchange sexual favours for rewards, it can also work in reverse. Women in positions of power can also be harassed sexually as a form of humiliation. This can occur where women occupy positions in what were traditionally considered male preserves (Kaplan, 2006). There are often allegations of sexual harassment of female lecturers by male students. Sexual harassment can also be performed as part of a regime of corrective punishment towards assertive women who are regarded as 'cheeky' or who 'play hard to get'. It is then done to diminish women's sense of empowerment and self-worth and to reinforce patriarchal relations (Keddie, 2009). This is often justified with comments like 'She was looking for it'. So far, the literature focuses on the sexual harassment in heterosexual contexts. There are research gaps pertaining to sexual harassment towards males in subordinate positions and sexual harassment in same-sex contexts.

FEMALE AGENCY AND SELF-OBJECTIFICATION

One of the reasons cited for not acting on sexual harassment allegations in universities is that female students use their agency to make sexual harassment work to their own advantage, in that they are not simply victims of patriarchy, but actively collude with it. Male lecturers accused of sexual harassment often transfer that blame onto female students. There are instances when males in positions of power, for example male lecturers, construct themselves as victims of sexual harassment when female students try to exploit the sexualised institutional relations to their own advantage. Women students may present themselves as sexual objects through dress codes, sexually charged behaviour or suggestive comments. This self-objectification, however, fits into a broader patriarchal narrative which constructs women as sexual objects. Sexual harassment erodes the culture of teaching and learning and commodifies the academic environment into a sexual market place where marks and academic rewards are traded for sexual favours (Moreley, 2011). If left unchecked, sexual harassment may become deeply entrenched in the institutional culture and part of normal conduct within the institution. In such institutional cultures, female students may use transactional sex to advance academically. In deciding how to deal with such instances, the power dynamics should not be overlooked. While the sexual advances by female students may be unwelcome, the relations of power remain unequal. The ability of male lecturers to use their positions or power to resist or refuse cannot be compared with that of female students in subordinate positions. The male lecturer is in a much stronger position to state unequivocally that the sexual advance is unwanted. The onus is on him to reassert the academic and professional nature of the student-lecturer relationship and not to exploit his position of power which has resulted in his being approached in a sexually-charged manner in the first place. The strategic use of sexual harassment by female students may serve the short-term interests of the individual student or lecturer. In the long-term it harms women as a group. It reinforces hegemonic masculinities, objectifies women's bodies and denigrates their academic achievements (Keddie, 2009).

EFFECTS OF SEXUAL HARASSMENT ON EDUCATIONAL ACHIEVEMENT

The known effects of sexual harassment are somatic (physical) symptoms like disturbed sleep, headaches, fatigue, nausea, neck pain, gastrointestinal disturbances, appetite loss and weight loss. This can be compounded by other psychological effects like feelings of guilt and helplessness, low self-esteem, humiliation, depression, anxiety and fear (Imonike et al., 2012; Kaplan, 2006; Penrod & Fusilier, 2011; Smit & Du Plessis, 2011). These psychological effects can cause students to disengage from their academic environments (Eliason, Hall, & Anderson, 2011). This disengagement can manifest itself in absenteeism and under-achievement (Eliason, Hall, & Anderson, 2011; Kaplan, 2006; Nwadigwe, 2007; Shumba & Matina, 2002; Smit & Du Plessis, 2011). Sexual harassment can also lead to outright failure or dropping out (Nwadigwe, 2007). Since women as a group are disproportionately affected by the negative effects of sexual harassment, it impedes their participation in academia. In an influential article, Benson and Thomson (1982) argued that the practice of sexual harassment both reflected and reinforced the devaluation of women's competence and eroded their commitment to competitive careers.

LEGAL AND POLICY ENVIRONMENT OF SEXUAL HARASSMENT

The Namibian Labour Act (No. 11, 2007) defines sexual harassment as unwanted conduct of a sexual nature towards an employee, which constitutes a barrier to equality in employment (Government of the Republic of Namibia [GRN], 2007). Although the act limits itself to employment, it clearly sees sexual harassment as an issue of democracy, since it is seen as a barrier to equality and therefore a violation of fundamental rights. In the context of higher education, it is good practice for universities to adopt sexual harassment policies to give effect to such non-discriminatory legislation. The University of Namibia (UNAM) in its sexual harassment policy commits itself to providing a safe and secure working and learning environment. The policy extends to all job applicants, employees, students and people who have dealings with the University. The policy explicitly prohibits sexual harassment in and out of the classroom, in the evaluation of academic performance and the allocation of marks (University of Namibia, n.d.). Despite its prohibition, allegations of 'sex for marks' or 'sexually transmitted marks' continue to surface. The matter was raised in a petition to the university management by the Action Research Team (ART) on 8 March, 2011 (ART, 2011). The matter received national and international attention when it was raised by members of the Student Representative Council (SRC) in a meeting with the Deputy Minister of Education in August, 2011 (Magadza, 2011; Nakale, 2011a; Smit, 2011a). The university ordered a probe into the allegations, and four months later concluded that there was no evidence to substantiate 'sex for marks' allegations (Nakale, 2011b; Smit, 2011b). The UNAM case is consistent with international studies on sexual harassment in institutions of higher education. Drawing on experiences from Israel, Kaplan (2006) argues that because of the one-on-one nature of sexual harassment, it is difficult for victims to complain since corroboration may not be possible. In addition, because the perpetrator may be a figure of authority, the event may be denied or repressed. Smit and Du Plessis (2011) have dubbed sexual harassment as the 'silent' problem in education to indicate an unwillingness to acknowledge the problem and to deal with it. In university communities women's voices have been silenced under confidentiality clauses.

RECOGNITION AND REPORTING SEXUAL HARASSMENT

It goes without saying that allegations of sexual harassment should be thoroughly investigated in order to safeguard those who are falsely accused. Leitich (1999) argues that there should be penalties for frivolous litigation to minimise possibilities of libel, slander or malicious accusations. This, however, should not stand in the way of the victim's right to redress. Morley (2011) argues that organisational cultures reproduce gender hierarchies which appropriate women's sexuality and protect male privilege. Institutions often deal with sexual harassment in ways which protect male perpetrators. Often educational institutions lack the mechanisms that would encourage victims to come forward and use the legal and policy provisions in place to protect themselves (Smit & Du Plessis, 2011). In the context of male dominance in these institutions, Keddie (2009) sees this bias as gender collusion which, in the end, has the effect of normalising sexual harassment. The international trends show that high levels of sexual harassment are accompanied by high levels of under-reporting (Bennet, 2009; Kaplan, 2006; Keddie, 2009; Merkin, 2008; Morley, 2011; Paludi et al., 2006; Smit & Du Plessis, 2011). It is estimated that only 15 percent of victims of sexual harassment file formal complaints (Smit & Du Plessis, 2011).

Why sexual harassment is under-reported

There are a number of reasons for not reporting sexual harassment:

1. Difficulties in recognising acts of sexual harassment: In certain cultural contexts certain actions that otherwise could be classified as harassment are not labelled or recognised as such and therefore are not reported (Merkin, 2008). Kaplan (2006) points out that cultural context and lack of knowledge may be critical aspects in the non-recognition and subsequent under-reporting of sexual harassment. Even when women have found certain experiences unwanted, distressful or even frightening, they hesitated to label it as sexual harassment (ibid.).

2. Top down approaches to policy-making: Smit and Du Plessis (2011) argue that where institutions use a top-down approach to policy-making on sexual harassment, the incidence of non-reporting is highest.

3. Lack of capacity and fear amongst university officials who ought to investigate sexual harassment charges: Often perpetrators are powerful individuals within university structures. Officials who are supposed to investigate allegations of sexual harassment may not want to confront these individuals. In addition, the officials may not have the capacity to conduct such investigations. This may cause stress to complainants and deter them from reporting incidents of sexual harassment (Bennet, 2009).

4. Fear of Victimisation: Morely (2011) points out that contrary to the democratic values universities are supposed to embrace, there is pervasive fear in universities. Victims often do not report sexual harassment to any authorities due to fear of victimisation. At times, levels of fear are so high that women refuse even to participate in studies on sexual harassment.

Bennet (2009) points out that this fear can be exacerbated if the victim and perpetrator live in close proximity to each other.

5. Social stigma: As is often the case with abuse and misuse of power, the victims are blamed, and perpetrators, who are often powerful individuals, go on repeating the abuses or merely get a minor reproof/warning. In the case of sexual harassment in Nigerian universities, Nwadigwe (2007) has argued that some victims want to prevent a sexual scandal and therefore remain silent. They fear being labelled and stigmatised. Some blame themselves for being chosen by the sexual predator. In certain cultures, the reputation of the victim is tarnished, which encourages silence. Sexual violence against women becomes a matter of family honour, and victims face severe penalties like intra-family femicide or stoning for having committed adultery. Bennet (2009) sees the discourses around reporting as the stigmatised zones of femininity, where the so called 'loss of honour' or 'soiled sexuality' becomes a source of deep private shame for victims.

6. Lack of confidentiality and anonymity: Some victims do not report sexual harassment because those from whom they seek redress may leak the complaints to others, or even inform the more powerful perpetrators. The victims may then face repeated victimisation. Some victims do not report matters because those they report it to may not have the courage to take matters further, and therefore nothing may come from the complaints. There may be evidence that those who reported it in the past did not receive any justice. It is therefore important to have impartial and independent bodies, not linked or paid by universities, to investigate instances of sexual harassment without fear or favour (Nwadigwe, 2007).

7. Lack of evidence: Obtaining evidence of sexual harassment is difficult, due to the nature of the transgressions. Acts of harassment are often done on a one-on-one basis and the victims have difficulty providing the proof or witnesses who can corroborate their claims (Kaplan, 2006). Often, perpetrators argue that relations were consensual, and it is difficult to prove the unwanted nature of the act, even when there is physical evidence of sexual activity. This legal loophole provides an escape route for perpetrators (Nwadigwe, 2007).

Responses from UNAM students to reporting sexual harassment
Female students expressed reluctance to report sexual harassment incidents, citing lack of confidentiality and fear of victimisation. In addition they argued that nothing was done about incidents of sexual harassment reported in the past and therefore reporting yielded no justice.

Vicarious liability
Rather than demonstrating zero tolerance of sexual harassment through swift investigation and subsequent punitive or remedial actions, institutions are often more interested in damage control (Penrod & Fusilier, 2011). The principle of vicarious responsibility asserts that universities can be held liable for harm caused by a peer or lecturer since they have a responsibility to ensure a safe environment for students and employees. In a much cited case in South Africa, Grobler verses Naspers, the court found vicarious liability because it is the employer's responsibility to protect employees' constitutional rights to dignity, freedom and security (Smit & Du Plessis, 2011). In this case, the court ruled that it was not only the individual perpetrator who could be

held legally responsible, but also the employers (Bennet, 2009). This is particularly clear in cases where institutions are seen to be indifferent to complaints (Hall, Graham, & Hoover, 2004).

CONCLUSION

Sexual harassment is an international phenomenon, and rather than denying its existence, universities should demonstrate a zero-tolerance approach, by putting in place policies and procedures that encourage prompt reporting and independent investigation of allegations by a competent body. In view of the fact that the majority of the victims of sexual harassment are female, it is deemed a form of sex discrimination. It violates the victim's fundamental human rights. Acts of sexual harassment hamper women's full participation in academic life and educational achievement. Universities should be at the forefront of protecting those rights, and therefore should swiftly eliminate any form of abuse and discriminatory actions. Acts of sexual harassment often go unpunished due to the difficulty victims have in recognising such acts as harassment. Institutions deny and trivialise sexual harassment.

Due to their nature, acts of sexual harassment are difficult to prove. This should, however, not provide an excuse for indifference. Institutions that ignore sexual harassment do so at their own peril, since it undermines the culture of teaching and learning inside those institutions. In addition, these institutions have an obligation to provide a safe working and learning environment in which everyone's human rights are protected. Failure to do so could result in litigation. With sexual harassment, prevention is better than cure. It is therefore important to raise awareness about what sexual harassment entails, its consequences, and the institutional policies and procedures which should be in place to deal with it. Guarantees of confidentiality and 'whistle blower protection' may encourage its exposure and deter would-be sexual predators from abusing power. Contrary to the openness of a democratic culture, institutions of higher learning often refuse to acknowledge the existence of sexual harassment. It is, however, a democratic imperative to tackle this phenomenon seriously and acknowledge its discriminatory nature.

References

Action Research Team (ART), University of Namibia. (2010). *Gender-based violence on UNAM campus.* Windhoek: Department of Sociology, University of Namibia. Draft Research Report.

Action Research Team (ART), University of Namibia. (2011). *Action research team (ART) petition against gender-based violence.* Windhoek: Department of Sociology, University of Namibia.

Bennett, J. (2009). *Policies for sexual harassment in higher education: Two steps forward and three steps somewhere else.* Retrieved from http://agi.ac.za/policies-and-sexual-harassment-higher-educationtwo-steps-forward-and-three-steps-somewhere-else-0

Benson, D. J. & Thomson, G. (1982). Sexual harassment on a university campus: The confluence of authority relations, sexual interest and gender gratification. *Social Problems, 29,* 236–251.

Eliason, K., Hall, E., & Anderson, T. (2011). Because God said so: Religious facets of sexual and gender harassment in Christian academia. *Journal of Psychology and Theology, 39*(4), 345–355.

Fals-Borda, O. (2001). Participatory (action) research in social theory: Origins and challenges. In P. Reason & H. Bradbury (Eds.). *Handbook of action research: participative inquiry and practice*. London: SAGE.

Government of the Republic of Namibia (GRN). (2007). *Labour act (Act NO.11)*. Windhoek: Office of the Prime Minister.

Hall, R., Graham, R., & Hoover, G. (2004). Sexual harassment in higher education: A victim's remedies and a private university's liability. *Education and the Law, 19*(1), 34–45.

Imonike, J., Alude, O., & Idoho, P. (2012). A survey of teacher's and student's perceptions of sexual harassment in tertiary institutions of Edo state in Nigeria. *Asian Social Science, 8*(1), 268–274.

International Community of Women Living with HIV/AIDS (ICW). (2005). *Sexual and reproductive health and rights briefing 1*. Retrieved from http://www.icw.org/files/SRH%20rights.pdf

Kaplan, O. (2006). Awareness instruction for sexual harassment: Findings from an experiential learning process at a higher education institution in Israel. *Journal for Further and Higher Education, 30*(3), 213–227.

Keddie, A. (2009). Some of those girls can be real drama queens: Issues of gender, sexual harassment and schooling. *Sex Education*, 9(1), 1–16.

Leitich, K. (1999). Sexual harassment in higher education. *Education, 119*(4), 668–692.

Magadza, M. (2011, September, 18). Namibia: Investigation into "sex for marks". *World University News*.

Menon, A., Shilalukey Ngoma, M. P., Siziya, S., Ndubani, P., Musepa, M., Malungo, J., & Serpell, R. (2011). University students' perspective of sexual harassment: A case study of the University of Zambia. *Medical Journal of Zambia, 36*(2).

Merkin, R. (2008). Cross-cultural differences in perceiving sexual harassment: Demographic incidence rates of sexual harassment/sexual aggression in Latin America. *North American Journal of Psychology, 10*(2), 277–290.

Ministry of Health and Social Services, Namibia. (2008). *The Namibia Demographic Health Survey (DHS) 2006-7*. Windhoek: Ministry of Health and Social Services.

Ministry of Health and Social Services, Namibia. (2014). *Namibia Demographic and Health Survey 2013: Main findings*. Windhoek: Ministry of Health and Social Services.

Morely, L. (2011). Sex, grades and power in higher education in Ghana and Tanzania. *Cambridge Journal of Education, 4*(1), 101–115.

Nakale, A. (2011a, August, 31). Sex for marks. *New Era*.

Nakale, A. (2011b, December, 12). Sex-for-marks probe lacks evidence. *New Era*.

National Planning Commission (NPC). (2013). *Millennium development goals: Interim progress report no. 4*. Windhoek: National Planning Commission.

Nwadigwe, C. (2007). Unwilling brides: "Phallic attack" as a barrier to gender balance in higher education in Nigeria. *Sex Education, 7*(4), 351–369.

Paludi, M., Nydegger, R., De Souza, E., Nydegger, L., & Dicker, K. (2006). International perspectives on sexual harassment of college students. *Annals New York Academy of Sciences, 1087*, 103–120.

Penrod, C. & Fusilier, M. (2011). Improving sexual harassment protections: An examination of legal compliance of U.S. university sexual harassment policies. *Journal of Workplace Rights, 15*(2), 151–167.

Reid, C. (2004). Advancing women's social justice agendas: A feminist action research framework. *International Journal of Qualitative Methods, 3*(3). Retrieved from https://journals.library.ualberta.ca/ijqm/index.php/IJQM/article/view/4462

Robinson, K. (2005). Reinforcing hegemonic masculinities through sexual harassment: Issues of identity, power and popularity in secondary schools. *Gender and Education, 17*(1), 19–37.

Robson, R. & Kessler, T. (2008). Unsettling sexual citizenship. *McGill Law Journal, 53*, 536–571.

Schlyter, A. (2009). Body politics and the crafting of citizenship in peri-urban Lusaka. *Feminist Africa,* (13), 23–43.

Siegel, R. (2003). *A short history of sexual harassment.* Retrieved from https://www.researchgate.net/publication/289005316_Introduction_A_Short_History_of_Sexual_Harassment

Shumba, A. & Matina, A. (2002). Sexual harassment of college students by lecturers in Zimbabwe. *Sex Education, 2*(1), 46–59.

Smit, D. & Du Plessis, V. (2011). Sexual harassment in the education sector. *Potchefstroom Electronic Journal PER/PELJ, 14*(6), 173–217.

Smit, N. (2011a, September, 7). UNAM knew about sex-for-marks claims. *The Namibian.*

Smit, N. (2011b, December, 14). UNAM sex probe finds nothing. *The Namibian.*

Uggen, C. & Blackstone, A. (2004). Sexual harassment a gendered expression of power. *American Sociological Review, 69*, 64–92.

University of Namibia (n.d). *HIV/AIDS and sexual harassment policy.* Retrieved from http://www.aau.org/sites/default/files/univ_namibia_AIDS_policy.pdf

Xoagus-Eises, S., Brown, E., & Makaya, M. (2012). *SADC gender protocol 2012 barometer: Namibia.* Windhoek. SADC Gender Protocol Barometer.

10

Conclusion: Democracy, education and social justice achieved?

Elizabeth Magano Amukugo

As you consolidate your thoughts on all the issues discussed in this book, ask yourself the following:

1. How would you define 'democracy' in your own terms? What does the author of this chapter give as the most important pillars of democracy? Do you agree? Have other authors in this book mentioned different main characteristics of democracy you think should be included in this list?

2. What kind of citizens are most needed for a democratic society?

3. How should the goals of democracy shape the education system of your country?

4. How do you explain the conflicts that can occur between education for a democratic and socially just society and a society with capitalist market policies?

5. How well is your country's education system addressing democracy and equity goals, and what shortcomings need to be addressed?

This book has two main objectives:

1. To explore the meaning of the concept democracy and its relationship to education
2. To reflect on what democracy means for justice in general society and in the Namibian context

TO WHAT EXTENT CAN EDUCATION ACHIEVE THESE AIMS?

The concepts of democracy and education mean different things to different people depending on divergent ideological viewpoints. The chapters in this book reflect this diversity at least in what they choose to emphasise. Thus Amukugo (Chapter 2) states that democracy is generally thought of as 'a system of governance in which members of an institution/organisation or society partake directly or indirectly in a decision-making process and, through their participation, can exercise control over decision making on issues that affect their lives'. She suggests, however, that this is not a very satisfactory definition as it raises questions of why participate, who participates, and what the participation entails.

Amukugo points to democracy existing at different levels: state and non-state levels. At state level, democracy must include a socially just society that delivers education and health and related public goods. It must include fundamental human rights and values, equity and justice. It is in this context that education is at the core of democratic values and governance as it is one of the most important instruments by means of which the goals of equity and justice can be attained.

One of the ways in which a society can be just and fair is to focus on issues of equity rather than on merely providing equal opportunities in legalistic terms. Mufune (Chapter 3) agrees with Amukugo that at the very least the term democracy is vague, and there has been intensive debate about what democracy is and how to achieve and maintain it. Mufune's take on this issue differs from Amukugo's in that he emphasises the distinction between what democracy means in theory and in practice. In theory, democracy is about participation in the polity through meaningful and extensive competition, through inclusion in the selection of policies and leaders, and through provision and facilitation of civil and political liberties guaranteed by rule of law.

Democracy as practice pertains to a cluster of rules, procedures and institutions permitting the broadest involvement of the majority of citizens in political affairs as well in the selection of representatives that make decisions. Education is crucial to upholding these rules and to exercising these rules that ensure participation and social justice. Mufune links democracy to education at the macro level and argues that although there is a relationship between education and democracy, it is not always apparent. Although evidence shows that countries that have more education are on average more democratic than countries with less education, at a macro-level it is also easy to point out countries with more education that falter when it comes to democracy. It is also not clear to what extent the relationship between education and democracy is confounded by other factors such as economic development and culture.

It seems that education plays different roles in different versions of democracy. Iijambo (Chapter 5) argues that 'there are many democracies to know in today's pluralistic world'. He lays emphasis, however, on participation, transparency, flexibility and tolerance as the pillars of democracy and this in relation to the political system. In particular he agrees with Diamond's conception that democracy as a concept must be limited to a system of governance that promotes meaningful and extensive competition among individuals and groups for positions of power. It is a system that denotes a high degree of inclusiveness in selecting leaders and policies, and the facilitation of civil and political liberties making participation possible. All this requires citizens (not subjects) who critically understand issues and act responsibly. It requires civic-minded citizens who are bound together by commitment to common institutions. Education is indispensable in equipping citizens with abilities and skills to engage critically, and act responsibly. Education does not exist simply to serve the market, but to serve society, and that means instilling in pupils and students a broad sense of values and norms that underpin institutions of democracy. It is in this context that he believes that the educated are core supporters of democratic rights, liberties, and institutions.

Notwithstanding positive developments within the education sector, Amukugo (Chapter 6) contends that Namibia's adoption of a mixed economy, based on capitalist ideals and with liberal democracy as a form of political governance, has meant that the post-colonial education system has, over the years, developed towards a 'positivist technical rationality' outlook which focuses on measuring knowledge in quantitative terms. As a result, teachers and students alike are inclined to delink the aims of education from the social, political and economic context. The IGCSE/HIGCSE paradigm, she argues, provided a good example of such educational orientation.

In many ways Lilemba (Chapter 7) is in sync with the others regarding what democracy is. He sees many systems of democracy, of which the main ones are direct and representative forms. His main concern is not with providing a definition of democracy per se but with understanding the barriers to democracy education in the Namibian context. Thus his focus is more micro than macro. Democracy has a relationship to education in the sense that educational institutions are arenas in which the 'public' and 'private' play out for many.

Brown and Haihambo's conception of democracy (Chapter 8), emphasises inclusiveness. According to them, in school contexts where children are looked upon as less human than adults, with limited rights to opinions, their democracy is inhibited. Where diversity is not considered, democracy is curtailed. Like Lilemba, they focus on micro barriers to participation in education institutions. They point out that some of the most salient barriers to inclusive education are related to attitudes and power relations between role players in education.

Edwards-Jauch and Namupala's view of democracy and citizenship (Chapter 9) is crafted in terms of citizens' rights in relation to the state. Theirs is a critical discussion from a feminist point of view of how women's bodies are used to assert power and control in public and private life. In particular, sexual harassment is perceived as an issue of democracy since it is a barrier to equality and therefore a violation of fundamental rights. Sexual harassment infringes on the rights mostly of women since it involves more women than men. Male dominance in decision-making positions within universities, and the resultant protectionism, as expressed through denial and trivialisation of sexual harassment, serve to perpetuate those institutional cultures. As such, sexual harassment is coercive, undemocratic and unjust. Labelling the term an international phenomenon, the authors underscore the need to raise awareness about these issues in order to find lasting solutions. Research is one way of making people aware of these pertinent gender issues. They thus think of democracy in terms of full participation in all aspects of human endeavour including sexuality.

All the authors in this volume agree that democracy has a relationship to education. They proceed from the premise that democracy needs education just as education needs democracy in Namibia. What is coming through in this book is that educational opportunities must be provided to the majority rather than to a select few – inclusion (accommodating everyone regardless of ethnicity, sex, race, religion and disability) is an absolute necessity if education is to play a meaningful role in Namibian democracy. Inclusive education itself must be based on a value system that recognises and celebrates diversity arising from gender, nationality, and language of origin, social background, level of education achieved or functional disability.

The authors emphasise that a democratic education must contribute to human rights which are necessary to secure freedom, social justice and equality to all. Educational systems, especially universities, should be open institutions that uphold the democratic values of equality, non-discrimination, transparency, accountability and freedom of expression if they are to meaningfully contribute to a democratic Namibia. This includes eschewing gender discrimination and sexual harassment.

Equality, autonomy, inclusion, social justice and freedom are values that are part and parcel of the democratisation project. It is imperative that these values and whatever is taught in schools must fit the reality of the Namibian society. This implies 'putting the right history back into the curriculum' by nurturing critical inquiry and forming a historical consciousness that avoids shortcomings of imported education systems that promote elites who disregard or look down on Namibian heritage while marginalising and excluding the majority from political decision-making processes. Social justice is about prioritising the concerns of the marginalised and the excluded.

Through interrogation of such concepts as inclusiveness, human rights, gender discrimination, freedom, non-discrimination, equality of opportunity, equity, etc. this book connects democracy to education and social justice. The various authors are unequivocal in seeing education as a means to create a socially just society. Although this is the case, there is a danger that the rhetoric of social justice and social inclusion do not match the realities of a capitalist society with market policies in which divisiveness and injustices resulting from competition have increased.

As Brown and Haihambo allude, continued calls for secluded schools for San children and requests for special schools for children with special needs may not bode well for social justice. Single-sex, single race or any form of sameness-schools are in total contrast with human rights and other principles of democratic inclusivity. Brown and Haihambo point to a series of pragmatic policies designed to include pregnant girls, orphans and vulnerable children, including street children, in Namibian education. These policies have been at the centre of heated controversy as both learners and teachers have rejected such learners.

An undercurrent running through the various chapters is the argument that it is difficult to associate undemocratic schools and educational systems with the promotion of democracy. As Freire (1998, p. 40) argued, an authoritarian education system, 'will at times cause children and students to adopt rebellious positions, defiant of any limit, discipline, or authority. But it will also lead to apathy, excessive obedience, and uncritical conformity, lack of resistance against authoritarian discourse, self-abnegation, and fear of freedom'. Thus schools can also represent oppressive government policies, irrelevant curricula taking students from agricultural work to urban employment, and leading to the relative exclusion of girls and women.

Indeed, as both Iiyambo and Lilemba argue, to develop education for democracy we must develop democratic education. An education system that is authoritarian and autocratic will likely face difficulties developing learners who adhere to the principles of democracy, human rights and freedom. Such a system produces students who fail to interrogate knowledge and power and who end up as passive consumers of whatever the political process puts out.

In this vein Edwards-Jauch and Namupala argue that sexual harassment is a form of gender-based violence that reflects broader societal level inequalities. It is also a phenomenon that pervades universities and educational institutions around the world, and in Namibia in particular. The very presence of sexual harassment does not bode well for democratic practice.

How democratic is the Namibian education system and how well does it nurture democracy and augment social justice? These questions are addressed in various chapters of this book, notably in Amukugo's, Iijambo's and Lilemba's chapters. Namibia has come a long way from the days of apartheid education when education was explicitly designed to reinforce racial inequality. Then, Bantu Education served to dehumanise the colonised. In post-colonial times the aims of education in Namibia included the anti-colonial struggle for freedom, justice and socio-economic emancipation. It reflected a vision of education that not only recognised human capacities and divergent views, it also promoted the democratic ethos of active participation. The four major goals of education in independent Namibia were access, equity, quality and democracy.

Despite these major goals, Namibian education is not yet fully promoting democracy and enhancing social justice. As Amukugo (in this volume) indicates, achievements during the past 27 years in this regard have been rather mixed, partly due to stark socio-economic inequities within the Namibian society. Both Iijambo and Lilemba argue that to develop education for democracy we must develop democratic education. In Namibia, school boards do not always operate as they should, students are not always consulted on the curriculum, teachers are not always familiar with the principles of democracy and human rights, the learner-centred approach is not accepted and practised by all teachers, and the like. Lack of inclusion of the San, Ovahimba and Ovatua does not speak well for democracy. Sexual harassment at tertiary institutions is also an issue of democracy, since it is a barrier to equality and therefore a violation of fundamental rights. It is in this context that Iijambo speaks of Namibia as semi-democratic, in that education does not necessarily promote effective power of elected officials or political competition.

Thus, slow progress in the education sector notwithstanding, Article 20 of the Namibian Constitution made provision for free primary education in 1991(Government of the Republic of Namibia [GRN], 1990). The introduction of free primary education in 2013, though delayed for 22 years, is a step in the right direction, and it will help to promote the goals of access, equity, quality and democracy within basic education in Namibia. This is especially the case against the backdrop of the provision made in the Education Act of 2003, implemented in 2016, that extends secondary schooling to all eligible learners, and emphasises that issues related to quality and equity at secondary school and higher education levels are comprehensively dealt with in order to realise the goals of democracy and justice within the education sector. As the Educational Pathways International (2010) rightly observed, universities produce '… trained individuals who develop the capacity and analytical skills that drive local economies, support civil society, teach children, lead effective governments, and make important decisions which affect entire societies'. This places higher education at the centre of social change and subsequently of democracy, and hence needs to be sustained by society. The Namibian Government has recently launched the Harambee Prosperity Plan (HPP) (GRN, 2016), with clearly pronounced objectives and implementation strategy on how to mitigate poverty and inequalities among other social ills.

This is a step in the right direction. As Amukugo (Chapter 6) observed, however, the suggested Vocational Education and Training (VET) programme would have more impact if it were linked to a VET curriculum within the secondary education system. This would encourage choice of VET pathways out of interest, as opposed to students who fail merely taking the first opportunity available in order to make it elsewhere. It would also generate a strong foundation for post-secondary VET education and training programmes. Nonetheless, the Harambee Prosperity Plan's positive impact will be best judged four years from now, pending results from a robust monitoring and evaluation system.

In the final analysis, conversely, education needs to move beyond the elitist function in order to meet the requirements for a just and inclusive society. The stage has been set upon which education can increasingly contribute to democratic consolidation.

Nonetheless, Amukugo has argued that liberal democracy, which is a form of governance in Namibia, emphasises abstract political rights at the expense of concrete economic rights and legalistic equal rights at the expense of social equity. As such, it consequently limits education's capacity to sustain democracy and social justice. To remedy the situation there is a need to implement what Ake (2000, p. 138) terms 'structural democratisation' at the level of the state, in a way that guarantees concrete economic rights, addresses economic inequalities and increases the democratic participation of the disadvantaged within society. Such a move would address key educational goals of quality and equity.

References

Ake, C. (2000). *The feasibility of democracy in Africa*. Dakar: Council for the Development of Social Science Research in Africa (CODESRIA).

Educational Pathways International. (2010). *The impact of university education in developing countries*. Retrieved from http://www.educationalpathwaysinternational.org/?page_id=99

Freire, P. (1998). *Teachers as cultural workers: Letters to those who dare teach*. Boulder, Colo: Westview Press.

Government of the Republic of Namibia (GRN). (1990). *The Namibian constitution*. Windhoek: Ministry of Information and Broadcasting.

Government of the Republic of Namibia (GRN). (2016). *Harambee prosperity plan 2016/17 – 2019/20: Namibian Government's action plan towards prosperity for all*. Windhoek: Office of the President. Retrieved from http://www.gov.na/documents/10181/264466/HPP+page+70-71.pdf/bc958f46-8f06-4c48-9307-773f242c9338

Contributors

Elizabeth Magano Amukugo is an Associate Professor in the Department of Educational Foundations and Management at the University of Namibia (UNAM). She holds a PhD (Education), an MSSc (Education) and a BSc (Sociology and Education) from Lund University (Sweden). She served as Head of the Department of Educational Foundations and Management at UNAM for six years, and as a member of the UNAM Senate. She was the founding Director of Research for the International University of Management (IUM). A former Member of Parliament for the Republic of Namibia (2000–2005), she served as the founding Vice-President of the Forum of African Parliamentarians for Education (FAPED); chaired the African Capacity Building Foundation's (ACBF) Technical Advisory Group (PARLIANET); was Senior Representative for the Commonwealth Parliamentary Association (CPA) Women (Africa Region); and a member of the UNESCO Working Group on Education for All. She is currently a member of the ACBF's Strategic Study Group which helps to shape Africa's Research and Policy Agenda. Her publications include *Teacher Education for an Independent Namibia: Problems and Prospects* (University of Lund, 1987) and *Education and Politics in Namibia: Past Trends and Future Prospects* (New Namibia Books, 1993 and Gamsberg Macmillan, 1995).

Anthony Brown is a Senior Lecturer in the Department of Educational Psychology at the University of Johannesburg. He is mainly responsible for Inclusive Education and Life Orientation in the teacher education programme. Brown's research is located in sexual diversity and inclusive education, social justice and transformation in the Namibian context. He holds an MA (Special Education) from Leeds University (UK), a BEd from the University of Namibia, and an EdD (Educational Disadvantage and Special Education) from the University of Birmingham (UK).

Lucy Edwards-Jauch is a Senior Lecturer in the Department of Sociology at the University of Namibia (UNAM). Her research interests are gender, violence, intersections between gender and other forms of oppression and the social-cultural context of HIV and AIDS. She is also the coordinator of an Action Research project that focuses on young women's leadership and sexual and reproductive rights. She holds a PhD (Philosophy) from UNAM, an MA (Philosophy) from the University of Cape Town (South Africa) and a BA from UNAM.

Cynthy K. Haihambo is a Senior Lecturer in the Department of Educational Psychology and Inclusive Education at the University of Namibia (UNAM). She has done extensive research and consultancies in the areas of special needs and inclusive education; early childhood, gender and HIV/AIDS; street children and other marginalized children; indigenous knowledge systems; and orphans and vulnerable children. She serves on various national and international education-related committees and platforms. She holds a PhD (Inclusive Education) from the University of South Africa, an MPhil (Special Needs Education) from the University of Oslo (Norway) and a BEd (Hons) from UNAM.

Tangeni C. K. Iijambo is a Lecturer in the Department of Educational Foundations and Management at the University of Namibia. He teaches Philosophy of Education, Comparative and International Education and Effective Leadership in Schools. He is an edutainor, educating through entertainment, and his research interests include philosophy for children and the

...on of ethnic groups through song and dance. He holds a PhD from Michigan State ...ıversity (USA), an MEd from the University of Bristol (UK) and an EdD from West Sussex Institute of Higher Education (UK).

John Makala Lilemba is a researcher, scholar and a winner of the Pamwe Literature Award in siLozi short stories. He is a Lecturer at the University of Barotseland in Zambia and was previously Head of Department of Educational Foundations and Management at the University of Namibia (UNAM). With 18 years of university teaching and research, he has read and researched widely, including reviewing journal articles, book chapters, conference proceedings and essays in educational sciences. He holds a PhD from UNAM, an MA (Educational Studies) from the University of Manchester (UK), a BEd and an EdD from the University of the North (now the University of Limpopo, Polokwane, South Africa). He is the author of three books used in secondary schools and one novel prescribed by the UNAM Language Centre.

Pempelani Mufune (deceased) was Professor of Environmental Sociology in the Department of Sociology at the University of Namibia (UNAM). He previously taught at the universities of Zambia (1981–1991) and Botswana (1991–1995). He joined the University of Namibia in 1995 and served as Head of the Department of Sociology for ten years and member of the UNAM Senate. Among his many professional activities, he served as President of the Southern African Universities Social Sciences (SAUSS) (2003–2006); editorial board member of *International Sociology: Journal of the International Sociological Association* (ISA) (1993–2004); and Member of The Population and Development Strategy Unit of the National Planning Commission of the Republic of Namibia (1998–2013). Among his writings are: *Debt relief initiatives and poverty alleviation: lessons from Africa* (Africa Institute of South Africa Publishers, Pretoria, 2003) and *The Rural in Namibia: An introduction to concepts and issues* (UNAM, 2011). Mufune's chapter is his last published work of research.

Ndeshi Namupala is a Lecturer in the Department of Sociology at the University of Namibia. She holds an MA (Sociology) from the University of Eastern Finland. She is currently pursuing her PhD at the University of Namibia. Her research interests include labour, gender, youth and urban studies.

Index

157

www.ingramcontent.com/pod-product-compliance
Lightning Source LLC
Chambersburg PA
CBHW052010270326
41929CB00015B/2863